afoot & AFLOAT

South Puget Sound
& Hood Canal

Fourth Edition

**MARGE & TED
MUELLER**

THE MOUNTAINEERS BOOKS

THE MOUNTAINEERS BOOKS
*is the nonprofit publishing arm of The Mountaineers Club, an organization
founded in 1906 and dedicated to the exploration, preservation, and
enjoyment of outdoor and wilderness areas.*

1001 SW Klickitat Way, Suite 201, Seattle, WA 98134

©2006 by Marge and Ted Mueller

First edition 1983. Second edition 1990. Third edition 1996. Fourth edition, 2006

Manufactured in the United States of America

Project Editor: Mary Metz
Copy Editor: Joeth Zucco
Cover Design: Mayumi Thompson.
Book Design: Marge Mueller, Gray Mouse Graphics
Layout: Marge Mueller, Gray Mouse Graphics
Cartographer: Marge and Ted Mueller, Gray Mouse Graphics
All photographs by Marge and Ted Mueller, except as noted.

Cover photograph: *Big leaf maples over Quartermaster Harbor, Vashon Island.*
©Donnelly-Austin Photography

Library of Congress Cataloging-in-Publication Data
Mueller, Marge.
  Afoot and afloat : South Puget Sound and Hood Canal / Marge and Ted Mueller.
—4th ed.
     p. cm.
  Rev. ed. of: South Puget Sound, afoot & afloat. c1996.
  Includes bibliographical references and index.
  ISBN-13: 978-0-89886-952-1 (alk. paper)
  ISBN-10: 0-89886-952-8 (alk. paper)
  1. Outdoor recreation—Washington (State)—Puget Sound. 2. Outdoor recreation—
Washington (State)—Puget Sound—Directories. 3. Puget Sound (Wash.)—Guide-
books. 4. Marinas—Washington (State)—Puget Sound—Guidebooks. 5. Outdoor
recreation—Washington (State)—Hood Canal—Guidebooks. 6. Hood Canal (Wash.)—
Guidebooks. I. Mueller, Ted. II. Mueller, Marge. South Puget Sound, afoot & afloat.
III. Mountaineers (Society) IV. Title. V. Title: South Puget Sound and Hood Canal.
  GV191.42.W2M84 2006
  796.5025'7977--dc22

                                      2006017244

 Printed on recycled paper

Contents

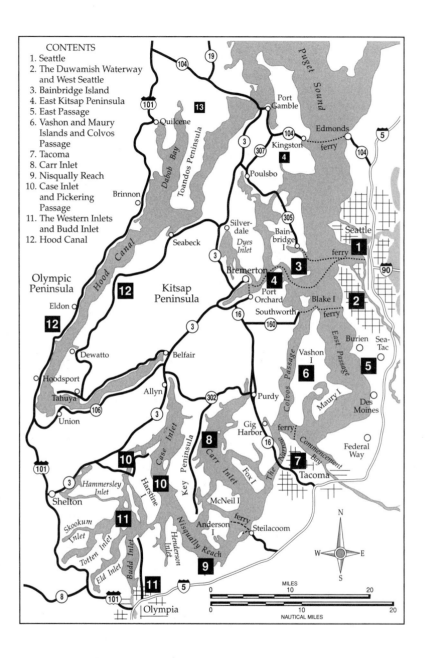

CONTENTS

Puget Sound

Port Gamble

Edmonds
ferry

Quilcene

104

307

Kingston

4

Toandos Peninsula

13

Poulsbo

305

Brinnon

Silver-dale

Bain-bridge I

Seattle

1

Dyes Inlet

Seabeck

3

Bremerton

3

ferry

Olympic Peninsula

12

Hood Canal

Kitsap Peninsula

4

Port Orchard

Blake I

2

Eldon

Southworth

160

East Passage

12

Dewatto

Belfair

3

16

Vashon I

6

Burien

Sea-Tac

5

Hoodsport

Allyn

302

Purdy

Maury I

Des Moines

Tahuya

106

Colvos Passage

Gig Harbor

16

ferry

Commencement Bay

Federal Way

Union

3

Case Inlet

8

Carr Inlet

The Narrows

7

Tacoma

Hammersley Inlet

10

Key Peninsula

Fox I

Shelton

3

10

Harstine

McNeil I

Skookum Inlet

11

Anderson I

ferry

Steilacoom

Totten Inlet

Henderson Inlet

Nisqually Reach

9

Eld Inlet

Budd Inlet

11

5

8

101

11

Olympia

N
W E
S

MILES
0   10   20

0   10   20
NAUTICAL MILES

List of Sidebars

MAP KEY

════════	freeway	🗼	lighthouse
──────	major road	⚓	navigational beacon
────────	minor road or street	⬭	reef
▬▬▬▬▬	service road	🐦	wildlife refuge
━·━·━·━	boundary	🛈	ranger station
───┼───	gate	⊼	picnic area
------------	trail	⌂	campground
)(	footbridge	⌂	primitive campsite
....	ferry route	⌂	Cascadia Marine Trail campsite
⟝⟝⟝⟝⟝	airstrip or airport	*	submerged or submerging rock
⚓	anchorage		lake
⚓	mooring buoy	⚘⚘	marsh
•–•–•–•	lineal mooring		

NOTE:

This book's sketch maps are not intended for navigation. Not all hazards, such as rocks or reefs, are shown.

The mileage scale indicates general distances. However, because nearly all the maps are drawn in perspective, as if seen from an airplane, front to back distances are somewhat greater than indicated, due to foreshortening.

Icons for mooring buoys and campsites are placed to show their general location, but the number of icons is not indicative of that item's total number. Refer to the text information blocks for more exact numbers.

Quick Reference to Facilities and Recreation

Some kinds of marine recreation, such as boating and beachcombing, are found throughout North Puget Sound and the Strait of Juan de Fuca. Others, however, are more specific to particular areas. The following table provides a quick reference to important facilities and activities. Some facilities listed might be at commercial resorts or marinas; some might close off–season. For detailed information read the descriptions of specific areas in the text.

Marine Services include marine supplies and repair; in some places they might be of a very limited nature.

Moorage refers to marinas that have guest moorage. It also includes public docks and buoys at marine parks.

Launch Facilities includes shore access only for hand-carried boats. Hoists and slings are always at commercial marinas. Ramps might be at either commercial or public facilities.

Groceries/Shopping might be of a very limited nature.

Camping is listed under recreation to avoid duplicating it as a facility. However, it also means that campsites, as a facility, are available.

Point of Interest includes educational displays, museums, and self-guided nature walks.

(•) = Nearby; [•] = Freshwater
Fuel: D = On Dock; S = Service Station
Launch Facilities: R = Ramp; H = Hoist; C = Hand Carry
Restroom or Toilet: S = Shower Also
Camping: M = Cascadia Marine Trail Campsite Also
Hiking/Beach Walking: B = Beach Walk

Facilities									Location	Recreation								
Fuel	Marine Pumpout	Marine Services	Moorage	Launch Facilities	Restroom or Toilet	Lodging	Groceries/Shopping	Restaurants		Fishing	Shellfish	Paddling	Scuba Diving	Camping	Picnicking	Hiking/Beach Walking	Wildlife Watching	Point of Interest
									1. SEATTLE									
					•			•	Golden Gardens	•		•	•		•	B	•	
				R	•			•	Eddie Vine Boat Launch	•		•						
•	•	•	•	H	•/S		•	•	Shilshole Bay Marina	(•)		•						
				C	•			•	Hiram M. Chittenden Locks	•					•		•	•
					•			•	Discovery Park			•				•/B	•	•

Fuel	Marine Pumpout	Marine Services	Moorage	Launch Facilities	Restroom or Toilet	Lodging	Groceries/Shopping	Restaurants	Location	Fishing	Shellfish	Paddling	Scuba Diving	Camping	Picnicking	Hiking/Beach Walking	Wildlife Watching	Point of Interest
•	•	•	•		•/S		•	•	Elliott Bay Marina			•						
									Smith Cove City Park			•			•			
					•			•	Elliott Bay Park	•						•		•
					•				Myrtle Edwards Park						•	•		•
	•		•		•/S	•	•	•	The Downtown Seattle Waterfront	•		•			•	•	•	•

2. THE DUWAMISH WATERWAY AND WEST SEATTLE

Fuel	Marine Pumpout	Marine Services	Moorage	Launch Facilities	Restroom or Toilet	Lodging	Groceries/Shopping	Restaurants	Location	Fishing	Shellfish	Paddling	Scuba Diving	Camping	Picnicking	Hiking/Beach Walking	Wildlife Watching	Point of Interest
									Terminal 23 Fishing Pier	•					•			
				C					Terminal 18 Public Access			•			•			
				C	•				Terminal 105 Public Access	•		•			•			
					•				Jack Block Park						•	•		•
			•		•		•	•	Seacrest Park	•			•		•			
				R	•		(•)	(•)	Don Armeni Park	•		•	•		•	•		
					•		(•)	(•)	Alki Beach Park and Lighthouse						•	•/B		•
				C	•				Parks South of Alki Point			•			•	•/B		
				C	•			•	Lincoln Park	•			•		•	•/B		
									Cove Park									•

3. BAINBRIDGE ISLAND

Fuel	Marine Pumpout	Marine Services	Moorage	Launch Facilities	Restroom or Toilet	Lodging	Groceries/Shopping	Restaurants	Location	Fishing	Shellfish	Paddling	Scuba Diving	Camping	Picnicking	Hiking/Beach Walking	Wildlife Watching	Point of Interest
			•	R	•		(•)	(•)	Eagle Harbor Waterfront Park			•			•	•		
	•		•		•/S		•	•	Eagle Harbor Marinas									
									Joel Pritchard Park			•				•/B		•
				C	•				Blakely Harbor Park			•			•	•/B		•
			•	R	•				Fort Ward State Park	•		•	•	M	•	•	•	•
									Point White Fishing Pier	•		•	•					
									Fletcher and Manzanita Bays			•						
									Fairy Dell Park		•					•/B	•	
									Reitan Road Access				•			B		

Fuel	Marine Pumpout	Marine Services	Moorage	Launch Facilities	Restroom or Toilet	Lodging	Groceries/Shopping	Restaurants	Location	Fishing	Shellfish	Paddling	Scuba Diving	Camping	Picnicking	Hiking/Beach Walking	Wildlife Watching	Point of Interest
									West Port Madison Nature Preserve							•	•/B	
									Inner Port Madison			•						•
			•		•/S				Fay-Bainbridge State Park	•	•	•	•	•/M	•		B	•
									4. EAST KITSAP PENINSULA									
				R	•		(•)		Manchester Launch Ramp	•	•				•			•
				C	•/S				Manchester State Park	•		•	•	•/M	•	•		
				C	•	(•)	(•)		Beach Drive East	•		•						
					•		•	•	Port Orchard									•
•	•	•	•		•/S	(•)	(•)		Port Orchard Marina and Waterfront Park			•				•	B	
				R	•	(•)	(•)		Port Orchard Boat Launch and Public Pier	•		•						•
				C					Sinclair Inlet Wildlife Viewing Area			•					•	
•			•		•/S	(•)	(•)	(•)	Bremerton Marina			•				•	B	
					•	(•)	(•)	(•)	Bremerton Waterfront							•		•
				R	•				Evergreen City Park	•		•				•		
				C					Bachmann Park			•			•			
				R	•			•	Lebo Boulevard Parks	•		•				•	B	
									Naval Ammunition Depot Marine Park							•	B	•
				R					Chico Launch Ramp			•						
•			•	R	•	(•)	(•)		Silverdale Waterfront Park	•		•				•	B	
					•	(•)	(•)		Old Mill Park								•	
					•				J. A. and Anna F. Smith Children's Park			•		M	•			•
				R					Tracyton Launch Ramp			•						
			•	R	•/S				Illahee State Park	•	•	•	•	•	•		•/B	•
			•			(•)	(•)		Illahee	•			•					
•		•	•	R	•/S		•	•	Brownsville Marina	•		•		M	•			•

| Facilities | | | | | | | | | Location | Recreation | | | | | | | | |
Fuel	Marine Pumpout	Marine Services	Moorage	Launch Facilities	Restroom or Toilet	Lodging	Groceries/Shopping	Restaurants		Fishing	Shellfish	Paddling	Scuba Diving	Camping	Picnicking	Hiking/Beach Walking	Wildlife Watching	Point of Interest
					•		•		Naval Undersea Museum									•
			•	R	•		(•)	(•)	Port of Keyport Marina			•				•		
•	•	•	•	R/C	•/S	•	•	•	Poulsbo	•		•				•	•/B	•
					•		•		Suquamish Museum							•	•	
				C	•				Old Man House Park			•	•			•		•
S				R	•		•	•	Suquamish			•						•
		•		R	•				Miller Bay and Indianola	•		•				•	B	•
									5. EAST PASSAGE									
					•/S				Ed Munro Seahurst Park	•		•	•			•	•/B	•
									Eagle Landing Park								•/B	
				C					Three Tree Point			•	•					
					•				Marine View Park							•	•/B	
•	•	•	•	H	•		(•)	•	Des Moines Marina	•		•						
					•				Des Moines Beach Park							•	•/B	
			•	C	•/S				Saltwater State Park	•		•	•	•		•	•/B	
				R	•		(•)		Redondo Waterfront Park	•		•	•			•		•
									Dumas Bay Park Wildlife Sanctuary								•/B	•
					•/S				Dash Point State Park	•		•	•	•		•	•/B	
				C	•		(•)		Dash Point Park	•		•	•			•		
									6. VASHON AND MAURY ISLANDS AND COLVOS PASSAGE									
					•				Winghaven Park		•	•		M		•	•/B	
									Point Heyer			•					B	•
									Tramp Harbor Fishing Pier	•		•				•	B	
				C	•	•			Point Robinson Park and Lighthouse	•		•	•	M		•	•/B	
					•				Maury Island Marine Park	•	•	•					•/B	
					•				Quartermaster Harbor	•	•	•						

Fuel	Marine Pumpout	Marine Services	Moorage	Launch Facilities	Restroom or Toilet	Lodging	Groceries/Shopping	Restaurants	Location	Fishing	Shellfish	Paddling	Scuba Diving	Camping	Picnicking	Hiking/Beach Walking	Wildlife Watching	Point of Interest
				R	•		(•)		Burton Acres Park	•	•				•	•	•	
	•		•	R	•/S				Dockton County Park	•	•				•	•		
					•				West Side Shore Accesses			•	•	M	•	B		
•			•		•/S			•	Blake Island Marine State Park	•	•	•	•	•/M	•	•/B	•	•
				R	•				Southworth and Harper Public Access	•		•	•			B		
					•				Anderson Point Park	•	•					•/B		
				R		•			Olalla	•	•							
					•				Sunrise Beach County Park	•					•	•/B		
•	•	•	•	R	•	•	•	•	Gig Harbor	•	•					•		
									7. TACOMA									
					•				Browns Point Park							•		•
		•	•	R/H	•			•	Tacoma Waterways Industrial Area			•						•
		•	•	H/C	•		•	•	Thea Foss Waterway			•			•	•		
			•	C	•	•		•	Ruston Way Waterfront Parks	•		•	•		•	•		
•		•		R/H	•	•		•	Point Defiance Park	•	•					•/B		•
				C	•				Narrows Park	•	•			M	•	B		
•					•/S		(•)	(•)	Titlow Beach Park	•			•			•/B		•
•		•		R/H					Day Island	•	•							
									8. CARR INLET									
				R					Wollochet Bay	•		•	•					
				R/C	•				Fox Island	•		•	•		•			
				R					Horsehead Bay	•		•						
			•		•/S				Kopachuck State Park			•	•	•/M	•	•/B		
			•						Cutts Island Marine State Park			•	•	•		B		
				R			(•)	(•)	Henderson Bay and Wauna	•	•					B		
				C	•				Glen Cove		•							

Fuel	Marine Pumpout	Marine Services	Moorage	Launch Facilities	Restroom or Toilet	Lodging	Groceries/Shopping	Restaurants	Location	Fishing	Shellfish	Paddling	Scuba Diving	Camping	Picnicking	Hiking/Beach Walking	Wildlife Watching	Point of Interest
(S)				R			(•)		Von Geldern Cove	•		•						
•			•	R	•		•		Mayo Cove									
			•		•/S				Penrose Point State Park	•	•	•		•/M	•	•/B		
9. NISQUALLY REACH																		
•	•	•	•	R	•		•	•	Steilacoom	•		•	•		•			•
					•	•		•	Anderson Island	•		•		M	•	•		•
			•						Eagle Island Marine State Park	•		•				B		
			•	R			(•)		Pitt and Drayton Passages	•	•	•						
					•				Nisqually National Wildlife Refuge	•		•				•	•	•
				R	•				Luhr Beach	•		•					•	•
			•		•/S				Tolmie State Park	•	•	•	•		•	•/B		
•		•		R	•		•	•	Johnson Point Marinas	•								
					C	•			Woodard Bay Natural Resource Conservation Area						•	•	•	•
10. CASE INLET AND PICKERING PASSAGE																		
					C				Devils Head and Taylor Bay	•		•						
			•	R	•				Joemma Beach State Park	•	•	•		•/M	•	•/B		
									Haley Property State Park	•	•	•		M	•	B		
				R					Vaughn Bay			•						
					•				North Bay Public Access		•	•				B		
(S)	•			R	•		(•)	(•)	Allyn	•		•			•			
•		•		R	•/S		•		Fair Harbor			•			•			
			•						Stretch Island	•	•	•					•	B
					•				Harstine Island State Park and DNR Beach 24	•	•	•	•		•	•/B		
			•		•				McMicken Island Marine State Park	•	•	•			•	•/B		
				R	•				Latimer's Landing	•	•	•						

Fuel	Marine Pumpout	Marine Services	Moorage	Launch Facilities	Restroom or Toilet	Lodging	Groceries/Shopping	Restaurants	Location	Fishing	Shellfish	Paddling	Scuba Diving	Camping	Picnicking	Hiking/Beach Walking	Wildlife Watching	Point of Interest
									Harstine Island DNR Beaches	•						B		
•	•		•		•/S			•	Jarrell Cove Marina		•			•	•		•	
•		•			•/S				Jarrell Cove State Park	•	•			•/M	•	•		
				C					Brisco Point		•							
		•			•				Hope Island Marine State Park	•	•	•		•/M	•	•/B		
11. THE WESTERN INLETS AND BUDD INLET																		
•			R	•		(•)	(•)	(•)	Shelton	•								
				•					Walker County Park	•				M	•	B		
			R						Arcadia	•	•							
			R	•					Jacoby Shorecrest County Park		•				•	B		
									Olympia Oyster Company									•
									Geoduck Beach							•/B		
				•					Frye Cove County Park	•	•		•		•	•/B		
•		•	R	•			•	•	Boston Harbor Marina		•			•				
				•					Burfoot County Park	•	•		•			•/B		
				•					Priest Point Park	•						•	•	•
		•		•		•	•	•	Olympia									•
•		•	•	R/H	•/S			(•)	East Bay		•					•	•	•
•		•			•/S		(•)	•	West Bay		•					•		
12. HOOD CANAL																		
					•				Indian George Creek Estuarine Restoration Site	•						B		
•	•		•	R	•/S				Quilcene Bay Marina						•			
			•	R	•				Point Whitney State Shellfish Laboratory	•	•				•			•
									Dabob Bay Public Tidelands		•							
				C	•				Seal Rock Campground	•	•	•		•	•	•/B		•

Fuel	Marine Pumpout	Marine Services	Moorage	Launch Facilities	Restroom or Toilet	Lodging	Groceries/Shopping	Restaurants	Location	Fishing	Shellfish	Paddling	Scuba Diving	Camping	Picnicking	Hiking/Beach Walking	Wildlife Watching	Point of Interest
					•/S				Dosewallips State Park		•			•	•	•/B	•	
									Anderson Landing Preserve		•	•					•	
•		•	•	H	•		•	•	Seabeck	•			•					
				R	•				Misery Point Launch Ramp	•		•	•					
					•				Scenic Beach State Park	•	•	•	•	•	•	•/B		•
					•				Guillemot Cove Nature Reserve		•	•		M	•	•/B		
				C					Anderson Cove			•						
				R	•				Kitsap Peninsula Public Tidelands		•	•		M				
•			•		•		•	•	Pleasant Harbor	•		•			•			
				R	•				Triton Cove State Park	•		•		M	•			
									West Shore Public Beaches		•	•					•	
S		•			•		•	•	Hoodsport	•		•			•			•
				R	•				Cushman Hydro Project Saltwater Park	•		•			•			
				•	•/S				Potlatch State Park	•	•	•	•	•/M	•	•		
			•	R	•		•	•	Union	•								
	•		•		•/S	•		•	Alderbrook Inn		•							•
	•		•	R	•/S			•	Twanoh State Park	•		•	•	•	•	•		
					•		(•)	(•)	Theler Wetlands Nature Trail						•	•	•	•
					•/S		(•)		Belfair State Park	•	•			•	•	B		
	•		•	R	•				Port of Allyn Dock and Launch Ramp			•						
			•	R	•/S		(•)		Tahuya	•		•		•				
				C	•				Menard's Landing		•	•			•	B		

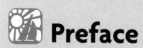 # Preface

NEW AND BETTER seems to always be what people strive for. It certainly is true for us, and we hope we have achieved that in this new edition of our *Afoot and Afloat* book. We have updated all the information, of course, but we also have reorganized it to make the book easier to use and more interesting. This edition includes

- Newly formatted lists of attractions to entice you to visit the sites.
- Complete "getting there" directions, both by car and boat, and those directions have been moved to the beginning of the site description.
- Additional maps and cross-referencing to maps.
- Sidebars with interesting facts and trivia about the South Sound.
- Navigation notes highlighted with a ✹.

A few new sites have appeared since we last surveyed South Puget Sound, and some of the old ones are gone. More important, many existing sites have been improved by repairs, updates, and expansions—giving you good reason to revisit spots you might have been to before, or to try new ones.

And instead of three volumes covering North, Middle, and South Puget Sound, we have merged them into two, North and South, to make them more compact and to make it easier for readers to find information about particular sites.

About the Afoot and Afloat Series

Many guidebooks are written with a specific activity in mind, telling people such as bicyclists, paddlers, or clamdiggers where to go to better enjoy their favorite recreation. Although the books of our *Afoot and Afloat* series do cover some activities and areas strictly limited to boaters, we know that boaters frequently leave their vessels to walk beaches, dig clams, or hike trails in nearby forests, and that some boaters even bring bicycles with them to widen their explorations.

At the same time, many people who do not own boats love roaming beaches, hiking bluff tops, and peddling quiet roads, enjoying the bite of salt air, the cries of seabirds, and the rush of waves. The one common thread in this book is shorelines, and all the activities associated with them, no matter how one arrives there.

Descriptions of facilities are kept brief because we feel that such things as marinas and campgrounds are not ends in themselves but merely places that enable one to enjoy the shorelines and water.

Buoys placed off Fay-Bainbridge State Park offer a nice spot to pause while cruising Puget Sound.

Attractions are described in order to entice visitors to out-of-the-way spots they might otherwise pass by. Because exploration of any region is more enjoyable if spiced with some of its history and ecology, we have included tidbits on the history and natural life of some of the areas.

The areas in this book were surveyed over a period of several years and rechecked just prior to publication of this new edition. Changes to facilities do occur, however. The authors and The Mountaineers Books would appreciate your letting us know of any changes to facilities so future editions can be updated. Please address comments to The Mountaineers Books, 1011 SW Klickitat Way, Suite 107, Seattle, Washington 98134 or e-mail us at *margeted@comcast.net.*

Marge and Ted Mueller

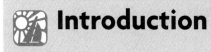

Introduction

BOATERS THINK OF SOUTH PUGET SOUND as teeming with the activity of giant freighters plowing up and down the channel, ferries churning back and forth, bevies of white-crowned sailboats being driven in the wind, cruisers of every size bustling about, and fishing boats bobbing on the tides. That is certainly true, to an extent. However, much of South Puget Sound will come as a pleasant surprise. Many inlets are as natural as those found in the San Juans and Gulf Islands. Expanses of tree-cloaked hills stretch down to meet the water. Flotillas of waterfowl dabble in quiet, shallow coves. Seals—even whales at times—inhabit the channels.

From cities and towns along the shores stream thousands of recreation seekers, some headed for distant vacation spots, but many looking for nearby diversions. And the diversions *are* here—beaches and parks draw people for an array of activities, ranging from fishing to sand castle building, from birdwatching to sunbathing. Parks and public shorelands are sandwiched between real estate developments and tucked in obscure crannies of quiet bays. These public areas range from multipurpose facilities of several hundred acres to narrow beaches offering only a chance to drag a boat to the water and toss it in.

These waters, along with channels to the north, were visited by British sea captain George Vancouver in 1792. He explored the area in two ships, the 90-foot sloop of war *Discovery* and the 60-foot brig *Chatham*. The expedition drew amazingly accurate charts of the area, and named many locations—most notably Puget Sound, for his lieutenant, Peter Puget.

Another historic name you will see frequently mentioned in this book is Lt. Charles Wilkes. In 1841 he commanded six vessels of the United States Exploring Expedition, with the mission of exploring and charting the region and, incidentally, to establish claims to the area for the United States government. Many Puget Sound names come from this expedition.

Where Is "Puget Sound"?

The broad seaway on which the major population centers of western Washington front, and on which thousands of boats travel daily, ought to have a nice all-inclusive name. Unfortunately, it doesn't. In precise geographic language, "Puget Sound" applies only to the channels south of a line drawn from Port Townsend on the Olympic Peninsula to Admiralty Head on Whidbey Island. That leaves a whole chunk of Washington's inland waters without a name. True, some of these, such as the Strait of Juan de Fuca, Colvos Passage, and Case and Carr Inlets have individual names, but the area as a whole still lacks an official name that weather reports, government agencies, the populace in general, and beleaguered writers (especially) can use.

Officialdom aside, however, many local people, as well as most state agencies, commonly consider Puget Sound to be all of Washington's inland waters that run north from Olympia to the Canadian border and west to the Pacific Ocean. Thus, we titled this book *Afoot and Afloat: South Puget Sound* and its companion volume *Afoot and Afloat: North Puget Sound*. There is no tidy division between north and south, so we set a very arbitrary dividing line for the purpose of these books. We consider North Puget Sound to be the area lying above a line drawn from Shilshole Bay to Kingston, continuing west and swinging south of the Hood Canal Bridge to include the area north of Bangor and including all of the south shore of the Strait of Juan de Fuca. That pretty group of islands sitting near the center of all this are covered in our third companion volume, *Afoot and Afloat: The San Juan Islands*.

Getting Around in South Puget Sound

Time was when the only way to travel around the Puget Sound area was by boat. Forests blanketed most of the shoreline so thickly that even walking was difficult; the communities that sprang up as the land was settled were linked by sailing ships and rowboats. Because waterways provided easy channels of travel, time was better spent clearing land for farming or cutting timber for mills than undertaking the Herculean task of road building.

Ferries both large and small, such as these little ferries that operate at Steilacoom, connect several points in South Puget Sound.

Using This Book

- This guide is arranged geographically, moving roughly from north to south and east to west. Chapters have an overview map and numerous detail maps. The maps are referenced at the beginning of each site description.
- Sidebars are our digressions of thought into something we found interesting. We hope you, too, will find them interesting.
- Attractions and facilities listed at the beginning of each site description are arranged, in general, with the most important attractions for that site first and lesser ones later.
- Access directions are given via car 🚐 and boat ⛴️, as is applicable. However, most sites can be reached from a variety of different points, so the access directions and distances are from the most likely spot.
- We have not noted places where fees are charged, because nearly all facilities charge a fee. Assume you will need to pay for their use. State parks recently dropped day-use fees, but they do charge for the use of camping, group, and boat-launch facilities.

Today, highways make the farthest points of South Puget Sound but a half-day's journey from any of the northern population centers. The major north–south arterial, I-5, provides the quickest route to most of the land-accessible points. The Washington State Ferry System provides a shortcut to the Kitsap and Key Peninsulas and a more leisurely approach than the longer highway routes through Tacoma or Olympia.

Ferries or private boats provide the only access to several of the islands—Vashon and Maury, Anderson, McNeil, Ketron, and Herron. Most of the other islands, except for the very small ones, are reached by bridges.

On the east side of Puget Sound, the Kitsap Peninsula can be reached from the south end by leaving I-5 in Tacoma and heading north on State Highway 16, reaching the peninsula via the Tacoma Narrows Bridge (soon to be bridges). Still another route is via US 101 from Olympia to Shelton, and then to the Kitsap Peninsula on either State Highway 3 or 106.

The east side of Hood Canal, which is lightly populated, is only minimally accessible by road. A county road extension of State Highway 300 west of Belfair skirts the north edge of the canal's "bend" as far as Tahuya. It then turns inland and wanders, sometimes paved, sometimes not, through dense forest to touch the east side of the canal at only a couple of small bays. Not until the vicinity of Seabeck, near the north end of the canal, are public recreational sites again accessible by land. North of Seabeck the huge Bangor Naval Base locks up the shore access until Lofall, the old Hood Canal ferry terminal.

The west side of Hood Canal can be reached from the south through Olympia and Shelton via US 101, a very scenic highway running along the complete length of the west shoreline of the canal. From the north end of

Kitsap Peninsula, the Hood Canal Bridge (on State Highway 104) provides a route to the west side of the canal.

Public Shorelines—Separating the Public from the Private

Parks—State, County, and City • "Public" beaches imply ownership by some public agency—city, county, state, or federal—and therefore are open for public use. State park beaches are generally associated with campgrounds, picnic areas, and other developed recreational features such as fishing piers. County and city parks are nearly always day-use, offering picnic facilities and play space.

On public tidelands, do not stray onto adjacent private land and uplands. Even if lands are unposted, do not assume they are public or that no one cares if you trespass. With the press of people moving to the area, beachfront properties command premium prices, and owners are becoming increasingly hostile to trespassers.

DNR Beaches and Other Public Accesses • Substantial stretches of public beach are owned by the Washington State Department of Natural Resources (DNR). The majority of these are accessible only by boat, and their usability varies. Most of these shorelands are public only up to mean high water line—this is the region just below the layer of driftwood or below the end of grass, trees, or other terrestrial vegetation.

The U.S. Fish and Wildlife Service controls most wildlife refuges. The state Department of Fish and Wildlife, which owns some boat launch ramps, and the U.S. Bureau of Land Management (BLM), which maintains Coast Guard–operated lighthouses, are responsible for some of the smaller segments of public shorelands.

City and County Road Ends • In some locations where a platted public road deadends into a beach, the road legally extends across the tidelands, is open to public access, and offers an easy place to launch hand-carried boats. However, do not assume that all road ends offer beach access. Those described in this book were checked by the authors and were legally open at the time of publication.

The Nature Conservancy • The Nature Conservancy, a private conservation organization supported by memberships and donations, has purchased some environmentally important property on the inland waters. In general, lands owned by this group are considered biological preserves and are open to the public for limited use—nature walks are fine, but camping and picnicking are not allowed. However, in some cases the area might be so sensitive that public visits are not permitted.

Cascadia Marine Trail • The Washington Water Trails Association, an organization of paddlers, has created the Cascadia Marine Trail (CMT), which links 150 miles of inland waterways from the southern reaches of Puget

Sound to the Canadian border. This marine trail system has set up a chain of campsites that are a reasonable day's paddle apart. Washington State Parks, the DNR, and several city and county park departments have designated primitive shoreside CMT campsites on their properties. An annual permit is required for their use, and in state parks a nominal fee is charged.

Boat Launching and Mooring Facilities

Since this book focuses on boat-oriented recreation, getting boat to water becomes extremely important; thus boat-launch sites are key to the enjoyment of the area. Both public and commercial launch facilities are noted. A fee is nearly always charged for the use of commercial facilities, and many public ramps have an honor box for depositing fees.

The quality and safety of launch facilities range from the sublime—with excellent surface, drop-off, and protection—to the ridiculously hazardous, where boaters risk getting stuck in mud at low tide or having boats reduced to splinters by ever-present winds or waves. Explore the surface of a ramp before launching, and exercise care using any launch facility until you are familiar with it. At times of wind or surges, extra care must be used to avoid damaging the boat or injuring boaters.

Launch facilities tend to change occasionally. Some are neglected and become unusable. Commercial ones close down for the season or even go out of business. On the plus side, sometimes new ones are built or old ones improved.

Commercial or port authority–run marinas normally set aside space for guest moorage, available for a daily fee. Some accept reservations. Marina facilities run the gamut from meager wooden docks clinging to ancient piers to posh resorts complete with full dockside utility hookups for boats, hot tubs for salt-encrusted crews, and attractions for stir-crazy kids.

Marine state parks are accessible only by boat; they all have mooring buoys and a few have floats, as do a few land-based parks. During busy times, rafting (two or more boats tied together, side by side) is encouraged on floats where possible.

Lineal mooring systems, installed in a number of heavily used areas, allows more moorage in a small area and is easier on the environment, as it greatly reduces the damage done to the seabed by dragging buoy anchor blocks and boat anchor chains. These 200-foot-long cables, strung between a pair of pylons, have mooring eyes along the cable to which boats can tie.

Park buoy anchor blocks are set reasonably solid, generally in 2 fathoms of water or more, with sufficient swing room to avoid collisions with neighbors; however, they are not designed in either strength or placement to accommodate a rafted fleet of boats. Follow these guidelines:

- Boats less than 24 feet long, four boats
- Boats from 25 to 36 feet long, three boats
- Boats from 37 to 45 feet long, two boats
- Boats more than 45 feet long must tie up singly on buoys

During severe weather, rafting should be significantly fewer.

Recreation on Washington's Inland Waters

One of the most remarkable aspects of Puget Sound is the variety of activities the water and shores engender. They offer something for all ages, from tots experiencing the first squish of sand through toes, to senior citizens enjoying retirement with leisurely beach strolls or boat cruises. Here you'll find boating to satisfy every taste from yachting to kayaking and canoeing as well as bicycling, camping, picnicking, birdwatching, beach walking, hiking, scuba diving, and more. Nature preserves, historical sites, and scenic vistas make this a destination to please nearly every visitor.

Boating and Paddling ... And Doing It Safely • Puget Sound residents do like their boating. You have only to take a quick look at the forest of masts in the many marinas, or glance at the parking lots full of boat trailers at the larger launch sites, to quickly establish that fact. Billowing sails and throbbing motors don't tell the whole story, however; peek into any secluded bay and you will probably find kayakers in search of shoreline sights that the crews of larger boats might never find.

Boating, as referred to here, runs the complete spectrum of conveyances that float, from kayaks and canoes to pleasure cruisers and sailboats. Regardless of the size or shape of your transportation, certain fundamentals and cautions apply to all who use these waterways. In many places throughout the text, comments refer to "paddlecraft" or "small boats," a vague category including dinghies, rubber rafts, canoes, and kayaks, or, in general, any watercraft that is muscle powered, or has minimal power. Safety cautions can also apply to boaters in larger boats who have had little experience in handling adverse conditions, whatever the size of the craft.

A boater's best ally in navigating safely is "sea savvy": a generous helping of common sense augmented by boating safety courses and instruction in safely operating one's vessel. Before committing your safety as well as that of a boatload of family or friends to your competence, take one of the excellent courses that are available through either the U.S. Power Squadron or the U.S. Coast Guard Auxiliary. Information can be obtained through the U.S. Coast Guard. Note that state law now requires that each occupant of a boat have available a wearable floatation device in case of emergency.

Be especially aware that these waters are frequently used by scuba divers. Use caution in the vicinity of known dive areas and be on the watch for the red flag with a white diagonal stripe that marks areas where scuba divers are working. When approaching beaches, cut boat speed to a minimum and watch for swimmers in the water.

Renting a boat for a day of fishing or exploration, or chartering one for an extended cruise, is common. This book notes places where such boats are available. No matter what size the craft, to attempt boating without somebody on board who is experienced is folly. Most charter operators will check out clients before turning a boat over to them; if prospective boaters are obviously unqualified to operate a vessel safely, the charter operator might give them a quick course, or might insist that an experienced skipper go along (for a fee). All required safety gear is included with the rental.

The text makes particular mention of places that are appropriate for paddling—that is, muscle-powered boating in kayaks, canoes, dinghies, or inflatables. While this is the ideal way to reach many of the beaches along the sound, extreme care must be used, with an eye to tide rips and currents, the weather, and even larger boats. Crossing channels can be quite hazardous for the inexperienced. Classes are available in larger cities; guided trips are an ideal introduction to the sport.

NAVIGATION. This book attempts to address major boating concerns, but it is not possible to cover all navigational hazards that might affect all kinds of boaters. In some places, water depths and particular current problems are noted; however, nothing can take the place of a good navigational chart, an accurate compass, and the knowledge of how to use both. The best chart for close-in navigating is the one with the largest scale—that is, showing the greatest detail.

ROCKS AND SHOALS. Most serious navigational hazards in this area, such as rocks and shoals, are marked with lights, buoys, or similar navigational devices. Another warning of a rock or reef is long streamers of bull kelp floating on the surface—approach any bed of kelp cautiously. However, with a potential tidal variation of 16 to 20 feet at extreme tides, normally submerged and safe rocks and reefs can come dangerously close to the surface at extreme minus tides, and underwater shoals and bars can become a four-hour or more resting place for the sailor who doesn't keep a wary eye on the chart, tide table, and depth sounder.

TIDAL CURRENT. Tidal current is not the same as the tide, although one does give rise to the other. *Tides* measure the vertical distance that water rises and falls above the sea floor due to the gravitational attraction of the sun and moon, as well as more obscure influences. *Tidal currents* represent the horizontal flow of water resulting from the rise and fall of the tide.

Tidal currents in Puget Sound vary from 1 to 10 knots. In addition, the various interconnecting waterways found in Puget Sound give rise to some rather illogical directions of tidal currents. The small-craft portfolio of charts indicate position, direction, and average speed of the current at maximum flood or ebb tide at specific, measured points. *Tidal current tables* (not tide tables), which are printed annually, are keyed to station points on the charts. The approximate time of maximum velocity of the current can be computed by referencing the tidal current tables to a chart's station point. Although many other factors enter into the actual surface velocity, and even the direction of the current, general knowledge of the predicted velocity is invaluable for safe navigation.

TIDE RIPS. Navigational charts typically bear notations of "tide rips" off points of land between channels. Tide rips are caused by either the impact of tidal currents meeting from differing directions or the upwelling of currents as they meet underwater cliffs. In either case the surface appearance is the same: the water appears to dance across an area in small to moderate choppy waves and appears to swirl like a whirlpool. A boat crossing a tide-rip area might have difficulty maintaining course when erratic currents spin the vessel first one way and then another. Persons in small boats such as kayaks might find rips an experience that should be avoided. The positive aspect of tide rips is that the upwelling current also brings to the surface food-chain elements that attract game fish and therefore are ideal fishing spots. They are also a likely place to spot seals and birds attracted by the good eating.

VESSEL TRAFFIC. Some sections of Puget Sound are heavily used by commercial vessels, naval vessels, ferries, fishing boats, and recreational boats, making it seem downright crowded at times. Rules of the road specify who stays clear from whom under what conditions; however, don't risk life, limb, and the hull of your boat assuming another captain knows those rules and will follow them. A sailboat skipper shouting "Starboard tack!" at a large power vessel closing at high speed might end up getting his satisfaction in court—after he has been fished from the sound.

To bring order to large vessel traffic, the Coast Guard has installed a Vessel Traffic Service (VTS) on Puget Sound. Northbound and southbound traffic lanes have been designated down the center of the sound; they are marked on all area charts. The ½-nautical-mile-wide traffic lanes lie on either side of a ¼-nautical-mile-wide separation zone, which has midchannel buoys marking every point at which the lanes alter direction. Radar stations are located at key points on Puget Sound to track vessel traffic; all radar signals feed into the Coast Guard VTS Center on Pier 36 on the Seattle waterfront.

Boating in South Puget Sound waters is usually a simple matter. Even so, skippers must follow boating regulations as well as use common sense.

Large vessels are required to participate in the system. Communication with the VTS Center is over VHF channel 14; boaters concerned with the location of large-vessel traffic, especially in fog, can monitor this frequency for information. Smaller commercial and recreational vessels generally don't participate in the VTS; however, they will probably appear on the center's radar, depending on their size and radar reflectance. These boats can contact the center in emergencies, and the center will provide assistance, if possible.

Another potential traffic problem, especially at night during commercial salmon fishing season, is dozens of fishing boats with nets deployed. Proper lights on fishing boats and nets should identify areas to avoid, but a sharp lookout is required to spot these lights and avoid snagging nets.

WEATHER. Summer favors Puget Sound and Hood Canal with mild temperatures, moderate weather, and light winds. However, sudden summer storms come up occasionally; in other seasons the waters in this area can at times be downright nasty and dangerous. Prevailing storm winds come from the southwest; the shift of wind to that direction, plus a falling barometer, bodes worsening weather.

In sections of North Puget Sound, steep terrain that forces winds along the direction of a waterway can produce an effect called "channeling," or "gap winds," which causes the speed of the wind to increase by as much as double. In the Strait of Juan de Fuca, winds near the west entrance have reached up to 65 knots as a result of channeling.

The middle section of Puget Sound has a particular weather anomaly known as a "convergence zone." Low-level winds from the west off the ocean split as they encounter the Olympic Mountains. A portion loops south around the mountain range and then goes back north, downsound. Another portion loops north through the Strait of Juan de Fuca and then heads south, up the sound. When these two fronts of winds meet head-on (generally in the area between Seattle and Everett), a violent local weather front is sometimes created, with localized high winds, rain, and at times thunder and lightning.

FOG. In the inland waters, the price often paid for warm sunny summer days is morning fog created by the temperature differential between the sun-warmed land masses and the perpetually chilly waters. Early departure plans should include a well-plotted compass course to destinations that might disappear in the sea-level morning mist. Although this fog generally lifts by midday, a planned early departure might have to be delayed.

CHOPPY WATERS. A phenomenon peculiar to long, open, relatively shallow channels such as East Channel or Port Orchard Channel are substantial seas with a very short, steep wave form, in contrast to the broader swells built in the deep channel of the Strait of Juan de Fuca or the open ocean. This generally occurs when wind-built waves are met by strong tidal currents from the opposite direction. The choppy seas chew away at forward boat speed and provide persons prone to seasickness an excellent opportunity to head for the lee rail. The conditions can be very dangerous for small boats, as they might be swamped or overturned. The best defense against being caught by adverse weather conditions is a regular monitoring of the NOAA weather channel, VHF channel WX1 (FM 162.550 MHz).

ANCHORING. When anchoring, whether in a marine state park or in another protected area, be sure your hook is properly set and that the swing of your vessel will not let you collide with others. In a tight anchorage it might be useful to also set a stern anchor, or row a stern line ashore and tie it to a tree in order to reduce swing.

Check predicted tide levels to make sure you have enough water under you for the duration of your stay and that the proper length of anchor rope has been payed out. Contrary to the rules proclaimed in some boating "bibles," an anchor scope of seven times the water depth generally is not necessary and is almost impossible to achieve in small coves. In all but the most severe weather, a three-to-one scope is adequate with a well-set anchor and considerably more courteous for others who might want to share a crowded anchorage. It is also more environment friendly, because dragging anchor chains damage the seabed—the shorter the chain, the less the damage.

Walking and Hiking • Very little of the footbound exercise described in this book is vigorous enough to be categorized as hiking. For the most part it involves easy strolls to viewpoints, short nature loops through forested glades, or walks along beaches. With time out for birdwatching, flower smelling, rock skipping, or any of many other diversions, most of the walks described are ample enough to fill an afternoon. For extended walks, many of the public areas can be linked by walking the beach at low tide or following city streets at high tide.

Do not approach too close to the top edge of bluffs because they might crumble. To compound the problem, the tops of many such bluffs are covered with a grass that is quite slippery, especially for smooth-soled shoes. At no time should hikers attempt to ascend or descend a bluff if there is no trail; when trails are present, use care because even they can become treacherously slippery.

Long walks on DNR beaches can be found in some locations. Many are very dependent on tide levels, because a wide, gradually sloping beach can disappear within four or five hours beneath an incoming tide. Note the time of the next tide change and plan your walk to avoid getting trapped in some uncomfortable or unsafe place such as below steep bluffs or impenetrable brush.

Bicycling • Nearly all the areas encompassed in this book are well suited to bicycle exploration. Many shoreline roads are quite popular for both one-day and extended bicycle trips. Because traffic tends to keep to the inland highways and freeways, many roads are lightly traveled yet are level and smoothly paved. Beware of logging trucks, especially on backroads of the Kitsap Peninsula. They travel fast, are not maneuverable, and require a long distance to stop.

US 101 along Hood Canal is popular for long trips and, with a few exceptions, has shoulders wide enough for safe and comfortable bicycling. Highway 106 along the south side of the bend of Hood Canal is another well-used bicycle route; however, the road is narrow and twisty and traffic is generally heavy. Follow all bicycling safety rules.

Picnicking and Camping • Picnic facilities, found in nearly all of the developed state, county, and city parks, are for day use only and cannot be used for overflow camping. These sites usually hold only picnic tables and either fire braziers, fireplaces, or fire rings. Usually water and restrooms are nearby. Most also have one or more picnic shelters, some with kitchens.

As funding has become available, park facilities have become increasingly barrier free. A number of the parks have restrooms, parking spots, and one or more picnic sites, shelters, or campsites that have been modified to eliminate access impediments. For more information, contact the individual park.

Toilet facilities are classified in this book as *restrooms, toilets,* and *composting toilets.* When you are in need of one, it probably doesn't matter to you which is which. *Restrooms,* by our definition, have flush toilets and running water for washing up. If they also include showers, it is noted. What we classify as *toilets* are little houses that sit over a dirt pit or have a holding tank that is pumped out at regular intervals. They do not have running water. *Composting toilets* are popular for remote parks because of their efficiency, safety, and decreased odor. In these, disease-causing organisms are destroyed and wastes are broken down by special bacteria and fungi to a compost similar to garden soil. *Note:* Boaters and campers should not empty portable toilets into these composting toilets because the addition of other chemicals and water might hinder bacterial growth.

Some state parks will accept campsite reservations online or via a telephone reservation system. Refer to appendix A for phone numbers and Website addresses. Camping at unreserved sites is on a first-come, first-served basis. Fees are collected nightly for all campsites, and campgrounds are closed after 10:00 PM In this book we note the different types of sites found in the parks.

- *Standard campsites* have a car pullout, either a fireplace (a ground-level metal enclosure on a concrete pad) or brazier (metal enclosure on a waist-high metal stand), picnic table, and a level tent pad. Water and toilets are nearby. If utilities hookups are available for RVs, they are noted by E (electricity), W (water), and S (sewer). If a trailer dump station is in the park, it is noted.
- *Walk-in campsites,* favored by bicyclists and hikers, are similar, but have no vehicle pullout and are a short distance from the road. Some walk-in, primitive, and group campsites have one or two Adirondack shelters. These are three-sided affairs with a sloping cedar roof and usually four wood-planked bunks.
- *Primitive campsites,* as defined by Washington State Parks, hold only a picnic table and fire ring (designated fire area surrounded by rocks), fireplace (low concrete enclosure topped with a metal grate), or brazier. Toilets are nearby, but water might not be available. This type of campsite is found in all of the marine state parks.

- *CMT campsites*, reserved for kayakers and other paddle-powered boaters, are near water's edge and are usually primitive. Toilets are available at or near the campsites, but other amenities are limited—often the site is just a spot level enough for a tent. Open fires are either not permitted or are strongly discouraged, and potable water is available only at those sites that are associated with other fully developed camping facilities.
- *Group campsites*, which usually require a reservation, have space for large groups to camp together and usually have a picnic shelter and dedicated restrooms.

Wildlife Viewing and Birdwatching • If you don't bring binoculars with you on your excursion, you probably will wish you had. You are almost certain to see some local wildlife. You might spot harbor seals or river otters. Sea lions often haul out on bell buoy platforms or beaches.

The San Juan Islands are well known for whale sighting; however, whales might also be seen at many places in the inland waters, even in Seattle's Elliott Bay. If you should see a group of whales while boating, move away, or move parallel to them, at the speed of the slowest ones. Look in all directions before approaching or departing. A minimum distance of 100 yards is required by law. Failure to heed this can result in a severe fine.

You could have a good time just trying to identify all the different gulls you see on the shores. However, birdlife extends far beyond gulls, from skittery little shorebirds to tuneful perching birds and soaring eagles and hawks. Grab a bird guide and go!

Harvesting Seafood: Beach Foraging, Fishing, and Scuba Diving • One of the greatest excitements of the seashore is the prospect of gathering food fresh from the water for a seaside feast or a quick trip home to the dinner table. Washington's inland waters are home to more than fifty varieties of sport fish, many of which make excellent eating. Salmon, the prize of Puget Sound sport fish, are frequently caught in areas where opposing tidal flows meet and form tide rips, concentrating food sources for the salmon.

Many state regulations cover seafood harvesting in Washington. Additional regulations cover specific parks, reefs, marine sanctuaries, and similar areas. *You are responsible for knowing the regulations, following them, and having appropriate licenses.* A pamphlet published by the state Department of Fish and Wildlife, available in most sporting goods stores, lists bag limits, seasons, licenses required, and other restrictions. Complete current information can be accessed on the DFW website at *wdfw.wa.gov/fishcorn.htm.* Local regulations for parks and similar areas are prominently posted at that site. *Before removing anything from a beach, check reader boards for any postings.*

Be especially aware that state regulations require that holes dug on a beach for purposes of gathering clams *must always* be refilled. The incoming tide might take three or four cycles to fill holes; in the meantime small marine animals trapped on top of the pile are exposed to the sun and might die of dehydration, and others trapped under the pile might suffocate.

All state parks and some county and city parks have regulations protecting nonfood forms of marine creatures, such as limpets, barnacles, starfish, and sand dollars. Although it is not illegal to take a small non-living souvenir of a beach trip, such as an empty seashell, small rock, or piece of driftwood, please use restraint in the quantity you take, or better yet, leave it. Even non-living beach objects such as driftwood and empty shells are an important part of the marine environment, forming growing sites for marine plants, providing homes for small creatures, and helping to control erosion. Many tidelands in populated areas along the sound were once a bright tapestry of marine life but are now virtually barren due to longtime abuse by beachcombers, coupled with the effects of pollution.

Beachcombers can occasionally find historical treasures washed up on shore, such as debris from shipwrecks, some nearly a hundred years old, and pioneer artifacts that were imbedded in eroding underwater cliffs near areas of early settlement. The removal of historical artifacts is prohibited in some areas. Before taking anything away, be sure to check if it is legal.

PARALYTIC SHELLFISH POISONING (RED TIDE OR PSP). The state Department of Health periodically issues a "red tide warning" and closes particular beaches on Puget Sound. The name "red tide" itself contributes to the public's confusion, for it is not always visibly red, it has nothing at all to do with the tide, and not all red algae are harmful.

PSP is a serious, and sometimes fatal, illness caused by *Gonyaulax catenella*, a toxic, single-celled, amber-colored alga that is always present in the water in small numbers. During spring, summer, and fall, certain environmental conditions might combine to permit a rapid multiplication or accumulation of these microscopic organisms. Most shellfish toxicity occurs when the concentrations of *G. catenella* are too sparse to discolor the water; however, the free-floating plants sometime become so numerous that the water appears to have a reddish cast—thus the name red tide.

Bivalve shellfish such as clams, oysters, mussels, and scallops, which feed by filtering seawater, might ingest millions of the organisms and concentrate the toxin in their bodies. The poison is retained by most of these shellfish for several weeks after the occurrence of the red tide; butter clams can be poisonous for much longer.

When the concentration of the toxin in mollusks reaches a certain level, it becomes hazardous to humans who eat them. *The toxins cannot be destroyed by cooking, and cannot be reliably detected by any means other than laboratory analysis.* Symptoms of PSP, beginning with tingling of the lips and tongue, might occur within a half hour of ingestion. The illness attacks the nervous system, causing loss of control of arms and legs, difficulty in breathing, paralysis, and, in extreme cases, death.

Shellfish on Puget Sound are under regular surveillance by the state Department of Health. Marine toxin/PSP warnings are issued, and some beaches are posted, when high levels of toxin are detected in tested mollusks. Warnings are publicized by the media; for current information as to which beaches are closed to shellfish harvesting, check the marine biotoxin Website at *www.doh.wa.gov/gis/mogifs/biotoxin.htm* or the phone hotline at (800) 562-5632.

POLLUTION. Both chemical and biological pollution have so thoroughly contaminated beaches in King County that harvesting of bottomfish, crab, or shellfish is not recommended along any of its shores. Similar problems afflict several beaches and bays in metropolitan areas of Kitsap and Snohomish Counties and some limited areas on Hood Canal in Mason and Jefferson Counties. Fish and shellfish from these areas have been found to have high levels of pollutants in their body tissues. A continuous diet of such animals can pose a health hazard. Hazardous beaches are generally posted. If in doubt, inquire.

Chemical pollution occurs near industrial areas, such as Harbor Island and Commencement Bay. Biological contamination occurs in areas where runoff from barnyards or sewage finds its way into the water or where large numbers of seals or sea lions congregate. In the far reaches of some of the inlets, where water movement is restricted, such pollution can occur.

Swimming ● Some beaches along the sound are shallow and therefore warm enough for saltwater bathing in summer, especially in the southern reaches. Because of the close confines, wave action is nominal except in foul weather, and with some notable exceptions such as the Tacoma Narrows, the current

Puget Sound and Hood Canal shellfish are sweet and succulent. In only a few areas and at a few times pollution and other contamination might be a problem.

is weak near beaches and poses little hazard. However, none of the public beaches, including those in the state parks, have lifeguards; swimming is at the participant's risk and should not be done alone or unwatched.

Using the Public Parks: Rules, Regulations, and Courtesy

Rules and regulations in the various areas are set up to preserve the natural environment and to maintain the safety and pleasure of all visitors, as well as park neighbors.

The following comments apply specifically to parks operated by the Washington State Parks and Recreation Commission. In general, these same rules, where relevant, also apply to county parks. When using any area, check for specific rules and regulations that are prominently posted or are found in pamphlets available at the entrance.

Some activities listed here might not be specifically covered by park rules but affect the aesthetics and environmental well-being of the area and the enjoyment of others. While visiting, be courteous and considerate of other park users and treat the park itself with care.

FEES. Fees are charged for use of many state park facilities. Campsite reservations can be made online at the parks website, *www.parks.wa.gov* or by calling (888) CAMPOUT or (888) 226-7688. Check the Website or contact the specific park for information on group areas. The Website also lists current fees.

CAMPING. Camp only in designated areas; camping is limited to ten consecutive days at any one park. Do not ditch tents, cut green trees or boughs, hammer nails into trees, or in any other way mutilate nature in the quest for a perfect campsite. Clean up your campsite after using it.

FIRES. Build fires only in designated fireplaces and fire rings. Fire hazard can be extreme in summer. Before leaving, be sure your campfire is completely extinguished and the embers are cold. Beach fires are prohibited.

Portable charcoal-burning barbecues or hibachis placed on the boat floats can badly char them; when using any such stove, be sure the wood is properly shielded from the heat. Some places prohibit the use of such stoves on docks.

Gathering fallen trees, branches, and driftwood for campfires is prohibited in all state parks. Decaying wood provides valuable nutrients to the forest ecology, and driftwood helps prevent beach erosion. Either bring firewood with you, or, where it is available, purchase it at a campground registration booth or at a store.

GARBAGE. Trash receptacles are provided at the larger state parks; please use them. Many of the smaller, more remote marine state parks have neither garbage cans nor garbage collection. In areas where garbage cans are not provided, all trash must be removed. Recycling is encouraged.

When on boats, do not "deep-six" debris, whether it is cans, bottles, orange peels, or chicken bones. It usually does not come to permanent rest six fathoms down, as the slang expression implies, but will eventually wash up on some beach as ugly litter.

LIVING THINGS. Feeding, hunting, or harassing of wildlife and discharge of firearms is prohibited within the state parks and most other parks. Plants may not be dug up, nor flowers picked.

VEHICLES AND BICYCLES. Motorized vehicles and bicycles are prohibited on service roads and trails. Observe posted speed limits on public roads within parks.

BOATS. In the moorage area of marine state parks, the boat speed limit is 3 mph (no-wake speed). In addition to being extremely annoying to other boaters, hot-rodding or racing, even in small outboard-powered dinghies, can create a wake that might swamp small craft, send hot food flying from a cruiser's galley range, or cause other damage. Boaters are legally responsible for any damage caused by their wakes.

Moorage on buoys, floats, and lineal mooring systems is on a first-come, first-served basis. The practice of individuals attempting to "reserve" space by tying a dinghy to a buoy or float space is not legal in the state parks. Continuous moorage is limited to three consecutive nights.

It is courteous to use the minimum moorage space possible on a float. Beach small boats whenever you can, instead of tying up to a float. Berth small cruisers or runabouts as far inboard as possible, leaving the end of the float for larger boats that require deeper water and more maneuvering space.

PETS. Pets must be on a leash no longer than 8 feet and must be under control at all times. They are not permitted on designated swimming beaches. Pet owners must clean up after their animals; violators are subject to fines.

NOISE. Because sounds carry greater distances over water, use care that radios or overly boisterous noise do not penetrate to nearby boats or campsites. Report disturbances to park rangers.

VANDALISM. It probably does little good to talk about intentional vandalism here. The damaging or removal of park property is, of course, illegal, and if you observe it, you should report it to the proper authorities.

Some acts of vandalism, however, are committed out of thoughtlessness or ignorance. Defacing park property or rocks or other natural features by spray painting or scratching graffiti is vandalism and will be prosecuted.

Digging into banks with shovels, picks, or any similar tool is also prohibited. Holes dug in beaches for clamming or for any other purpose must be refilled.

Safety Considerations

Boating and beach travel entail unavoidable risks that every traveler must be aware of and respect. The fact that an area is described in this book is not a representation that it will be safe for you. The areas described herein vary greatly in the amount and kind of preparation needed to enjoy them safely. Some might have changed since this book was written, or conditions might have deteriorated. Weather conditions can change daily or even hourly, and tide levels will also vary considerably. An area that is safe in good weather at low or slack tide might be completely unsafe during inclement weather or at times of high tide or maximum tidal current. You can meet these and other risks safely by exercising your own independent judgment and common sense. Be aware of your own limitations, those of your vessel, and of conditions when and where you are traveling. If conditions are dangerous, or if you are not prepared to deal with them safely, change your plans. Each year many people enjoy safe trips on Washington's shores and inland waters. With proper preparation and good judgment, you can, too.

The Mountaineers Books

Emergency Assistance and Other Concerns

In parks where rangers or managers are not on duty, the proper authority can be reached by marine or citizens band (CB) radio if immediate action is necessary. From cell phones, the quick-dial number, *CG, immediately connects the caller to the Coast Guard Vessel Traffic Center in Seattle. The center coordinates marine safety and rescue activities in the region. Be prepared to explain the nature of the emergency and your exact location.

The U.S. Coast Guard has primary responsibility for safety and law enforcement on the water. Marine VHF channel 16 is continuously monitored by the Coast Guard and should be the most reliable means of contact in case of emergencies on the water. The Coast Guard monitors CB channel 9 at some locations and times, but it has no commitment to full-time radio watch on this channel. Several volunteer groups do an excellent job of monitoring the CB emergency frequency and will assist as best they can by relaying emergency requests to the proper authorities

Overall legal authority in all unincorporated areas of the state rests with the county sheriff. The emergency number is 911. Complaints or other business should be referred to the sheriff's office. A list of phone numbers and addresses for parks and legal agencies is included in appendix A. In matters of less urgency, park rangers should be contacted by telephone or in writing.

chapter one

Seattle

SEATTLE STRETCHES ALONG THE EAST SHORE of Puget Sound for more than 20 miles, filling shore, bluff, and ravine with residences and commercial enterprises. The city once fronted only on Elliott Bay, but today it has extended so far north and south that it dominates much of Puget Sound's midsection, and its skyscrapers and Space Needle have become navigational landmarks from miles away.

Amid the city's metropolitan sprawl are an array of public facilities and

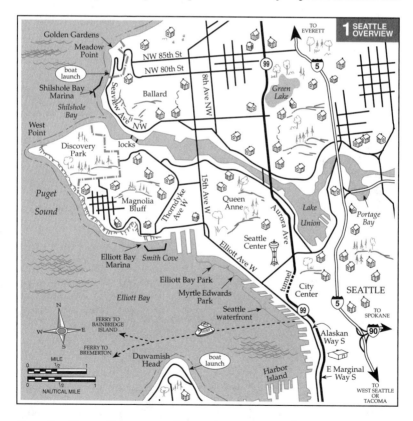

Opposite: *Masts of boats moored at Smith Cove Marina frame the Space Needle and skyscrapers of downtown Seattle.*

accesses—some sublime, some fascinating, and some deliberately obscure. Here can be seen nearly every facet of the city—historical, natural, recreational, and scenic as well as workaday.

SHILSHOLE AND SALMON BAYS
Map 2

Golden Gardens (City of Seattle)   Map 2
Beach walking • Swimming • Picnicking • Wading • Paddling • Fishing • Sailboarding • Scuba diving • Birdwatching • Kite flying

Facilities: Picnic tables, firepits, picnic shelters, restrooms, concession stand, teen center, volleyball courts, basketball court, children's play equipment, off-leash dog area

Area: 87.8 acres; 3850 feet of shoreline

Lower (beach) entrance: From Aurora Avenue (SR 99) head west on N 46th Street, which becomes NW Market Street as it drops downhill into Ballard. Follow Market through Ballard, and then take NW 54th Street west past the Hiram Chittenden Locks. 54th bends north and becomes Seaview Avenue NW, which passes Shilshole Bay Marina and deadends at the park.

Upper entrance: Continue west on NW Market Street past NW 54th Street for two blocks, and turn north on 32nd Avenue NW. At NW 85th Street continue north on Golden Gardens Drive NW, which winds down to the park.

Paddlecraft can be beached at the park, which is immediately north of Shilshole Bay Marina. The nearest launch ramp is Eddie Vine ramp, immediately south of the park.

During sunny summer weather, hordes of Seattle sun worshipers are lured to Golden Gardens. For over eighty years the beaches of Meadow Point, north

Kite flying is just one of many ways to have fun at Golden Gardens.

of Shilshole Bay, have seen a succession of youths engaged in the courting rituals of the time, picnickers on family outings, and mothers tending toddlers enthralled with building fantasies in the sand. The former bathhouse has been renovated to create a teen and community activity center. Named in 1907 by its owners, Harry and Olive Treat, the beach was then the terminus of a trolley line that offered city dwellers a salt-air retreat—surely it was only a coincidence that the route passed through adjoining areas of prime real estate huckstering.

The park is split by the railroad tracks; to the east is an off-leash dog area and a wooded sidehill threaded by trails, while west of the tracks is the 3/4-mile-long golden strand of sand topped by silvered driftwood for which the park is so well known. Icy Puget Sound waters, flowing over the shallow bottom, warm in summer to temperatures pleasant enough for swimming and wading.

Although the beach throng in itself might be enough entertainment for the day, there's also the stream of boats in and out of the north entrance to the marina, the tug and freighter traffic on the sound, and the rugged peaks of the Olympic Mountains. Fly a kite, launch a sailboard, watch a sailboat race, or just hunker in the driftwood and beach grass for a tan and a semblance of solitude.

The park is a nice place to visit even on a blustery winter day when the beach crowd has departed and the bite of wind across the sand brings refreshing memories of our common saltwater origin. Take along binoculars to watch for loons, black brant, and other seabirds on their migratory routes.

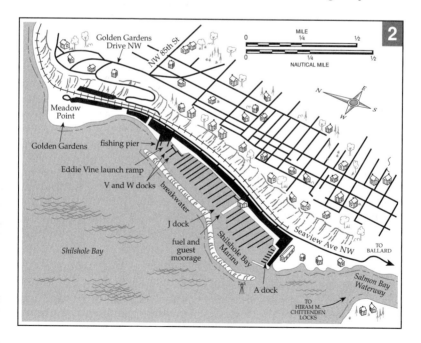

Eddie Vine Boat Launch (City of Seattle)   Map 2

Fishing • Boating • Paddling

Facilities: 4 paved launch ramps with boarding floats, toilets, bait, concession stand, fishing pier

Immediately south of Golden Gardens on Seaview Avenue NW is the Eddie Vine launch ramp, a 95-foot-wide asphalt ramp with boarding floats along either side and down the middle. It is busy year-round as a launch point for the hordes of anglers plying the sound. There is ample parking for about a hundred cars and trailers in two large lots north of the ramp. A concession stand/bait shop is just south of the ramp. The wavebreak at the north side of the launch area has a walkway on top (disabled accessible), which allows it to be used as a fishing and crabbing pier.

Shilshole Bay Marina (Port of Seattle)   Map 2

Boating • Paddling • Restaurants

Facilities: Guest moorage with power, phone, and water, diesel, gas, propane, wireless broadband, boat launch (cranes, hoist), limited groceries, ice, fishing piers, bait, tackle, marine supplies and repairs, dry storage, marine pumpout station, portable toilet dump, restrooms, showers, laundry, restaurants

See directions to the lower entrance to Golden Gardens, described above.

The marina lies on Shilshole Bay. There are entrances at either end of the breakwater, and guest moorage is alongside the central pier between I and J docks.

The vast boat "parking lot" on the north shore of Seattle is a certified tourist attraction, agleam with fiberglass, mahogany, teak, brass, chrome, aluminum, and acres of bright blue canvas. It's the place to bring visitors to show them a little of what boating on Puget Sound is about or the place for locals to go to dream about their first boat—or their next one.

Shilshole Bay Marina is the second largest saltwater moorage on Puget Sound, surpassed only by the Port of Everett Marina. A multiyear waiting list for permanent moorage attests to its popularity. Permanent moorage is not the only attraction, as the marina also offers full services for visiting boaters, as well as nautical-related shops and a restaurant with spectacular views over a forest of masts in the basin to profiles of distant Olympic peaks. The marina has provided moorage to Seattle residents and visitors for more than thirty years. Work began on the breakwater in 1957, and the marina itself was built over a period of twenty years. Today it has nearly fifteen hundred permanent slips and about seventy-five guest moorages, plus areas for dry storage. The port plans to repair and add to existing piers and slips between 2005 and 2008.

The main guest moorage area is alongside the central pier between I and J docks, and rafting is permitted up to five boats deep. There is also limited guest moorage at the north end along the north side of W dock. A boat repair yard with hoists is at A dock. Restrooms and showers are along the parking area; the buildings above J and L docks also have laundry facilities. Most of

Shilshole Bay Marina, with around fifteen hundred slips, is one of the largest such facilities on the West Coast.

the marina shops, restaurants, and facilities are in the administration building near the center of the marina. Fuel, groceries, supplies, and a marine pumpout station are near the end of the central pier between I and J docks. For visitors arriving by boat, the Metro bus runs at regular intervals along Seaview Avenue. The Ballard district, with dozens of shops and services, is a few minutes' ride away; downtown Seattle is a little farther.

Walk the promenade along the bulkhead at the head of the docks and choose the boat of your dreams from those tethered at the moorages below; however, except for guest docks, all dock gates are locked and accessible only by tenants. Fishing is permitted from the end section of A dock and from the pier forming the wavebreak at the far north end of the marina, north of the launch ramps.

Hiram M. Chittenden Locks (U.S. Army Corps of Engineers) Map 3

Boating • Sightseeing • Museum • Fish ladder • Picnicking • Fishing

Facilities: Boat locks, restrooms, museum, gardens, fish ladder. *Commodore Park:* Boat launch (hand-carry)

🚗 From Aurora Avenue (SR 99) head west on N 46th Street, which becomes NW Market Street as it drops downhill into Ballard. Follow Market through Ballard, and then take NW 54th Street west for a block to the entrance to the lock's parking lot.

🚤 The west end of the two locks is the range-marked channel southeast of Shilshole Bay. For safety reasons, people arriving at the locks by boat are not permitted to leave their vessels to go ashore in the locks or in temporary mooring areas, and those on shore may not board boats.

The transition from salt- to freshwater, from tidal to nontidal, and from the outer shores to the heart of the city takes place in a 6-mile-long, east–west channel dividing Seattle in two. Two sets of locks near the west end of the channel permit boat access from Shilshole Bay into Salmon Bay.

The locks are the best free show in town; every year more than a million visitors watch the tos and fros of commercial tugs, barges, fishing boats, tour boats, military vessels, and hordes of recreational craft. Although there are other locks in the United States larger than these, none handle more vessel traffic. The locks are in operation continuously; however, the best boat-watching is on the weekend during good weather.

The lock complex, operated by the U.S. Army Corps of Engineers, consists of two parallel locks—the larger 825 feet long and 80 feet wide, and the smaller 150 feet long and 28 feet wide. Both are capable of lifting boats a vertical distance of 6 to 26 feet, depending on the level of the tide on the saltwater side. To the south of the small lock is a spillway dam constructed to control the level of the water in Lake Washington and the navigational channel.

Carl S. English Jr. Ornamental Gardens • At the entrance to the lock grounds is a 7-acre arboretum containing native and exotic trees, shrubs, and flowers. In spring, the rhododendrons and azaleas add a swath of bright color to the nautical scene. A terraced lawn is designed as a spot to watch lock traffic and perhaps enjoy a midday picnic.

Visitor Center • Adjacent to the gardens, a visitor center features displays on the history and operation of the locks and the role of the Corps of Engineers in the Pacific Northwest. Hours are May 1 through September 30, 10:00 AM to 6:00 PM daily; October 1 through April 30, 10:00 AM to 4:00 PM, closed Tuesday and Wednesday.

Fish Ladder • Because the inland freshwater lakes and streams were vital spawning grounds for over a third of a million salmon and seagoing trout,

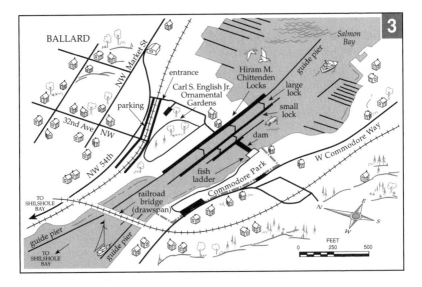

Boats, seen here loading into the large locks, are raised a vertical distance of 6 to 26 feet, depending on the tide level.

a fish ladder allows fish to move gradually up the grade. A viewing gallery with windows into a portion of the ladder is located along the south side of the locks; displays in the gallery identify the various species of fish and explain their migratory cycles and the operation of the ladder. Salmon can be seen from June through November; steelhead and cutthroat trout from September through February. The gallery can be reached from the grounds of the locks by crossing the lock gates and the walkway adjacent the dam.

Commodore Park (City of Seattle) • On the south side of the locks, adjoining the fish ladder is a fine grassy park that also can be reached by car from W Commodore Way. Hand-carry access to the water is behind the wooden guide pier on the southwest side of the locks. Stairs and disabled-accessible concrete ramps lead down to the waterfront promenade, where there are a few benches sheltered by concrete roofs and some nearby fire braziers in the grass. Because of the closeness of the fish ladder, particular fishing restrictions are posted.

MAGNOLIA BLUFF
Map 4

The freshwater side of Seattle is described in a companion volume: *Lakes, Bays, and Waterways, Afoot and Afloat*. In this book we remain on the saltwater side and the 200-foot-high, handsome bluff that dominates the city shoreline. Although much of Magnolia Bluff is residential, the very best part of the area—the extreme tip—has become a fine park. Here, within a short bus ride from most metropolitan areas, is a grand wilderness for all to enjoy.

Discovery Park (City of Seattle)   Map 4

Hiking • Picnicking • Beach walking • Birdwatching • Bicycling • Historical site • Lighthouse • Nature programs • Native cultural center

Facilities: Environmental Learning Center, Native American cultural center, trails, bicycle paths, nature trail, picnic tables, restrooms, fitness trail, sports fields (volleyball, soccer, basketball), tennis courts, museum, children's play area

Area: 512.5 acres; 12,000 feet of shoreline

🚌 *East entrance and Visitor Center:* Use exits from 15th Avenue W at either the Magnolia Bridge, Dravus Street W, or W Emerson Street, which angles northwest as West Emerson Place. From the west end of the Magnolia Bridge, turn northwest on Thorndyke Avenue W, which becomes 20th Avenue W, Gilman Avenue W, and then W Government Way, which ends at the park gate. From the Dravus Street exit, turn north on 20th Avenue W and follow the preceding route. The W Emerson exit leads to this route at Gilman Avenue W. *South parking lot:* Drive to the main park entrance, as described above, and turn south onto 36th Avenue W, west on W Emerson, and then north into the park at 43rd Avenue W. *North*

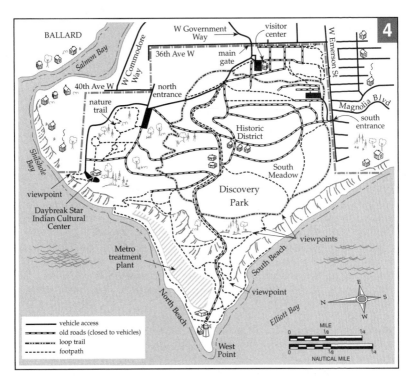

Entrance: Turn north from W Emerson Place onto 21st Avenue W, which shortly becomes W Commodore Way. Follow W Commodore Way to 40th Avenue W, and turn south to reach the park entrance.

🛶 Paddlecraft or beachable boats can land on the park beaches on either side of West Point.

Discovery Park, the largest and most choice of Seattle's city parks, is also one of its newest. For nearly ninety years the park was locked up as a military reservation, which explains why such prime real estate on Magnolia Bluff went undeveloped for residential or commercial use. Like numerous parcels of land along the sound, the property became available for public use after the government no longer needed it. Although decidedly urban, the park is visited by more than 200 species of birds and includes a dozen varieties of trees, an equal or greater selection of shrubs, 40 or more types of herbs, ferns, and mosses, more than 50 species of beach life, and a showcase-lesson in Puget Sound geology in its beach bluffs.

To keep the grounds as natural as possible, most roads that had been built for the fort are closed to traffic. Many of the areas must be reached by walking; some routes are old roads, others are trails that are wide, well maintained, and (for the most part) gentle. On summer weekends, from noon to 5:00 PM, the park runs a shuttle bus every half hour between the Discovery Park Visitor Center and the beach at West Point.

Environmental Learning Center ● The informational hub of the park is the Environmental Learning Center, open Tuesday through Sunday, 8:30 AM to 5:00 PM, except holidays. It offers environmental classes, naturalist-led tours, and park-related publications and displays.

Discovery Park Trails ● More than 7 miles of trails, ranging from ½ mile long to nearly 3 miles long intertwine in the forests, in the meadows, and on the beaches of the park. Some are genuine footpaths, while others follow old roads. Brochures available at the Environmental Learning Center describe the sights along the trails—birds, plants, beach life, and points of geological interest. Take along field glasses, pause frequently, and try to identify some of the species of birds that might be seen at the park.

West Point ● The lighthouse at West Point, on the far western tip of Discovery Park, has one of the most scenic settings on the sound. Jumbo cargo ships lumber by, sailboats with brightly colored spinnakers race in the offshore breezes, the Olympic peaks frame the western horizon, and Mount Rainier rises above the city's skyscrapers. The lighthouse has been overseeing the passing scene since 1881, eight years before Washington became a state. It is now on the National Register of Historic Places.

North Beach ● North Beach offers a ¾-mile-long beach walk until uprising cliffs block your progress. The rock and gravel shore is home for a wide variety of intertidal life ranging from chitons, limpets, barnacles, and mussels to sea stars, urchins, and tiny crabs. A sewage treatment facility between the

Sailboats race off Magnolia Bluff's West Point.

shore and the bluff is hidden by landscaping and earthen mounds, and not even a sensitive nose should be aware of its size or function. An adjacent lagoon and wetland marsh, a popular gathering spot for gulls, ducks, and other waterfowl, were created as part of a beach restoration project.

South Beach • South Beach, stretching for more than a mile southeast from West Point, offers a marked contrast to the rocky shoreline of North Beach. Here is sand extending well out into the sound on a minus tide. Driftwood and dune grass define the high tide line at the western end. The beach supports sea pens, moon snails, sand dollars, and other sand-loving marine life.

To the east, steep cliffs rising from the beach to the bluffs above provide an interesting geology lesson on the formation of the area. Clearly defined bands show sediments from lakes and streams, topped by dark gray clay that settled out of a huge freshwater lake. Higher up, loose, yellowish sand was deposited by streams and glacial meltwater. This is topped by till—a collection of boulders, rocks, sand, silt, and clay deposited directly by the glacier that last covered this area, roughly 12,000 years ago. Scan the cliffs for the hollows of kingfishers and other birds that have made their nests in the soft sand.

Reach South Beach from the Visitor Center or south entrance by following the Loop Trail to its intersection with the South Beach Trail, and then take this trail down to the beach. Alternatively, continue on the Loop Trail to its intersection with the road to the Metro plant and follow the road downhill to the beach.

Daybreak Star Indian Cultural Center • The Daybreak Star Indian Cultural Center, northwest of the north parking lot area, houses a library, museum, and a gallery of Indian art (some on display, some for sale). The center also

From Fort to Footpaths

In 1894 Magnolia Bluff was one of eleven sites designated as potential military reservations for the Coast Artillery to protect the naval station that had just been built at Port Orchard. The army concluded that it would be wise to have troops permanently stationed close to the two population centers of Seattle and Tacoma; the proposed Magnolia Bluff reservation seemed an excellent location for an infantry garrison until it might be needed by the Coast Artillery.

In 1896 acquisition of land for the post began, quarters for officers and non-coms, barracks, a hospital, stables, a quartermaster building, and other units were constructed, and the site was officially named Fort Lawton. Although the fort served alternatively as a post for infantry and Coast Artillery, no artillery was ever installed here. Military activity wound down during the Great Depression, and the army offered the land to Seattle for the price of one dollar; however, the city declined, feeling it could not afford the maintenance costs.

During World War II the fort sprang back to life—more than a million troops were processed here, a prison camp on the fort held 1150 German POWs, and another 5000 Italian POWs passed through here en route to Hawaii. After the war, the fort remained a debarkation point for a time, and then became a processing center for civil service employees and military headed to the Far East, and finally was a reserve training center. In 1970 the army surplused 85 percent of the fort property, and the city acquired it for a park (this time willingly assuming the maintenance costs). However, this was the beginning of the city's headaches. Local Native American tribes demanded the property be returned to them under the provision of early treaty rights; a compromise was reached, and 19 acres were set aside for a Native American cultural center. Special interest groups, ranging from golf buffs to hang-gliding enthusiasts, came out of the woodwork with plans and demands. The parks department, wisely, maintained that the park should be a sanctuary where people could escape for quiet and solitude. Although some areas were to be developed for conventional recreational use, the bulk of the park was to remain nature oriented. In October of 1973, the land was formally dedicated as Discovery Park, named for the ship of George Vancouver, the explorer who first charted Puget Sound.

The dust has not completely settled however, as the navy had retained about 30 acres of the old fort for naval housing. With the creation of Naval Station Everett, the navy found that the commute of its personnel from Discovery Park to Everett was too long and consolidated all its Puget Sound housing in a joint privatization venture, with a developer taking title to current naval property in return for construction of new housing closer to the naval bases. This opened the possibility of a private developer building an upscale residential neighborhood right in the heart of Seattle's most prized park. As of fall 2004, the issue has not been resolved, and local neighborhood groups and an array of politicians are trying to find a solution to retain the property as a part of the park.

hosts touring shows by native artists, cultural heritage programs, and other special events celebrating Native American history and spiritual traditions. A wooden overlook north of the center faces expansive views north over Shilshole Bay to distant Mount Baker.

ELLIOTT BAY
Map 1

Elliott Bay, with its deep, protected waters, triggered the birth of the city of Seattle in 1852, and it has continued to nurture the city's growth over the past 150 years. The first settlers in the area landed on the shallow shore at Alki Point in West Seattle; however, it didn't take them long to recognize that a site closer to deep water was essential for creating the port city of their dreams. With a few horseshoes tied to a clothesline, they sounded the east shore of Elliott Bay and to their delight found the spot that answered all their needs. Claims were staked out, families established homesteads, and, thus (with a slight oversimplification of time and events) Seattle came to be.

The world port that the original settlers envisioned has materialized, although certainly not in the form they could ever have anticipated. Today, Seattle is one of the largest container ports in the world. An average of five ocean-going vessels per day call on the commercial piers along Elliott Bay, and the value of goods passing through the port exceeds $25 billion annually.

The giant wharves of Smith Cove lie along the north edge of Elliott Bay. The first piers here were used for loading coal on ships. In 1892 two huge piers (now Piers 88 and 89) were constructed, from which railroad-owned steamers linked transcontinental rails to trade with the Orient. Shipments of raw silk valued as high as $1000 dollars a bale were off-loaded from ships

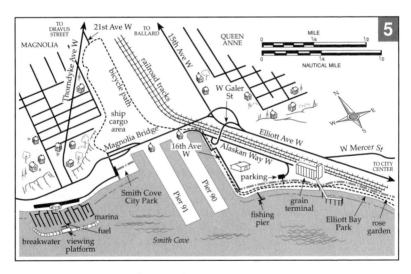

to waiting special freight trains for a high-speed, direct run to the garment factories of the East Coast.

Piers 90 and 91 were constructed at the head of the cove by the Port of Seattle. At the time of their completion in 1921, these 2530-foot-long earth-fill piers were the longest of their kind in the world. The piers were sold to the U.S. Navy in 1942 for use as a major supply depot but were repurchased by the port in 1976. As of 2006, a proposal is being considered to move one of the cruise ship terminals to Pier 90.

Elliott Bay Marina   Map 5

Boating • Paddling • Viewpoint • Fishing

Facilities: Guest moorage, power, phone, cable TV, wireless broadband, restaurants, groceries, fuel dock, restrooms, showers, laundry rooms, marine pumpout station, portable toilet dump, shops, hazardous waste disposal, chandlery, marine repair, observation platform

🚐 From Elliott Avenue W take the on-ramp to the Magnolia Bridge. Midway up the span take the off-ramp to the right. The ramp Ts into 23rd Avenue W under the west end of the bridge. In two blocks 23rd bends west and becomes W Marina Place and ends at the marina.

The fine new 1200-slip marina lies on the north side of Elliott Bay. The facility is protected by a 2700-foot-long rock breakwater along the south side of Magnolia Bluff and a concrete wavebreak at the west end of the breakwater. Fuel, groceries, and a pumpout station are at the end of G dock, in the center of the marina. An observation platform atop the center of the breakwater provides terrific views across Elliott Bay; it is accessible from the channel behind the breakwater by boat or via a shuttle boat from the end of G dock.

Check with the dockmaster for guest moorage in unoccupied slips. Buildings at either end of the marina contain necessities such as laundry and showers; offices and shops are near the end of G dock.

Smith Cove City Park (Port of Seattle)   Map 5

Picnicking • Viewpoint • Paddling

Facilities: Picnic tables
Area: 2.5 acres; 500 feet of shoreline

🚐 See directions to Elliott Bay Marina, above. The park is at the junction of 23rd Avenue W and W Marina Place.

🛶 Paddlers can land at the park, with care. It is 2 n.m. north of Don Armeni Park, near Duwamish Head.

Squeezed between Pier 91 and the Elliott Bay Marina is delightful little Smith Cove City Park. Small, a bit hard to find, and not long on amenities, the park is nonetheless a pleasant waterfront alcove from which to watch the shipping activities of Elliott Bay and enjoy a picnic lunch spiced with a stiff,

Smith Cove City Park affords close-up views of cargo ships. In the future, cruise ships might be docked here.

salt-air breeze. Massive Pier 91 is immediately to the east, and picturesque Mount Rainier caps the end of Elliott Bay to the south.

A bicycle path that leads north from Elliott Bay City Park ends here. This route follows along the east side of the Pier 90-91 fence, then goes around the north end of the piers' loading area, and joins 21st Avenue W about 1/2 mile from the park entrance, where it again heads south, and ends at the park

Elliott Bay Park (Port of Seattle)   Maps 5 and 6

Sightseeing • Walking • Jogging • Skating • Bicycling • Fishing • Picnicking • Points of interest

Facilities: Foot and bike paths, fitness course, picnic table, fishing pier, concession stand, bait, tackle, restrooms, children's play areas, rose garden
Area: 10.5 acres; 4100 feet of shoreline

🚗 From Elliott Avenue W, at the on-ramp to the Magnolia Bridge, take the overpass ramp signed to Piers 86–91. The overpass loops down to Alaskan Way W, which heads south between the railroad tracks and Amgen's Seattle campus. Between fences at the north end of the Pier 86 grain terminal is a parking lot for a dozen cars. A path leads to the park. From the south, the park is a continuous extension of the city's Myrtle Edwards Park.

The massive concrete silos of the Port of Seattle grain terminal mark Pier 86, between Smith Cove and downtown Seattle. From here, freighters take on grain for export to foreign markets. At the base of the silos, the grass strip of narrow Elliott Bay Park runs along the shore for nearly a mile. The bicycle path continues north from the park, along the east and north sides of the Pier 90–91 fence, eventually reaching 21st Avenue W, which leads to Smith Cove Park.

The park's walking/jogging path is immediately above the rock-ribbed beach; a bicycle route runs inland along the fence. The pedestrian path has a number of adjacent fitness exercise stations, as well as several benches from which to leisurely watch the marine traffic or see a passing sea lion scouting for lunch.

Near the north end of the park, a 400-foot-long, T-shaped concrete fishing pier extends into the bay. Two orange-striped `s 100 feet offshore mark an artificial underwater reef. Fishing near the reef must be done from the pier—angling from boats is prohibited here. Surf perch, flat fish, salmon, cod, cabezon, and rockfish might be caught. The pier is open 7:00 AM to 11:00 PM daily in the winter and 6:00 AM to midnight in the summer.

Myrtle Edwards Park (City of Seattle)   Map 6

Picnicking • Jogging • Walking • Bicycling • Skating

Facilities: Picnic tables, toilets
Area: 4.8 acres; 2000 feet of shoreline

🚗 A parking lot is north of Pier 70, at the intersection of Alaskan Way and Broad Street.

The public shoreline and its bicycle and walking paths continue south from the grain terminal silos in an unbroken swath. The southern portion, Myrtle Edwards Park, honors a former city councilwoman. Benches and picnic tables along the shore offer pleasant resting spots with views to the maritime activities of Elliott Bay and, beyond, Bainbridge Island and the Olympic range.

Near the center of the park is one of Seattle's interesting sculptures, part of the city's program providing 1 percent of development costs for artwork. The sculpture, *Adjacent, Against, Upon,* by artist Michael Heizer, consists of three massive pairs of carved stone slabs and concrete platforms, each

At Myrtle Edwards Park, toddlers find a field of daisies more interesting than the massive sculpture of Adjacent, Against, Upon, *or the tall silos of the grain terminal.*

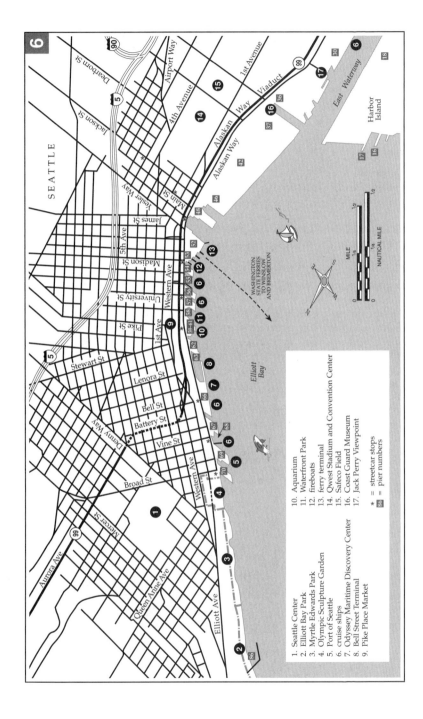

1. Seattle Center
2. Elliott Bay Park
3. Myrtle Edwards Park
4. Olympic Sculpture Garden
5. Port of Seattle
6. cruise ships
7. Odyssey Maritime Discovery Center
8. Bell Street Terminal
9. Pike Place Market

10. Aquarium
11. Waterfront Park
12. fireboats
13. ferry terminal
14. Qwest Stadium and Convention Center
15. Safeco Field
16. Coast Guard Museum
17. Jack Perry Viewpoint

★ = streetcar stops
86 = pier numbers

slab and platform related, according to the title of the work. It provides an interesting contrast of human scale versus the monumental.

The south end of Myrtle Edwards Park connects with the lower end of the Seattle Art Museum's 8½-acre Olympic Sculpture Park, which holds architectural-scaled works by noted artists such as Richard Serra and Alexander Calder. A glass bridge spans the railroad tracks, connecting the upper and lower portions of the park.

The Downtown Seattle Waterfront   Map 6

Shopping • Sightseeing • Picnicking • Fishing • Paddling • Parasailing • Tours

Facilities: Marina, shops, restaurants, parks, restrooms, maritime museum, cruise ship terminal, aquarium, tour boats, guest moorage, points of interest

The waterfront that edges downtown Seattle is a colorful, fascinating mélange of commercial and tourist-oriented facilities. On this mile-long stretch are found activities ranging from the sedate to the sensational. Visitors can sample such things as horse-drawn carriage rides, pedi-cab rides, sailing trips, cruise-boat tours, fishing trips, kayak excursions, and parasail flights. During the summer a variety of vessels that stop by, ranging from historic square riggers to modern navy ships, are open to the public at times. The port has recently developed a burgeoning Alaska cruise ship trade, and these mammoth vessels regularly visit the port facilities at Pier 66 and Terminal 30.

In early times the waterfront was a bustling center of commerce focused on shipping and fishing. As the shift to containerized cargo caused the working waterfront to move to Smith Cove and Harbor Island, warehouses on the downtown waterfront were abandoned. Several of these house small shops and restaurants. Piers are used by cruise ships, tour boats, and the state ferries.

Alaskan Way runs the length of the downtown waterfront. The central portion of the waterfront is cut off from downtown Seattle by a steep hill and a freeway viaduct. At several points sets of stairs and elevators rise from the waterfront to the upper street level. The Pike Place Hillclimb, east of Pier 59, leads up stairs and terraces to the historic Pike Place Market, one of the

The colorful food, flower, and craft stalls of the Pike Place Market are a major Seattle attraction.

best-known public markets in the country. A staircase/elevator combination at Lenora Street takes visitors to the street level two blocks north of the market. At the end of Bell Street, at Pier 66, a pedestrian bridge links to upper city streets. *Visitors to the area should be aware of one problem that might be encountered, especially at the south end of Alaskan Way, where there is a concentration of vagrants. Although most are harmless panhandlers, a few might become aggressive and threatening, especially if encountered in secluded spots. Use care and common sense.*

Major attractions of the waterfront are described here, from north to south.

The Waterfront Street Car •

The Seattle waterfront gained a novel attraction with the arrival of four 1927-vintage electric trolleys that had been retired from service in Melbourne, Australia. The picturesque streetcars make their fifteen-minute run along the waterfront, stopping at several stations along the way. Leaving the waterfront, the streetcar tracks head east through Pioneer Square on S Main Street to 5th Avenue, and the end of the line at Jackson Street. Car conductors frequently add their personal commentary to make the trip even more fun. The streetcar is out of service as of 2006, but it will return.

Cruise Ships •

The downtown waterfront is the terminal for several cruise ships. For persons wanting a quick trip to Victoria, British Columbia, the *Victoria Clipper* ships are high-speed jetfoils operating out of Pier 69 that provide passenger-only service year-round. The boats can also accommodate a few bicycles and kayaks. Check with Clipper Navigation, Inc., for information.

Four cruise ship lines have weekly sailings to Alaska between April and October. The Norwegian Cruise Line and Celebrity Cruises sail from the Bell Street Pier Cruise Terminal at Pier 66, and Holland America Line and Princess Cruises leave from the Terminal 30 Cruise Facility.

Argosy Cruises, at Pier 55, provides an Elliott Bay Harbor tour package, trips through the Hiram Chittenden Locks, narrated tours of Lakes Union and Washington, and cruises to Blake Island State Park's Native American Tillicum Village. Brunch and dinner cruises aboard the *Royal Argosy* operate from Pier 56. Land tours are coordinated with Gray Line buses.

In recent years, the *Lady Washington*, a reproduction of the first American vessel to explore the Pacific coast, has stopped at the Seattle waterfront in summer, providing visitors an opportunity to sail for an hour or two aboard an eighteenth-century square rigger. In addition, two 70-foot sailboats operating out of Pier 54 offer day-sails, sunset sails, and group charters between May and October.

Pier 69: The Port of Seattle •

The spiffy new headquarters for the Port of Seattle includes public shoreline viewpoints along the outside rim of the pier that offer outstanding views of nearby Pier 70, the grain loading facilities at Terminal 86, Elliott Bay, Harbor Island, and distant mountains. The lobby of the port offices displays scale models of various ships and a gantry crane, as well as models of aircraft that fly out of the port's SeaTac International Airport. Kiosks tell of the port's activities, and an interactive computer terminal allows visitors to access more information about the port.

Pier 66: The Bell Street Terminal • Recent major reconstruction of this part of the waterfront has added a first-class marina, restaurants, an international conference center, a maritime museum, and docks that serve cruise ship traffic. At the Odyssey Maritime Discovery Center, an interactive nautical museum, kids or adults can play longshoreman in a container crane simulator, listen to the radio traffic of ships in the sound, ride the bridge of a fishing vessel in the stormy Pacific, enjoy a magic kayak ride, or get splashed while learning about fish.

The roof of the conference center is a view plaza with benches, telescopes, and an outstanding panorama of the Olympic Mountains, Puget Sound, the waterfront, and the Seattle cityscape. For security reasons, the plaza is closed when cruise ships are in port.

At the Bell Harbor Marina, more than thirty-seven guest moorage slips with power and water lie in a basin protected by a huge cruise ship pier. A marine pumpout station is provided, there are restrooms with showers, and

Pleasure boats rub shoulders with a giant cruise ship at Bell Harbor Marina.

the entire area is under security protection. Maximum stay is seven days in peak season, and fourteen days off-season. The deck above the marina has a restaurant and a fish-shaped fountain that invites kids to splash in it. At the entrance to the marina stands a 100-foot-high metal column that is an abstract representation of a lighthouse.

Piers 62 and 63 • The broad wooden deck of these two piers is a city park, with picnic tables and ample space for viewing the city skyline and the bay. Community activities and special events frequently use the incomparable venue.

Piers 60 and 61: The Seattle Aquarium • Elliott Bay and Puget Sound are important not only for what occurs on their surfaces, but also for what exists below. The Seattle Aquarium provides a glimpse of this underwater world. One of its displays, a unique underwater dome, allows visitors to go beneath the waters of the sound and view marine life much as Captain Nemo would have seen it. On view in traditional glass tanks are nearly every kind of marine life found in Puget Sound. Displays provide information to help visitors better understand the various species and their environments.

Probably as popular as the fish displays are the tanks containing harbor seals and sea otters. Other displays include a "touch tank," where children can examine the crusty skin of a starfish, the squishy body of a sea cucumber, or other characteristics of fascinating marine animals.

In 2005 the city began a $37.6 million project to update and expand the facility. It is scheduled for completion in spring of 2008, but the aquarium will remain open during most of this time.

Piers 59 to 55: Waterfront Park • A large semicircular deck between Piers 57 and 59 forms Waterfront Park. Picnic tables along the terraced deck are favorite haunts of Seattlites who enjoy a splash of salt air as they share their lunches with scrounging pigeons and seagulls. Landscaping, a marvelously splashing fountain, and what is possibly the ugliest statue in Seattle (Christopher Columbus with a hole through his bronze head) add to the park's charm. Distinctive, open-air viewing towers can be reached from the deck below via stairs or ramps or via walkways leading from the second level of buildings on the adjoining piers.

The Bay Pavilion, on Pier 56, houses a collection of small shops and restaurants. The open end of the pier offers a scattering of tables and benches from which to watch waterfront activity. This pier end is a public fishing area; rod holders are mounted along its perimeter fence for the convenience of anglers. Pier 55 is companion to Pier 56 that houses still more restaurants and tourist-oriented shops. One gets the impression that both residents and visitors can never get their fill of seafood and outside dining in this purportedly rainy city.

Piers 56 and 55 are the base for a variety of harbor tours, sailboat tours, parasailing flights, bicycle rentals, saltwater fishing charters, and similar adventures.

Pier 54: Ye Olde Curiosity Shop and Ivar's Acres of Clams •

Two commercial enterprises on the waterfront have become Seattle institutions. Ye Olde Curiosity Shop, which has been a waterfront fixture since 1899, relocated to the north side of Pier 54 when Pier 51, its home of many years, was found structurally unsound. The store houses an eclectic assortment of artifacts, curios, and tourist kitsch—most are for sale, but some are just for display.

Pier 54 is also the home of one of the best-known waterfront restaurants, Ivar's Acres of Clams. On display in the restaurant are more than 500 historical photos of the waterfront. On the sidewalk in front, a bronze statue of the late Ivar Haglund feeding seagulls is a fitting tribute to a man who spent his life promoting the Seattle waterfront. An annual Fourth of July fireworks display in Elliot Bay sponsored by the corporation that now operates Ivar's restaurants also commemorates his life.

The Fitzgerald Fountain cascades prettily at Waterfront Park.

Pier 53: Fire Station Number 5 and Fireboats •

Fire Station Number 5 not only provides protection for the land side of Elliott Bay, it also acts as the home base for the two fireboats stationed on the bay. As well as fighting fires, the vessels often take part in marine parades and other special events on the bay. They provide a breathtaking scene when their water cannons send plumes of water arching high into the air.

The historic old fire bell outside the station was used in the 1800s to sound alarms to all fire stations in the north end of the city. Inside the building is an antique fire engine that answered the alarms in Seattle of the past.

Pier 52: The Colman Ferry Terminal •

From this Seattle terminus of the Washington State Ferry System, ferries serve Bremerton, on the Kitsap Peninsula, and Winslow, on Bainbridge Island. From balconies in the Colman Terminal, visitors can watch the flurry of activity as the huge vessels dock, then unload, load, and depart.

Pier 36: The Coast Guard Museum Northwest and the Vessel Traffic Service Center • Many of the interesting features at the Coast Guard Support Center at Pier 36 are not open to visitors for security reasons. The pier is home to the United States' two largest icebreakers, which see duty in arctic seas. Three high-endurance cutters are stationed here. The Puget Sound Vessel Traffic Service Center (VTS), also closed to visitors, is in the main building on the pier. This center maintains radar surveillance of about 2500 square miles of waterways in the Strait of Juan de Fuca and Puget Sound. It controls and tracks over 18,000 commercial vessel movements a month in these waters.

The one facility open to visitors is the Coast Guard Museum Northwest, on the north side of the pier, which houses marine memorabilia. Its collection includes several models of Coast Guard vessels, historic photos, and vintage uniforms. A post-mounted lantern on display was at Alki Point in 1887; it was a predecessor to later lighthouses. A fourth-order Fresnel lens now in the museum was installed at Admiralty Head in 1903 and later saw duty at New Dungeness Lighthouse.

The museum is open Monday, Wednesday, and Friday from 9:00 AM to 6:00 PM Group tours at other times can be arranged by telephoning the museum. All visitors enter the base via the main gate at S Massachusetts Street, two blocks south of the museum. Park on the street along Alaskan Way. Sometime in the future the perimeter fence might be modified to permit easier access to the museum.

Terminal 30: Jack Perry Viewpoint (Port of Seattle) • The Seattle waterfront ends at the East Waterway, the heart of commercial activity for the Port of Seattle. A public access provided by the Port of Seattle just north of Terminal 30 has a viewing site where the bustling activity of the port can be watched close at hand. To reach the site, follow Alaskan Way south from the central waterfront to where it jogs southwest and becomes E Marginal Way S. Follow the stub end of Alaskan Way straight ahead to the viewpoint; it is signed at the main road. The short road ends in a parking area at the edge of the East Waterway. Hand-carried boats can be put in here at high tide for a tour of the bay. Terminal 30 is the port's second cruise ship terminal, and these huge vessels can often be seen tied up here.

chapter two

The Duwamish Waterway and West Seattle

THE DUWAMISH WATERWAY
Map 8

FROM ITS SOURCE at the confluence of the Black, White, and Green Rivers, the Duwamish River originally meandered 8 miles through sixteen serpentine curves to the tideflats of Elliott Bay. In 1906 the White River was diverted to the south, and in 1916 the Black ceased to exist when the completion of the ship canal lowered Lake Washington, its source. Lack of flat land for industry led to extensive reshaping of the Duwamish; between 1913 and 1917 the river had ten of its curves eliminated by the Corps of Engineers, as it was dredged to its present relatively straight, 50-foot-deep channel. As it approaches Elliot Bay, the river splits and flows on either side of Harbor Island in two channels named, appropriately, East Channel and West Channel.

Looking south along the West Waterway, the Duwamish River is edged by a variety of industries.

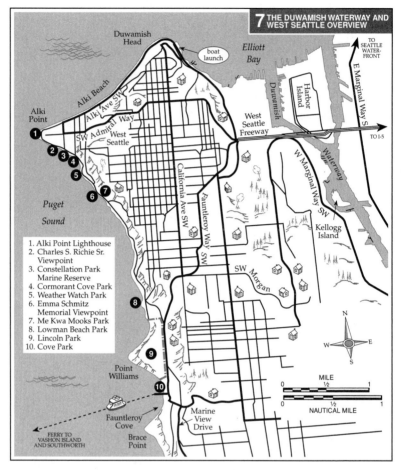

7 THE DUWAMISH WATERWAY AND WEST SEATTLE OVERVIEW

1. Alki Point Lighthouse
2. Charles S. Richie Sr. Viewpoint
3. Constellation Park Marine Reserve
4. Cormorant Cove Park
5. Weather Watch Park
6. Emma Schmitz Memorial Viewpoint
7. Me Kwa Mooks Park
8. Lowman Beach Park
9. Lincoln Park
10. Cove Park

Terminal 23 Fishing Pier (Port of Seattle)   Map 8

Picnicking • Fishing • Viewpoint

Facilities: Picnic tables, fish cleaning stations, toilet

🚗 From the westbound lanes of the West Seattle Freeway (Spokane Street viaduct) take the 11th Avenue SW exit to SW Spokane Street. Just beyond the end of the off-ramp find a driveway into a parking area on the north side of the street (easily missed). There is also some parking under the freeway at the intersection of SW Spokane Street and E Marginal Way S.

Sandwiched between the south gate of Terminal 18 and a cold storage plant at Terminal 25, with views out to cranes and cargo ships, the public fishing pier at the end of the East Waterway puts a human perspective in this otherwise industrial area. Benches (some covered) lining the 500-foot frontage of the pier provide pleasant spots to watch the waterway activity while waiting for a hit on the fish line. Note that bottomfish, shellfish, and crab might be unsafe to eat, due to pollution.

Terminal 18 Public Access (Port of Seattle)   Map 8

Picnicking • Paddling • Viewpoint

Facilities: Picnic shelters, picnic tables, information panel
Area: 1.1 acres; 310 feet of shoreline on the Duwamish River

From the westbound lanes of the West Seattle Freeway (Spokane Street viaduct) take the 11th Avenue SW exit to SW Spokane Street. Drive west on Spokane in the lane signed Terminals 3 and 4, which turns north on SW Klickitat Way. Keep right of the overpass to Terminal 4, staying on Klickitat, and in ¼ mile, at the entrance to Terminal 3, turn west on 13th Avenue SW, cross the tracks, and head south on SW Florida. At the junction with SW Lander from the northwest, turn west and immediately south on W Frontage Road (unmarked). Reach the park in four blocks; there is parking at either end.

This small waterfront park lies along the east side of the West Waterway (the mouth of the Duwamish River), just north of the West Seattle swing bridge. Three pitched-roof shelters, each with a picnic table, line the edge of the waterway. Huge colored panels on the south-facing roofs of the shelters identify the park as Terminal 18. A historical panel describes the creation of Harbor Island. The activities at Terminal 5, across the waterway, provide entertainment during a picnic lunch. Hand-carry boats can be launched here along the boulder bulkhead at high tide (with due regard for marine traffic).

The West Waterway is navigated by vessels ranging up to huge container cargo ships. Three bridges span the channel: one a fixed freeway bridge that soars high above, the second a railroad drawbridge, and the third a unique swing bridge

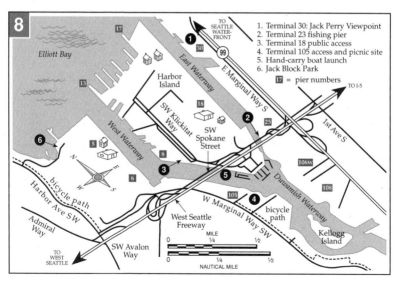

1. Terminal 30: Jack Perry Viewpoint
2. Terminal 23 fishing pier
3. Terminal 18 public access
4. Terminal 105 access and picnic site
5. Hand-carry boat launch
6. Jack Block Park

17 = pier numbers

Harbor Island

During the late 1800s, when the federal government was quibbling over a route for a ship canal to access Lake Washington, Seattlites grew tired of waiting and took matters into their own hands. In 1890 they obtained approval from the state legislature to construct a canal from the south end of the lake via a cut through Beacon Hill. Although the canal was never constructed, preliminary design work by the Army Corps of Engineers led, in 1895, to dredging of two channels in the Duwamish tideflats. Dredged material that was dumped between the two channels in the Duwamish tideflats formed the beginnings of Harbor Island. Augmented by rock ballast from lumber barges and from regrades at Beacon Hill, the island took the shape it has today.

The island lay virtually unused until 1910 when local business interests, spurred by visions of burgeoning trade through the soon-to-be-completed Panama Canal, sought East Coast financing to build piers and terminals at Harbor Island. Financing attempts failed, but by the 1920s some commercial development was noticeable, mainly along the edges of the adjoining waterways. A major burst of industrial growth that started shortly before World War II has continued and turned the island into the bustling industrial area of today.

The numbers associated with it are staggering: The East Waterway alone has 10,634 linear feet of berthing space and 187 acres of adjoining marine terminal yards, it can accommodate up to fourteen deep-draft vessels simultaneously, and over 4 million metric tons of cargo are transshipped yearly from its terminals.

for vehicle traffic. The swing bridge, in which two halves rotate horizontally on two huge concrete pivots, is the only one of its kind in the country.

An unofficial, unmarked hand-carry boat launch is on the opposite side of the waterway, directly under the swing bridge. Here a small backwater pond around the west pivot for the bridge is protected from waterway traffic by a sturdy wing wall of pilings. A paved parking lot under the bridge can be reached via W Marginal Way SW. A short road leads to a no-bank put-in site. It is usable only at high tides.

Terminal 105 Public Access (Port of Seattle)   Map 8

Picnicking • Paddling • Fishing • Views

Facilities: Picnic tables, picnic shelter, pier, toilets, hand-carry boat launch
Area: 1 acre; 500 feet of shoreline on the Duwamish River

🚗 On the west side of the Spokane Street swing bridge, take W Marginal Way SW south from SW Spokane Street, and in ¼ mile look for the Terminal 105 Viewpoint sign on the east side of the street. A gravel road leads to limited parking.

🚣 The hand-carry boat launch is on the south side of the viewpoint pier, directly across the Duwamish Waterway from the Harbor Island Marina. Low-tide launching involves a long slog through mud.

The picnic shelter at Terminal 105 Public Access is a fine spot to watch marine traffic in the Duwamish Waterway.

A little park just south of the tip of Harbor Island is a nice spot to fish or just to watch the marine traffic in the busy Duwamish channel. It's especially pleasant on summer evenings when river traffic is heavier and Mount Rainier is bathed in the glow of the setting sun. The gravel road into the park heads east between a chain-link fence and a shallow channel excavated by the Port to create an intertidal habitat. As a part of this restoration effort, all introduced vegetation has been removed from the area and replaced by native plants. A walkway leads to a 40-foot-long concrete pier, some picnic tables, and a picnic shelter. The Harbor Island Marina is directly across the river. A gravel path leading to the southeast corner of the park ends at a hand-carry boat launch site on the shallow channel.

WEST SEATTLE
Map 7

West Seattle has always seemed a bit apart from the rest of Seattle—partially because of its physical separation by the broad channel of the Duwamish River, and partially because it is a little bit different (and perhaps better) than the rest of the city, with its combination of extensive saltwater shoreline, outstanding beaches, and fine water-oriented views.

Jack Block Park (Port of Seattle)   Map 8
Viewpoints • Picnicking

Facilities: Restroom (disabled accessible), view platforms, view tower, pier interpretive displays, children's play areas, walking paths

Area: 15 acres; 4300 feet of shoreline

🚗 After crossing the Spokane Street swing bridge take the lane marked to West Seattle, Terminal 5. In the confusing spaghetti of roads at the end of the bridge, head northwest briefly on W Marginal Way SW, then west on SW Spokane Street, which Ts into Harbor Avenue SW in ¼ mile. Go north on Harbor Avenue for 1 mile, and turn east at the sign "Jack Block Public Access," ¼ mile south of Salty's Restaurant.

When the Port of Seattle expanded the container cargo area to use the wedge of land between Harbor Avenue SW and Terminal 5, part of the project package was a new shoreline park. The result is an outstanding park that offers visitors a plaza at the edge of Elliott Bay with raised platforms, beach-like play areas for kids, and a place to picnic with an appetite whetted by the snap of salt-air breezes.

Because the park is interwoven with the working waterfront, it has pedestrian ramps and bridges across active rail spurs to connect its various sections. These raised vantage points, as well as a viewing tower, provide spots to watch the industrial activities of the terminal and to see the Seattle skyline and Elliott Bay. A broad pier plaza holds picnic tables and interpretive signs explaining various activities of the port. A public accessible pier extends into Elliott Bay north from the plaza. The port plans to restore the remainder of the north shoreline of Terminal 5 to a nature habitat. There is no water access to the park.

Jack Block Park provides unique vantage point of Seattle waterways.

Seacrest Park (City of Seattle) Map 9

*Viewpoint • Picnicking • Bicycling • Fishing • Boating • Scuba diving • Skating •
Bicycling*

Facilities: Restrooms (disabled accessible), picnic tables, bicycle path, boathouse,
restaurant, fishing piers, guest moorage, concession, tackle, bait, boat rental,
outboard fuel

Area: 6.4 acres; 2200 feet of shoreline, passenger ferry to Seattle

See directions to Jack Block Park, above to reach the intersection of SW
Spokane Street and Harbor Avenue SW. Seacrest Park is on Harbor Avenue, 1 mile
north of this intersection.

The park is on the southwest side of Elliott Bay, ¾ n.m. southeast of Duwamish Head. Public moorage is on the inside of the float off the inner pier.

In 1971 the city of Seattle envisioned a premium waterfront park, complete
with a 700-boat marina, fishing pier, boathouse, promenade, and salmon-
rearing pens, along Harbor Avenue SW, southwest of Duwamish Head, Plans
for the marina ran afoul of Native American fishing treaty rights, and, in
addition, the total package substantially exceeded available funding.

Plans were scaled down, but even in their final form the breathtaking
views of the downtown Seattle skyline against a background of rugged Cascade summits make Seacrest a gem of a park. Shoreline restoration began
with the creation of a promenade along the inner rim of three small coves,
with grass enclaves and benches between them on which to enjoy the views.
In 1989 a boathouse was added.

The continuation of the Spokane Street Bicycle Path runs along the edge
of Harbor Avenue. Two fishing piers extend into the bay, one at the south
end of the park, and a second L-shaped one at the boathouse. Inside this
latter pier is a second float for guest moorage. The jumble of decaying
offshore pilings from wharves long forgotten is a favorite spot for scuba
diving, although diving is not permitted within 150 feet of the fishing pier.

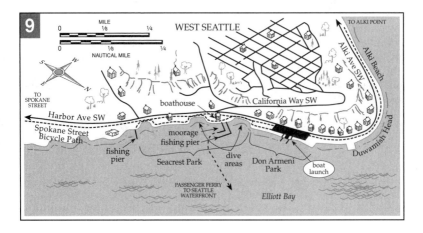

An underwater trail has been installed around the pier to help divers identify the off-limits area.

In summer Metro runs the Elliott Bay Water Taxi, a passenger boat, between Seacrest Park and Pier 55 on the Seattle waterfront. Crossing time is about twelve minutes, and sailings are hourly or less, depending on the time of day. A free Metro shuttle bus runs past the park about every twenty minutes on a route between the west end of Alki Beach and West Seattle Junction at California Avenue SW and SW Alaska.

The Seacrest Park area is reknowned for its excellent fishing, either from the pier or nearby waters.

Don Armeni Park (City of Seattle)   Map 9

Viewpoint • Picnicking • Bicycling • Boating • Paddling • Fishing • Scuba diving

Facilities: 12-lane launch ramp with boarding floats, restrooms (disabled accessible), picnic tables, bicycle path, boat trailer parking
Area: 4.8 acres; 1400 feet of shoreline

🚐 See directions to Seacrest Park, above. Don Armeni is immediately north of Seacrest.

🛥 See directions for Seacrest Park, above. Don Armeni is immediately north of Seacrest; the launch ramps are in the center of the park.

Don Armeni Park is a continuation of the theme of Seacrest Park, with similar fishing and beachfront attractions. The park, which lies along the shore just north of Seacrest Park, was named in 1955 for a popular deputy sheriff, active in youth fishing, who was killed in the line of duty.

Two pairs of launch ramps are in the center of the park; each pair has a loading float between them. The ramps to the south are to be used when launching, and the ones to the north when returning. Parking lots on either side of the ramps are for cars with boat trailers. A small area at the north end of the park is for general parking, or park along Harbor Avenue.

The shoreline not occupied by launch ramps has a landscaped walkway and park benches above a bulkhead. Concrete viewing platforms are at the ends of the park and at either side of the launch ramps.

DUWAMISH HEAD AND ALKI:
SEATTLE'S VACATION SPOT
Maps 7 and 9

To early Seattlites, the beautiful beaches of West Seattle were a vacation getaway. As early as 1899 the Coney Island Baths opened on the beach west of Duwamish Head, and by 1905 large stretches of the beach were lined with rustic summer cottages. The Coney Island Baths were replaced in 1907 by Luna Park, an amusement site built on a deck over pilings extending into the bay, which boasted a natatorium (indoor swimming pool) filled with saltwater, a dance pavilion, carnival rides, shows, restaurants, and a tavern. In 1931 the park was torched by an arsonist and it burned to the water. Recreation shifted westward three years later when the city opened a new natatorium at Alki Beach; Luna Park was never rebuilt.

In 1947 the city of Seattle acquired the beach north of Don Armeni Park, formerly occupied by Luna Park, as an extension of the public beaches lying west of Duwamish Head. The badly deteriorated ninety-five-year-old seawall has been rebuilt.

This is the only access point to the beach in this area. At extreme low tide an enormous tideflat is revealed, extending all the way to Duwamish Head and out into Elliott Bay for nearly a quarter of a mile; the stubs of the pilings that supported the park stand out above the tideflat. City dwellers throng here to search with metal detectors for treasures, or just to squish sand between their toes. ❋ Boaters approaching the head should be aware of the shoal, marked by a light and fog signal, which extends out for ¼ mile.

Alki Beach Park (City of Seattle) and Lighthouse   Maps 7 and 9

Swimming • Wading • Beach walking • Picnicking • Walking • Biking • Beach sports

Facilities: Restrooms, picnic shelter, fire rings, art studio, bicycle path, volleyball stanchions

Area: 135.9 acres; 10,000 feet of shoreline

🚗 From the junction of SW Spokane Street and Harbor Avenue SW, drive north on Harbor Avenue for 2½ miles to Duwamish Head where it becomes Alki Avenue SW. The park runs from Duwamish Head southwest to Alki Point, a distance of 2½ miles. Parking is in numerous spots along the street.

🛥 Hand-carried boats are easily launched and landed anywhere along the shore.

In 1851 the settlers of Alki Point called their community New York. When they were chided about this pretentious name, they would respond in Chinook jargon *al-ki*, which meant "by-and-by" or "someday"—someday it would equal New York. By 1853 the term had become so commonly used that the area was renamed Alki. Thankfully, it has not yet equaled New York.

Alki Beach has long been a favorite Seattle saltwater playground. As early as 1905 the area had a hotel, a swimming pool, and a dance pavilion. In order to assure availability of prime saltwater beach, in 1909 the city condemned buildings on 3000 feet of beach front northwest from Alki Point and erected a bathing and recreation pavilion. An indoor swimming pool, opened at the beach in 1934, was a popular spot for many years before falling into disrepair and finally being razed. Today the public beach extends along the peninsula in a continuous strip from Alki Point to the southern extremity of Seacrest Park.

The noisy crowds and parking problems make the lovely public beach

Sun and sand at Alki Beach Park—the best in Seattle

a mixed blessing for the local residents. The row of charming old beach cottages that once lined the waterfront is giving way to block after block of high-priced condominiums, which forebode the future of the remaining cottages as property values (and taxes) skyrocket.

Alki Beach Park is one of the most beautiful sand-covered expanses on Puget Sound, with exhilarating views across the sound to the Olympics and north to Whidbey Island and Admiralty Inlet. The shore tapers off gradually, and as a result the shallow waters heat enough in the summer to permit reasonably comfortable saltwater bathing. At minus tides the wide sand strip bares some distance out into the sound, exposing a menagerie of underwater life, including moon snails, starfish, anemones, and perhaps a clam or two. Because the intertidal life is now so sparse, please look but don't touch, leaving it for others to enjoy also.

Beach volleyball courts at the east end of the beach attract pick-up games. Restrooms are above the beach at 57th Avenue W, 60th Avenue SW, and 62nd Avenue SW. Toilets are at other beach accesses to the east. The building at 60th also houses a Seattle Parks Department art studio. A picnic shelter is near 62nd Avenue SW.

Alki Point Lighthouse • The prominent location of Alki Point, along the main channel of Puget Sound, makes it ideal for a navigational light. The first settlers to live on the point kept an oil lantern burning as a service to passing mariners. In 1887 the government authorized the placement of a kerosene-lit lens-lantern suspended on a wooden scaffold. This primitive but effective signal served until 1918 when the present lighthouse was commissioned.

Alki Point was the best possible duty for the lighthouse keeper stationed here. While other keepers were stuck on remote islands and far-flung beaches, the one stationed here at Alki enjoyed all of civilization's amenities, as well as the social life of the nearby city. The lighthouse is open for public tours on summer weekends and holidays from noon to 3:30 PM.

Parks South of Alki Point (City of Seattle)   Map 7

Views • Bicycling • Paddling • Nature interpretation • Marine preserve • Information panels • Tennis

Facilities: Beach access points, hand-carry boat launches; *not all the following facilities are at all parks:* Toilets, interpretive panels, picnic tables, tennis court, children's play equipment

🚗 From Alki Avenue SW at Alki Point continue southeast on Beach Drive SW. *Charles Richey Sr. Viewpoint:* Between Alki Point and 63rd Avenue SW. *Constellation Park Marine Reserve:* At 63rd Avenue SW. *Cormorant Cove Park:* At the intersection of 61st Avenue SW and SW Orleans Street. *Weather Watch Park:* At SW Carroll Street. *Emma Schmitz Memorial Viewpoint and Me Kwa Mooks Park:* Between SW Genesee Street and SW Jacobsen Road. *Lowman Beach Park:* Intersection of 48th Avenue SW and Lincoln Park Way.

🚣 Paddlecraft can be put-in or landed at most of the parks.

Turning the corner of Alki Point and heading south, a number of pretty little parks, some of them shoulder-to-shoulder, offer beach accesses. The gentle shore ends in some 6 miles with the uprising bluffs of Lincoln Park. A bicycle route begins at the east end of Harbor Avenue SW and follows the waterfront west around Alki Point and south to Lincoln Park via Beach Drive SW.

Charles S. Richie Sr. Viewpoint • Here, a beachfront promenade along 2000 feet of shoreline offers wide views across the sound to Vashon and Bainbridge Islands. The concrete bulkhead that runs south for several blocks to 63rd Avenue SW is interrupted by ramps leading down to the rocky beach; benches are scattered along the grassy strip that edges the bulkhead. Midway along the viewpoint the narrow lawn widens to encompass a group of three sculpted boulders. A wide concrete shelf provides an excellent place to snooze or bask in the afternoon sun while watching boat traffic in East Passage. A little streetside parking is available.

Constellation Park Marine Reserve • What a wonderful way to hide a Metro sewage pumping station! And it is all disabled accessible too. At the street level is a ceramic pool with bas relief octopus, starfish, and other marine life, and rails and a bench. At the base of a ramp is an elaborate mural depicting the plants and creatures of the intertidal world. Another ramp ending at the beach lets you explore for the real thing at minus tides.

Cormorant Cove Park • This delightful little pocket beachfront park is a joint project by the Alki Community Council and the Seattle Parks and Recreation Department. The park, a 200-foot-wide wedge of grass and landscaping that tapers down to a sand and cobble beach, lies just north of

A ceramic tidepool at Constellation Park Marine Reserve hints at the wonders that lie offshore.

a long condominium-topped pier that juts into Puget Sound. Views across the sound look into the throat of Rich Passage and beyond to peaks of the Olympic Mountains.

Weather Watch Park • In the early 1900s the little steamer *Eagle* provided quick transportation between West Seattle and the Seattle waterfront. When better roads made the service obsolete, the 100-foot-wide section of street-end from which the ferry ran lay fallow, the dock and steamer but memories. West Seattle residents have created a small park on the site—a perfect spot from which to watch changing weather over the sound.

A three-sided obelisk above the beach holds a tall pole that is topped by a flight of sheet metal ducks. Brass plates on the obelisk describe various cloud formations and tell historical vignettes of the region. A semicircular concrete bench offers a spot to sit and look across the sound to Blake and Vashon Islands and Colvos Passage. Plantings at street level give way below to large chunks of driftwood that decorate a 100-foot-wide cobble beach.

Emma Schmitz Memorial Viewpoint and Me Kwa Mooks Park • A mile south of Alki Point a pair of adjoining parks encompass a long strip of beach and adjacent hillside. A grassy strip, narrowing as it heads south, fills the six-block-long area between the road and the beach bulkhead. Several park benches offer spots to relax and watch the ferries ply the sound. Below the northern half of the grassy strip is a terraced walkway with a two-block-long concrete bench that invites leisurely afternoon sunning. Tidelands are rocky, with scattered boulders. The beach strip provides a pleasant stop on the bicycle route and jogging path that run along Harbor Avenue SW, Alki Avenue SW, and Beach Drive SW between Spokane Street and Lincoln Park.

Me Kwa Mooks was the name of a Nisqually village in the area. The term, meaning "shaped like a bear's head," refers to the entire area, including Alki Point and Duwamish Head. The parks represent two of three parcels of land given to the city by Ferdinand and Emma Schmitz, a pioneer couple who arrived in Seattle in 1887 and settled on this property in 1907. The third area of their bequest, 50-acre Schmitz Park, is a few blocks inland.

East of Beach Drive SW, the upland section of Me Kwa Mooks Park complements the beach strip with a picnic area and paths that lace dense woods that cover the adjacent hillside. This is the remains of the extensive grounds of the Schmitz estate, which at one time included elaborate flower gardens, an orchard, and a large, well-stocked trout pond.

Picnic tables dot a football-field-sized lawn. Short trails leave from both the north and south ends of the picnic area and duck through holly arches, raspberry thickets, and ivy patches as they meander across creeks and uphill through a woods of ivy-clad oak.

Lowman Beach Park • This urban meadow, scarcely 150 yards square, offers a bit of grass, a few trees, a tennis court, and a short strip of shorefront. The north two-thirds of the beach is framed by a concrete bulkhead. South of it, beach grass borders a sandy strip of shoreline that gives way to a gently sloping gravel beach at low tide. The Beach Drive bicycle route runs past the park and in a block connects to the north end of the Lincoln Park beach trail.

Lincoln Park (City of Seattle)   Map 10

Beach walking • Tidepools • Swimming • Picnicking • Group sports • Hiking • Fishing • Scuba diving

Facilities: Swimming pool (saltwater), sports fields, children's play equipment, wading pool, picnic shelters, picnic tables, restrooms, concession stand
Area: 135.4 acres; 10,500 feet of shoreline on Puget Sound

🚗 From the west end of the West Seattle Freeway take Fauntleroy Way SW to the south (with jogs west) for 2½ miles to reach the north end of the park. Parking is available off Fauntleroy at the center of the park at SW Monroe Street, or at the south end of the park at 46th Avenue SW. There is disabled parking at the beach at the south end of the park.

🚤 For land-to-water access, lightweight boats can be carried to the beach from the south parking lot.

This gem of the Seattle city parks system covers choice waterfront property above the beaches of Point Williams and Fauntleroy Cove. Although Lincoln

Park offers something for everyone and attracts throngs of people annually, it still retains a bit of intimacy, with vegetation and steep hillsides separating many of the activities. Red-barked madronas and heavy brush cling to clay banks above the beaches.

The park property was a private summer resort, established in 1904. It was acquired piecemeal by the city between 1925 and 1930 to form the park. Bulkhead and beach improvements benefited from Works Progress Administration funding in the Depression years of the 1930s.

❈ Visitors arriving at the park in large boats should anchor well out and dinghy ashore, but be aware that the beach slopes outward very gradually and it might be necessary to wade a bit and drag the dinghy in. A fringe of kelp beds 50 yards offshore that often plays host to seabirds marks the inner

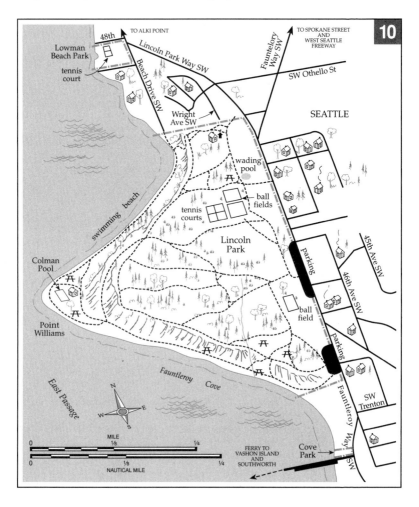

safe limit of approach for deep-draft boats. The rocky tideflats of Fauntleroy Cove can be hard on bare feet and the bottom of an inflatable. There are no public buoys; the several buoys south of the park near the Fauntleroy ferry terminal are private.

The upland areas of the park consist of large, grassy fields shaded by huge, old-growth fir and divided into people-sized units by smaller trees and shrubs. You'll find enough picnic tables to host your entire family reunion and playfields to keep everyone busy. The greatest concentration of picnic facilities is at the south end, although picnic tables are scattered throughout the park, and a shelter is in the north end. Play areas rimming the east edge of the park, just a short walk from the parking areas, include two baseball diamonds, a little league field, tennis courts, children's play equipment, and a wading pool. If that's not enough, there's ample space for Frisbee tossing or a quick game of catch.

Four and a half miles of trails lace the forest, reaching all corners of the park. The beach below the north bluff can also be reached by bicycle or on foot from the dead end of Beach Drive SW. This section of beach is sand and driftwood, with gravel exposed at low tide. Halfway between the north park boundary and Point Williams, a protective bulkhead separates the beach from the path. The wooded banks above the beach are occasionally scarred

Overhanging trees frame the beach and a picnic area at Lincoln Park.

A picnic shelter along the beach walk at Lincoln Park is shaded by tall madronas.

with scrambled trails—definitely not encouraged, and very unsafe.

Point Williams is the site of Colman Pool, an outdoor, heated, saltwater swimming pool, open only in summer. Grassy picnic areas are north of the pool; a children's play lot is to the south. On the south side of Point Williams the beach is rocky, scattered with boulders; kelp beds show it to be shallow some 200 yards out from shore. The Fauntleroy ferry adds action to the view with its regular departures from the terminal immediately south of the park.

Cove Park   Map 10

Views

Facilities: Art works
Area: 0.5 acre; 50 feet of shoreline on Puget Sound

🚐 From the west end of the West Seattle Freeway take Fauntleroy Way SW south (with jogs west) for 3 miles to the Fauntleroy ferry landing. The park is immediately north of the ferry pier.

This formerly vacant lot adjoining the Fauntleroy ferry pier has become a tiny beachfront park, notable for its art. The paved drive to the beach turn-around is rimmed with objects imbedded in aggregate, some painted or carved with phrases and thoughts by the artists. At the beach is more art: a large boulder with an etching of the brig *R. H. Fauntleroy*, a metal replica of a Nootka sealing canoe, and a whimsical iron crow perched atop a bleached driftwood tree with shiny glass in its beak. A gradually sloping sandy beach below the driftwood line invites lolling in the sun to watch the ferries come and go, or while waiting to board a ferry.

chapter three

Bainbridge Island

THE NEXT BEST THING TO LIVING ON AN ISLAND is visiting one, and Bainbridge Island is especially easy to visit. Those who don't have a boat of their own need only to saunter aboard the ferry or load kayak, canoe, bicycle, or auto onto the ferry, and, before the hour is over, they will be soaking up island atmosphere. One ferry from downtown Seattle goes directly to Bainbridge Island. Another leaves from Edmonds and runs to Kingston on the Kitsap Peninsula, and from there it's just a short drive south to the Agate Passage Bridge and across the bridge to the island.

The 24-nautical-mile circumnavigation of the island by boat makes a nice leisurely day excursion, with plenty of time for side trips into Dyes Inlet, Liberty Bay, or the island's inviting harbors, as the mood strikes. Boating facilities on the Kitsap shore of the Port Orchard channel, as well as navigational considerations in the channel and Rich Passage, are described in chapter 5.

Bainbridge Island is a favorite with bicyclers. Many roads are level, following the shoreline and offering spectacular marine views, but a few inland roads provide a real hill-climbing challenge—most notably Toe Jam Hill Road on the southeast point of the island, and Baker Hill Road, which cuts across the island's south end. Boaters or walk-on ferry passengers wanting to tour the island can rent bicycles in Winslow.

The parks department of the City of Bainbridge Island (which incorporates the entire island) has placed interpretive panels at various shoreline points around the island that describe the history or ecology of each site. A brochure available from the department locates each of these displays, and traveling to see the entire collection will provide visitors with a fascinating and enriching tour of the island.

THE EASTERN SHORE
Map 11

Eagle Harbor and Winslow Map 12

It's hard to imagine that more diverse activities could possibly be packed into a harbor of such small size. Eagle Harbor houses a ferry terminal, ferry maintenance facilities, boat repair yards, condominiums, yacht clubs, marinas, waterfront parks, private homes with docks, and a small fleet of live-aboard vessels. Only 2 miles long (and some of that taken up by mudflat) and averaging ¼ mile wide, the harbor and the business district along its north shore are the center of activity for all the island.

✵ When entering Eagle Harbor, boaters must use care, as a shoal and rocks extend south for about 500 yards from Wing Point on the north side of the harbor. Follow the channel markers, avoiding the natural desire to head straight into the bay. Good anchorages can be found in 30 feet of water near the west end of the bay, away from the flow of traffic. Anchoring in the bay is limited to seventy-two hours at a time.

A lineal moorage system in the center of the harbor accommodates more boats in a given space than individual mooring buoys can. For a fee, visiting

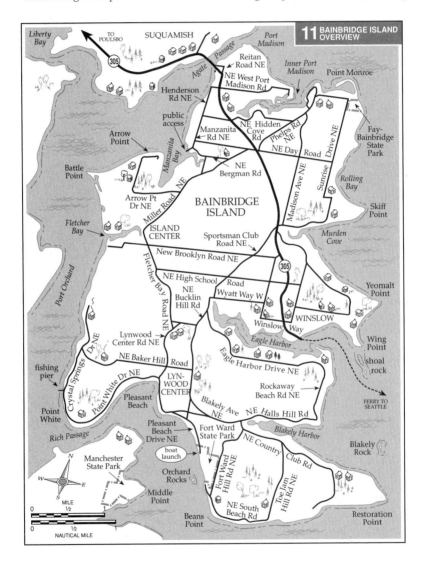

Eagle Harbor has moorages at several marinas and yacht clubs.

boats can tie to the eyes along the lines. Overnight moorage is permitted at the float at Waterfront Park, but there is no power or water on the pier, and the inboard portion of the float lies on the bottom at minus tides. Commercial marinas, described following, offer other moorage options.

Although the Agate Passage Bridge on the north end ties the island to the Kitsap mainland, lives are regulated by the comings and goings of the ferry headed for Seattle and big-city jobs. Early weekday mornings might find business-suited commuters, both male and female, rowing boats from Eagledale on the south shore of the bay to Winslow on the north, stepping ashore, briefcase in hand, and dashing for the ferry.

Eagle Harbor was one of the most polluted bays in Puget Sound, with bottom sediments containing a high percentage of toxic chemicals. An underwater sill near the entrance to the harbor slows tidal flows that flush the harbor, permitting sediments and pollutants to settle out within the bay. Contributing to the problem were failed septic tanks, animal wastes, storm drain run-off, and poor industrial practices; a former creosote plant was named a major culprit. Many of the pollutants have broken down chemically over time, and recent cleanup efforts included dumping a 3-foot-thick cap of soil over the contaminates, but fish, crabs, and shellfish in the bay are still considered unsafe to eat.

Winslow does it best to entice travelers to stop and enjoy the town before rushing on to distant destinations. The shopping district is uphill and to the west of SR 305, immediately after leaving the ferry. A host of stores and businesses along Winslow Way offer opportunities to browse, buy, dine, or wet your whistle. A complete circuit of downtown is just an easy stroll, ending with the green glade of the waterfront park.

Eagle Harbor Waterfront Park (City of Bainbridge Island) Map 12
Walking • Boating • Views

Facilities: Picnic tables, fireplace, picnic shelter, restrooms, dock, 1-lane paved launch ramp, boat rentals, marine pumpout station, portable toilet dump, children's play equipment, tennis courts

Area: 5.5 acres; 1000 feet of shoreline

From the Winslow shopping district, almost any turn to the south leads to the waterfront park. To drive to the launch ramp, turn off Bjune Drive onto Shannon Drive, and drive past the Queen City Yacht Club outstation to a road-end parking lot.

The business district of Winslow occupies the hillside above the bay. By some stroke of good fortune a stretch of waterfront below the town remained undeveloped and now is a pretty little park where tourists and townsfolk can recreate. To reach the park by foot from the ferry landing, walk down a road to the left that serves as an entrance to some condominiums; shortly it intersects a gravel path heading west, signed to Waterfront Park. A short extension of the path continues east, between Scotch broom and a yew hedge bordering the condo property, to the shore just west of the ferry landing. On the route to the west, a wooded ravine and a small backwater bay, crossed by a footbridge, lead to the east end of the park.

Madrona trees overhang the banks, and ivy-covered firs and alders reach upward. Picnic tables and benches at scenic spots provide plenty of excuses to while away some time and watch harbor activity. Kayaks and dinghies weave calmly among the yachts, ships, barges, and ferries. Ducks and seagulls eye visitors, hoping for a handout, crows complain about their presence, while cormorants look on.

The gravel and mud beach is not inviting for walking, but nice paths continue along the bank and through the heart of the park to its western

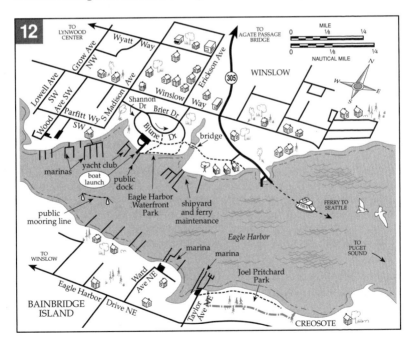

Eagle Harbor Waterfront Park offers nice boating facilities for visitors.

edge. Tennis courts, restrooms, and a picnic shelter with fireplace are a block uphill. A community center, more picnic tables, and children's play equipment are in the north portion of the park.

On the west side of the park is a launch ramp and a 300-foot-long float. Moorage on the float is limited to forty-eight hours per week; rafting is not permitted. The zero-tide level is marked on the dock; check the depth and tide level before securing your boat, as a tideflat extends for some distance from the shore. Although the launch ramp is excellent, it might not be usable at an extreme low tide. There is a small boat and kayak rental shop on the dock.

Eagle Harbor Marinas   Map 12

Facilities: Guest moorage with power and water, wireless broadband, restrooms, showers, laundry, marine pumpout stations, portable toilet dump, marine supplies and repair, restaurants, groceries, ice, fishing tackle, bait. Not all facilities are available at all marinas. There is no boat fuel available anywhere on the island.

Winslow Wharf Marina ● This facility, on the north shore west of the yacht club, has guest moorage, showers, laundry, a chandlery, groceries, a coffee shop, and a couple of restaurants on the wharf. The marina has no designated guest dock—all slips are permanent, and empty ones are sublet to visitors. Reservations for guest slips are accepted, or check with the dockmaster for available moorage on arrival.

Harbour Marina ● A few docks to the west, another tenant moorage offers guest slips on an "as available" basis. For open slips, check with the moorage manager on a live-aboard at the dock. Parking and a pub are nearby on shore.

Eagle Harbor Marina ● On the south shore, across from the ferry terminal, at the foot of Ward Avenue NE, this 150-slip marina includes showers, laundry, exercise equipment, and a recreation room. Although it was developed as a condominium dock, there are generally several slips that are available for guest moorage. Check with the dockmaster; all floats have power and water. There are no restaurants or stores on this side of the harbor, but downtown shopping is only a short row away at Winslow.

Joel Pritchard Park (City of Bainbridge Island)   Map 12
Hiking • Paddling • Beach walking • Historic interest

Facilities: Trails. *Planned:* Nikkei Exclusion and Internment Memorial, visitor center, garden
Area: 50 acres; 2000 feet of shoreline on Eagle Harbor
One block northwest of the ferry landing turn west on Winslow Way, and in ½ mile turn north on Grove Avenue NW. In two blocks turn west on Wyatt Way W, which becomes Eagle Harbor Drive NE at a sharp corner to the south in ¾ mile. Follow Eagle Harbor Drive southeast for 2 miles, and turn north on Taylor Avenue NE; the park is two blocks downhill.
The park beach lies on the south shore of Eagle Harbor, between the farthest east marina dock and the tip of the point that once held the Wycoff Creosote plant.

The narrow tip of land guarding the south entrance to Eagle Harbor was once the site of the Wycoff Creosote plant that disposed of waste byproducts from its wood treatment process into Eagle Harbor—an acceptable practice at the time. Current technology and environmental awareness realized that large portions of the harbor and shore were contaminated. The site is in the process of being cleaned up.

The City of Bainbridge plans to make 50 acres of the site's beach and uplands a park. A few upland trails have been laid in, and an abandoned road along the shore provides access to the broad sandy beach.

The west end of the park was once the location of the Eagledale ferry landing, the spot from which, in 1942, nearly 300 Bainbridge Islands residents, U.S. citizens of Japanese ancestry, were forcibly evicted and sent to wartime internment in inland prison camps. Plans for the park include a memorial and visitor center telling of this historic injustice. The book *Snow Falling on Cedars*, by David Guterson, was centered on this event. It later became a movie. The park is named in memory of Joel Prichard, the local congressman who was instrumental in obtaining the Superfund legislation to clean up the site.

BLAKELY HARBOR
Map 13

South along the Bainbridge Island shoreline, 1½ miles from Eagle Harbor, is the quiet little inlet of Blakely Harbor. Pleasure boaters enjoy the harbor as a good overnight anchorage and an interesting cruising diversion. Private residences rim the bay—some are the remodeled buildings of the old mill and shipyard; all shorelands are private, with the exception of a Bainbridge City Park at the west end of the Harbor. Numerous rotted piles and the concrete shell of an old generator building at the far northwest end of the bay are testimony to the previous life at Blakely Harbor.

Although the bay is exposed to winds from the east, some anchorages can be found along the south shore. The view east to Seattle is stunning, with the Space Needle and downtown skyscrapers looming large.

❋ Blakely Rock, which is marked by a light, lies ½ mile east of the entrance to Blakely Harbor and due north of Restoration Point. A rocky shoal extends 250 yards to the north. The reef is a popular scuba-diving site.

Blakely Harbor Park (City of Bainbridge)   Maps 11 and 13

Hiking • Picnicking • Beach walking • Paddling • Historic interpretation

Facilities: Trails. *Planned:* Additional trails, picnic areas, hand-carry boat launch, toilets, interpretive center, interpretive signs

Area: 38 acres; 4000 feet of shoreline on Blakely Harbor

🚗 One block northwest of the Bainbridge ferry landing turn west on Winslow Way, and in ½ mile turn north on Grow Avenue NW. In two blocks turn west on Wyatt Way W, which becomes Eagle Harbor Drive NE at a sharp turn to the south in ¾ mile. In about 3 blocks bear south on Bucklin Hill Road NE, and at a junction in another ½ mile continue south on Blakely Avenue NE. Follow it for 2¼ miles, and turn southeast on 3 T Road NE. The park entrance sign is on the right in about 100 yards. (The park entrance will be moved to Blakely Avenue when the park is further developed.)

🚣 On the west end of Blakely Harbor. A hand-carry boat launch area is planned for the northeast end of the park.

Blakely Harbor Park is a work in progress. The City of Bainbridge Island has acquired 38 acres of property at the west end of the harbor, the site of its once-flourishing sawmill. Development probably won't be completed until 2007 or later.

As of now, there is streetside parking for a few cars along 3 T Road. Short paths into the park reach either the beach or a wetland. At the north beach, stubs of rotted piles march west into the harbor. The beach is gradually

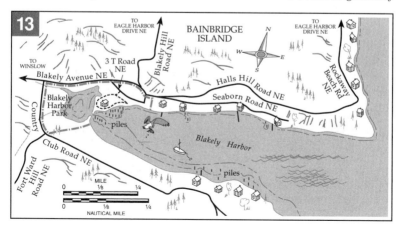

Rotted piles at the former sawmill site now mark Blakely Harbor Park.

tapering gravel with a low bank of beach grass above. Near the partially filled wetland is a concrete building shell that once housed the mill's power generators. East of it are rock jetties framing a mini-harbor that was used as a log pond. A steel gate between the jetties confined the logs.

Plans are for extensive wetland restoration and several short trails to viewpoints with historic and ecological interpretation. A hand-carry boat

The Hall Brothers Shipyard

Blakely Harbor wasn't always as tranquil as it is today. The harbor once held a booming sawmill that, during the 1880s, was claimed to be the largest in the world; lumber shipped from here graced fine mansions from San Francisco to London.

In 1881, the Hall Brothers Shipyard moved their operation here from Port Ludlow when problems at the Ludlow sawmill threatened the ready supply of finished lumber at that location. The Hall Brothers' yard built seventy-seven ships in the years they were in Port Blakely. It was a convenient cycle of events—ships were built of lumber from the mill, and then many of them carried lumber from the mill to markets throughout the world. The five-masted, 225-foot *H. K. Hall*, launched here, could hold 1.5 million board feet of fine Puget Sound lumber.

A 1907 fire devastated the mill, and it was rebuilt to only half its former size. The decline in readily available logs, combined with a depressed lumber market, finally led to the mill's closing in 1914. As the mill foundered, the Hall shipyard was moved north in 1903 to Eagle Harbor. For a time Blakely Harbor still held some importance as a ferry landing, but that too was moved to Winslow in 1937, and the harbor settled into a quiet existence as a residential community.

launch is planned at the northeast corner of the park, and the old generator building is scheduled for an interpretive center.

RICH PASSAGE AND PORT ORCHARD CHANNEL
Map 11

Bainbridge Island forms the northern boundary of Rich Passage, the narrow channel the ferry must thread through on its way to Bremerton. The passage is heavily traveled by pleasure boats; ⚓ on rare occasions an enormous ship or navy vessel heading for or leaving Bremerton fills the channel. Between Point White and Point Glover, at the west end, the channel makes a sharp turn and squeezes down to less than 500 yards wide before opening up into the expanse of the Port Orchard channel. Large vessels will sound one long blast when within ½ mile of Point Glover as a warning to approaching craft.

West of Rich Passage an arm of the Port Orchard channel bends southwest, ending in Sinclair Inlet and the gargantuan Erector Set of the navy shipyards. The main body of the channel sweeps steadily northward for 9 unobstructed miles between Bainbridge Island and the Kitsap Peninsula, before squeezing into Agate Passage and finally pouring into Port Madison. Navigational considerations and facilities in Rich Passage and Port Orchard are described in chapter 4.

Fort Ward State Park   Map 14

Historical displays • Boating • Paddling • Fishing • Birdwatching • Hiking • Scuba diving

Facilities: Picnic tables, fireplaces, toilets, 2-lane paved launch ramp, trail, 2 mooring buoys, underwater park, bird blind, CMT campsite, historic gun batteries, interpretive displays

Area: 137 acres; 4300 feet of shoreline on Rich Passage

🚐 One block northwest of the Bainbridge ferry landing turn west on Winslow Way, and in ½ mile turn north on Grove Avenue NW. In two blocks turn west on Wyatt Way W, which becomes Eagle Harbor Drive NE at a sharp corner to the south in ¾ mile. In about three blocks bear south on Hill Road NE, and at a junction in another ½ mile continue south on Blakely Avenue NE. Follow it south for 1½ miles to a junction with Blakely Road West NE. *Northwest park entrance:* Take Blakely Road West south for ½ mile to a T intersection, and then follow Pleasant Beach Drive NE southeast to the park entrance. *Upper east entrance:* Continue southeast on Blakely Avenue for ¾ mile, and turn south on Country Club Road NE. In ¼ mile head southwest on Fort Ward Hill Road NE, and reach the upper park entrance in 1 mile. *Lower south park entrance:* Fort Ward Hill Road NE can be followed as it continues steeply downhill to the water and the eastern end of the gated park road; however, there is no parking at the end.

⛴️ Fort Ward is on the northeast side of Rich Passage about 1 n.m. north of Beans Point. ⚓ There are offshore fish pens just south of the park, and Orchard Rocks, marked by a navigation beacon, are about 300 yards offshore. The park mooring buoys are near the launch ramp at the north end of the park.

Battery Vinton lies along the road at Fort Ward State Park.

It wasn't until recently, when lands on the south end of Bainbridge Island were developed as a state park, that many people even knew there had been a military fortification in the area. Visitors are now gradually discovering this history-rich corner of the island and the forested day-use state park overlooking Rich Passage.

Just inside the northwest park entrance is a launch ramp. Launching can be difficult due to the strong tidal current and wakes from passing boats, especially ferries churning through Rich Passage. The mooring buoys offshore, north and south of the ramp, are also subject to channel turbulence.

The bottom offshore is frequented by scuba divers who explore the abundance of sea life on the steep walls. To the south are Orchard Rocks, with anemone-filled grottos and perhaps an octopus. *Dive with extreme care; use a dive flag and watch and listen for boats when ascending.*

Walk the beach or the gated road south, passing the park office and a pretty, shoreside picnic area with tables and fireplaces. The brush along the beach at the picnic area screens a CMT campsite, the only camping available in the park. From the water a sign marking the site can be spotted on shore near a line of pilings south of the park buildings. South along the road from the picnic area is Battery Vinton, with an informational display and a tip-toe view over a growth of Scotch broom across Rich Passage to Middle Point.

A unique wooden structure with benches, midway down the road, is a bird blind for watching waterfowl in the channel. Along the shore three sets of moldering pilings topped by horizontal beams, are "cormorant parking lots," frequently holding a phalanx of these birds craning their necks to watch activity in the channel or spreading their wings to dry.

Trails through the forest connect the various entrances and lead to the ivy- and moss-encrusted Battery Thornburgh, where four 3-inch rapid-fire guns were once mounted. A complete loop hike, including all the sights, is about 2 miles. Do not stray off the paths, as there is poison oak in the area.

Continue driving or bicycling south on NE South Beach Road, which follows the shoreline, and a sharp turn to the north brings you to the fabled Toe Jam Hill Road NE. The name of the hill, it is said, comes from a particularly

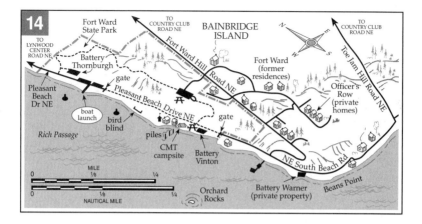

seedy tavern that was in the area in early times. The libation served by this establishment, instead of being called Rot Gut, was given the even more derisive term of Toe Jam. The tavern burned in 1903 or 1904, but the name remained forever for the hill on which it stood. The steep road is so challenging that it is included as part of island bicycle races. You might also think that the road is so steep that you must jam your toes in to climb it.

Point White Fishing Pier (City of Bainbridge Island)   Map 11

Fishing • Paddling • Scuba diving

Facilities: Fishing pier, informational sign

One block northwest of the Bainbridge ferry landing turn west on Winslow Way, and in ½ mile turn north on Grow Avenue NW. In two blocks turn west on Wyatt Way W, which becomes Eagle Harbor Drive NE at a sharp corner to the south in ¾ mile. In about three blocks bear south on Hill Road NE, and at a junction in another ½ mile continue south on Blakely Avenue NE. Follow it south for 1 mile, and turn west on Baker Hill Road NE. Follow it west for 3 miles to a T intersection, and turn south on Crystal Springs Drive NE. The pier is ½ mile to the south. *Alternatively:* From Lynwood Center go west on Point White Drive NE, which becomes Crystal Springs Drive NE at Point White, and reach the pier in 2¼ miles.

The pier is on the east side of Port Orchard (west side of Bainbridge Island) 1 n.m. north of Point White.

On the southwest corner of Bainbridge Island, in the small community of Crystal Springs, a long pier was formerly used by the Mosquito fleet. The pier is a city park open to the public for fishing. Even if fish are not interested in being caught some days, the dock is a nice vantage point, with miles of views up and down the channel to Port Orchard and across to Illahee State Park. The Suquamish Indians, less taken with the esthetics of the spot, called it *Tux'waxa'detc*, which translates to "goose droppings." This descriptive name came from the tideland boulders that were stained white by guano from the birds fishing the offshore waters. The pier has no float, but the adjoining beach is quite gentle, so small boats could be beached or hand-carried ones launched. An interpretive sign tells more of the history and ecology of the spot.

Fletcher and Manzanita Bays   Maps 11 and 15

Boating • Paddling

🚗 Take SR 305 north from the ferry landing for 4¾ miles, and turn west on Day Road West NE. At a T intersection in 1 mile head south on Manzanita Road NE. When this road bends eastward in ¼ mile look for the sign for Dock Street. This road stub ends at a bulkhead above the beach; parking is minimal. Property adjacent to the road and the beach on either side of the road end itself is private.

🛥 The bays are directly across from the entrance to Poulsbo's Liberty Bay on the Kitsap Peninsula, and 2 n.m. south of the Agate Passage Bridge.

Gunkholers take note! Two small bays along the west shore of Bainbridge Island offer boaters a quiet overnight anchorage or a spot to drop a lunch hook. Only one tiny stretch of shoreline on Manzanita Bay is public. Battle Point, the tip of the triangular peninsula separating the bays, was named for a battle of long ago when the local Suquamish Indians and their chief, Kitsap, fought off a band of marauding northern hostiles.

❉ A gravel bar blocks the entrance to Fletcher Bay at midtide, and the bay itself is quite shallow. Boats should enter it only during high tide, and then with extreme care. Manzanita Bay, to the north, offers the best overnight stops, with good protection from southerly blows or, in good weather, placid, star-filled nights. The main body of the bay extends due south for ¾ mile; a short "thumb" trends east. Good anchorages in up to 30 feet of water can be found in either section. ❉ The only hazards are submerged pilings about halfway in from the entrance on each side of the bay.

A sliver of public access exists on the north side of Manzanita Bay at a road end, the site of a ferry landing between 1895 and 1927. This is a good spot to launch hand-carried boats for exploration of the bay.

Fairy Dell Park (City of Bainbridge Island)   Map 15

Hiking • Beach walking • Birdwatching • Shellfish

Facilities: Parking, trail
Area: 0.5 acre; 100 feet of shoreline on the Port Orchard channel

🚗 Take SR 305 north from the ferry landing for 3 miles, and turn west on Koura Road NE. In 1½ miles turn southwest on Miller Road NE, and in ¼ mile go west on Arrow Point Drive NE. In ¾ mile, at Battle Point Park, this road turns north, and in another ½ mile head west, along the north side of Battle Point Park, on NE Frey Avenue. The Fairy Dell parking lot is on the northwest corner of the park, just east of the junction of Frey Road NE and Battle Point Drive NE.

🛥 The park beach is on the Port Orchard channel, on the northwest side of Bainbridge Island, midway between Battle Point and Arrow Point.

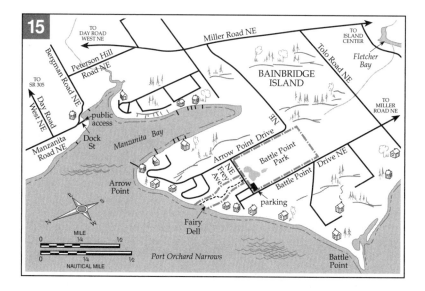

The park is aptly named Fairy Dell, as the trail descends an ever-deepening gully through second-growth timber and old-growth cedar stumps, with a carpet of ferns covering the bordering slopes. Tiny mushrooms sprouting from decaying stumps surely must be fairy food, and a seasonal streamlet trickling down the base of the gully might hold fairy wine. In a quarter mile the trail breaks out onto a shallow mud/sand beach with views across the Port Orchard channel to Keyport and north to the Agate Passage Bridge.

The obscure trailhead is on the north side of Frey Road about a block east of the parking lot. Its only identification is a small "Public Shoreline Access" sign.

AGATE PASSAGE AND PORT MADISON
Map 11

The Agate Passage Bridge, at the northwest tip of Bainbridge Island, is the island's only permanent tie to the mainland, freeing it from total dependence on the ferry. Since the completion of the bridge in 1950, old plans for building additional bridges have been periodically dusted off, but the increased cost of such a project, coupled with the islanders' satisfaction with the status quo, always causes plans to be shelved once again.

The call for more bridges usually comes from people on the Kitsap Peninsula, frustrated by ferry service, who want bridges to Vashon Island and the south end of Bainbridge, so they can have easier access to ferry terminals on those islands and can swear at three ferries instead of just one.

After their rapid trip through 300-yard-narrow Agate Passage, the waters of the Port Orchard channel pour into Port Madison, a broad, round bay bounded on the south by Bainbridge Island. Point Monroe, a curving sand spit marked by a navigational light, lies at the south point of the entrance to the bay. The spit encloses a lagoon that boats can enter at its west end; however, it is quite shallow and the entrance dries at low tide. Several private homes are on the spit, and there are docks on the inner edge.

Reitan Road Access   Map 11

Viewpoint • Scuba diving

Facilities: None

🚗 Head west on SR 305 and, just before crossing the bridge, turn north on Reitan Road NE. The narrow, paved road drops downhill and under the bridge footings. Parking for a few cars is at the side of the narrow road near a powerline tower, just northeast of the bridge.

This primitive access, directly under the bridge on the Bainbridge Island side of the channel, gives a unique water-level perspective on activity in Agate Passage. From the powerline tower a dirt path leads to a cobble beach dropping off abruptly to the water. The beach south of the bridge is private, but about 300 feet of shorelands to the north are open to public walking, although on power company property.

Traffic roars overhead, water swirls around the concrete abutments, boats sweep by grandly, given an overdrive assist by the rushing current, and an occasional black head, dripping with water, bobs to the surface. Seals? No—scuba divers!

The access is used by divers who explore the bridge abutments, offshore rocks, and steep walls of the channel. Because the tidal currents can reach 6 knots, only experienced divers should use the area. Those skilled enough to handle the flow thrill to a roller coaster ride around and over rocks and past the encrusted pilings of the bridge.

West Port Madison Nature Preserve (City of Bainbridge Island)

Map 16

Hiking • Picnicking • Beach walking • Nature study

Facilities: Trail, kitchen shelters, beach ladder

Area: 13 acres; 210 feet of shoreline on Port Madison

🚗 Take SR 305 north from the ferry terminal for 6½ miles, and turn east on NE West Port Madison Road. This road turns north in ½ mile, and turns east as NE County Park Road. The park is on the north side of the road in a couple of blocks.

⛴ The narrow park beach is on the south side of Port Madison (north side of Bainbridge Island) about ½ n.m. west of the entrance to Madison Bay (Inner Port Madison).

A tiny slice of county property just west of Inner Port Madison, once a park, is now a nature preserve. The beach, just west of some private homes, offers the only public access on the Bainbridge Island side of Port Madison.

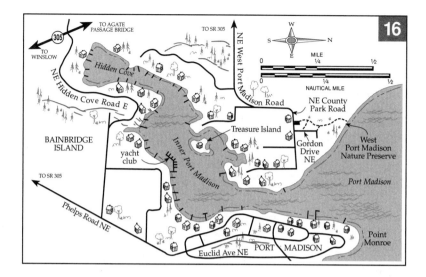

A signed parking lot for a dozen cars marks the head of a trail that winds north into the heavy growth of old cedar and fir. Short spurs lead east to the park caretaker's house and to Gordon Drive NE. Along the way to the beach, two old shake-roofed kitchen shelters hold fireplaces and picnic tables. Imagine the festive picnics of yesteryear that the little park must have seen.

The steep 75-foot clay bank above the beach is negotiated by a shaky ladder made of 4-by-4s threaded on cables lashed to an upland tree, with an adjoining (hang on for your life!) braided rope. This is not the spot to take small children (although they would probably enjoy it more than many adults). For your return, remember where the trail comes out of the brush at the beach, as the spot is not easily found. At low tides the beach is gradually tapering cobble; high tide brings water right up to the tree line.

Inner Port Madison   Map 16

The mile-long watery arm extending south from Port Madison is unquestionably one of the loveliest boating stops on Bainbridge Island, and perhaps all of South Puget Sound. Names around here are a little confusing—to some *this* narrow inlet is Port Madison—nevermind that big chunk of water hovering to the north; to others this arm is Madison Bay. But the name by which it is known locally, and by most knowledgeable boaters, is Inner Port Madison. The community on its shore is also named Port Madison.

Port Madison (the community) was once the major commercial center on the island. Not only was it the county seat, complete with a courthouse and jail, but it also had a large sawmill, shipyards, a foundry, a fish oil rendering plant, and a population of 400 to 600. A geography book published at the time described Seattle as "a lumber town across the bay from Port

Madison." Because this was a company town, residences were owned by the mill and rented to employees. When the company fell on hard times because of a depressed lumber market, it became heavily mortgaged by the Seattle First National Bank. Eventually the bank foreclosed and took over everything owned by the mill.

Because virtually all the property on the harbor was then in the hands of Seattle First, the bank conceived the idea of developing the property as an exclusive summer resort area. All but the best of the mill buildings were torn down, lots were sold for fashionable summer homes, and metal gates were installed on the road to keep cows from wandering through and destroying the ambiance (or depositing their own ambiance).

Over the years the summer homes gave way to the gracious permanent homes now found along the shore today. The Port Madison Yacht Club has moorages on the bay, and there is an outstation for the Seattle Yacht Club here. The small island midway along the north shore was used as a cemetery during days of the mill and so was known as Deadman's Island. When a cemetery was established elsewhere on Bainbridge Island, the human remains were moved. High society hit the bay, and the islet was renamed Treasure Island.

✸ Boats entering the bay should hold to the middle of the channel to avoid an old ballast dump along the east shore, a reminder of the days when this was a lumber port. Ships arriving in the harbor without cargo carried a load of rock as ballast to steady them; the rock was dumped when they were ready to take on a load of lumber.

Inner Port Madison is a nifty anchorage, but beware of a submerged rock southwest of Treasure Island.

✸ Inside the mile-long bay the only navigation hazards are shoals extending from Treasure Island and a submerged rock marked by a day beacon lying southwest of the small island. Good anchorages can be found throughout the bay, out of the way of traffic, in up to 20 feet of water.

In its last ⅓ mile the bay takes a dogleg turn to the south. This far end is known as Hidden Cove. Navigable water continues almost to the end of the bay; all shorelands are private.

Fay-Bainbridge State Park   Map 17

Camping • Boating • Paddling • Picnicking • Fishing • Beach walking • Scuba diving • Shellfish • Historical interpretation

Facilities: 36 campsites, picnic tables, fireplaces, picnic shelters, restrooms, showers, 2 mooring buoys, volleyball court, horseshoe pits, children's play equipment, trailer dump, CMT campsite, historical display, interpretive signs
Area: 16.8 acres; 1420 feet of shoreline

🚗 Take SR 350 north from the ferry landing for 4¾ miles, and turn east on Day Road East NE. At a T intersection in 1½ miles head north on Sunrise Drive NE and arrive at the park in 1¾ miles.

🛥 The park is on the west side of Puget Sound (east side of Bainbridge Island) 1 n.m. south of Point Monroe.

The only campground on Bainbridge Island, aside from the CMT campsite at Fort Ward State Park, is on the island's northeast shore at popular Fay-Bainbridge State Park. The park includes some nicely wooded uplands and one of the prettiest beaches on the island. The beach faces directly on the main channel of Puget Sound, so at times wind and wave action can be severe, and even on hot summer days the water is chilly for swimming. The sandy beach, topped by a row of driftwood and tufts of seagrass, is always a delight, however. At low water the long tideflat holds promise of a few clams for the lucky. The park is heavily used by island residents and on nice summer days can get very crowded.

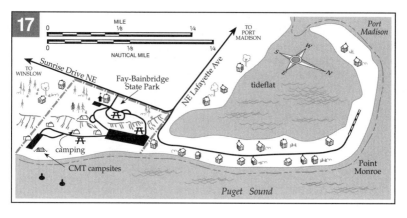

The beach at Fay-Bainbridge State Park holds some stunning driftwood. Point Jefferson on the Kitsap Peninsula lies in the distance.

The historic highlight of the park is the large brass bell on display near the entrance. The bell, which was brought from San Francisco about 1883, was purchased by private subscription by the people of Port Madison and was used in the courthouse.

For its relatively small size the park packs in a lot of activities. The upper portion of the park has a few picnic sites and some tent camping in grassy areas among the trees. Most of the camping is just above the beach at rather tightly spaced campsites for RVs along the southern side of the park. Two tent pads on the beachgrass flat at the south end of the park are CMT campsites.

Two mooring buoys offshore are usable for a lunch stop, but lack of protection from waves and wakes could make them quite uncomfortable for an overnight stay.

chapter four

East Kitsap Peninsula

THE KITSAP PENINSULA HAS THE DISTINCTION of being bounded on the west by one major waterway, Hood Canal, and on the east by a different large body of water, Puget Sound. With the exception of the large indentation of Port Gamble Bay, the western shoreline of Kitsap Peninsula rolls smoothly along the canal. The eastern edge of the peninsula, however, is heavily convoluted, with numerous bays and inlets pushing deep inland. These sheltered bays, with their miles upon miles of shoreline, lure boaters and beach walkers bent on marine diversions.

Several state and city parks along the shore offer recreation facilities, and a number of towns have marine accommodations and supplies. The shores are heavily populated—even in the parks one would be hard pressed to find a pristine beach, but the interesting villages and towns along the way compensate for this.

Land travelers usually arrive at the Kitsap Peninsula via ferry, either from Seattle to Bremerton, or from Seattle to Bainbridge Island, and then drive or bike over the Agate Passage Bridge. Either route is exquisitely scenic, with views of boating traffic on the busy marine highways, the sparkling skyline of the city, and the ethereal presence of Mount Rainier. The peninsula can also be reached from the south via SR 16 from Tacoma or SR 3 from Shelton.

Beyond Indianola the Kitsap shoreline takes on a different look. Gone are the sheltered beaches and forest-edged channels, as the peninsula sweeps north to its climax at Foulweather Bluff. Beaches here are wild and wind torn, with mounds of ragged beach grass and a strand of silvered driftwood deposited by the waves of Puget Sound. Shores north of Kingston are described in this book's companion volume, *Afoot and Afloat: North Puget Sound.*

Manchester Launch Ramp (Port of Manchester) Map 18

Boating • Paddling • Fishing • Picnicking

Facilities: Dock with float, paved launch ramp with boarding float, picnic tables, picnic shelter, disabled-accessible restroom, historic displays. *Nearby:* Groceries, ice, service station, bait, tackle

🚐 From the Southworth ferry landing take SE Southworth Drive west and north for 3½ miles to Colchester Drive SE. Turn north on it to arrive at Manchester in another 1¾ mile. The launch ramp is one block east at the end of E Main Street. Alternatively, from Port Orchard take Beach Drive E east for 6½ miles to E Main Street in Manchester.

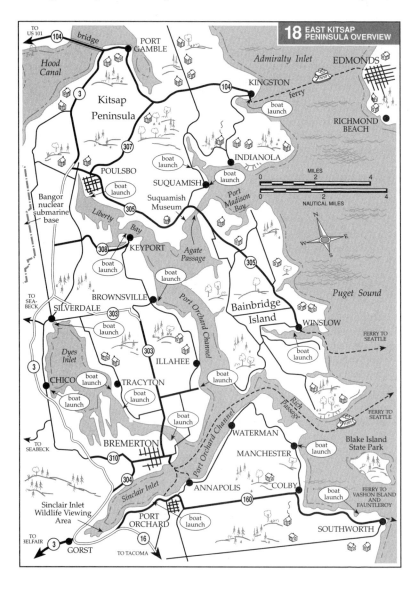 Manchester is on the northwest shore of Yukon Harbor, ½ n.m. south of the east entrance to Rich Passage (1 n.m. west of the west tip of Blake Island).

The only public water access between Harper and Rich Passage is at the community of Manchester. Here the Port of Manchester dock, with its 150-foot-long float, is available for day use by boaters and anglers; overnight moorage is not permitted. Adjacent to the dock on the north is a single-lane concrete launch ramp with a long boarding float. The docks also afford expansive views west to the Seattle cityscape, the West Seattle shoreline, nearby Blake Island, and south to Mount Rainier. Picnic tables line the beach between the two docks; a pair of information panels here tell the history of the Puget Sound Mosquito Fleet and of the town of Manchester.

Just south of the dock is tiny Pomeroy Park: a patch of grass above the beach with picnic tables and a small picnic shelter. The heart of Manchester is a cluster of stores around the intersection of Colchester and Main.

RICH PASSAGE
Map 18

Rich Passage is one of the most scenic spots along the route of the Bremerton ferry. Here the channel squeezes at its most slender point to a mere 500 yards wide, and passengers are treated to close-up views of salty beachfront homes tucked into green-clad shoreline. ❋ Pleasure boaters should be wary of stiff tidal currents that can be encountered in the channel, especially at the west end. Several rocks lying just offshore are well marked with lights or daymarkers. The largest of the obstacles, Orchard Rocks, lying on the north side of the channel just inside the east entrance, are partially exposed at low tide. Boaters will encounter no problems if they stay in the marked channel but should keep an eye over their shoulders for ferries bearing down on them.

Manchester State Park   Map 19

Camping • Picnicking • Historical displays • Hiking • Swimming • Fishing • Boating • Paddling • Scuba diving

Facilities: 15 RV sites (EW), 35 standard campsites, 3 hiker/biker primitive sites, CMT campsites, group camp with 12 RV sites (EW), picnic tables, fireplaces, picnic shelters, restrooms, showers, bathhouse, group day-use area, trails, nature trail, historic fortifications, trailer dump station, horseshoe pits, volleyball court, hand-carry boat launch

Area: 111 acres; 3400 feet of shoreline on Rich Passage

🚙 *From Bremerton:* Follow SR 304 west until it joins SR 3 southwest of the city, and then continue on SR 3 to its junction with SR 16. Follow SR 16 and then SR 160 to Port Orchard. Turn onto Bay Avenue, which becomes N Bay Street and then Beach Drive E. Turn north on E Hilldale Road 5¼ miles from Port Orchard, and reach the park in ¼ mile.

From the Southworth ferry landing: Head west on SE Southworth Drive, and in 3¾ miles turn north on Colchester Drive SE. In 1¾ miles, at the community of Manchester, continue north on Beach Drive E to reach E Hilldale in another ¾ mile.

🛥 The park is on the south side of Rich Passage, just west of Middle Point.

Although the United States was not at war at the turn of the century, the army feared foreign ships could sneak into Puget Sound and attack the vital naval shipyards at Bremerton. A military station was built at Middle Point on the south shore of Rich Passage to operate a minefield that was to be laid across the channel. By 1910, even before World War I broke out, the technology of the type of mine installed here became obsolete and, because there was no dire threat of attack, the fort was deactivated; the site was then for a time used for testing mines (or torpedoes, as they were then called).

During World War II anti-submarine nets were stretched from here across the channel to Fort Ward. The nets were lowered whenever ferries passed. After the installation was no longer needed, part of the military land was taken by the navy for a supply depot; the balance of the property was eventually surplused, and the public got lucky and gained another prime beachfront state park.

The park fronts on a small, shallow cove—not especially good for swimming, but an adequate spot to launch hand-carried boats. Underwater rocks off Middle Point are an attractive scuba diving site. The campground, on the hillside above the cove, lies in tall cedar, fir, alder, and maple with an undergrowth of sword fern and salal. Two CMT campsites are tucked in the brush just above the picnic area.

Especially interesting are two old remaining structures of the fortification, a torpedo (mine) warehouse and mining casemate. Informational displays describe the system of placing and detonating the mines and the tracking of ships in the channel. The huge brick torpedo warehouse, with gracefully arched windows and doorways, is now what is probably the state's biggest picnic shelter.

Several trails lace the park, connecting the campground with the picnic area and beach; most follow old service roads. A short loop interpretive nature trail is immediately north of the park entrance. Stay on trails and avoid brush near the shore because of a heavy growth of poison oak.

A trail leads west from the beach and picnic area to the concrete pit of

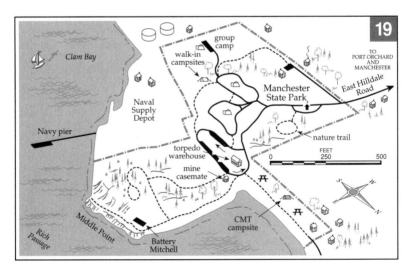

The former torpedo warehouse at Manchester State Park now serves as a grand picnic shelter.

Battery Mitchell. The army had planned for the Middle Point fortification to have two 3-inch guns to protect the minefield, but the four batteries at Fort Ward on Bainbridge Island, immediately across Rich Passage, offered ample protection, so the guns were never installed.

PORT ORCHARD CHANNEL AND SINCLAIR INLET
Map 20

Geographical names are supposed to be to clarify locations; unfortunately this is not the case with Port Orchard, as the name refers to the 9-mile north-south-flowing channel separating Bainbridge Island and the Kitsap Peninsula, the baylike continuation of that channel that runs southwest to Bremerton, and the small town on the shore of, not Port Orchard, but Sinclair Inlet.

Beach Drive East   Map 20
Fishing • Bicycling

Facilities: Public fishing pier, toilet, restaurants, hand-carry boat launch

🚗 From the east side of Port Orchard head east on Bay Street, which becomes Beach Drive E at the community of Annapolis. Continue east on Beach Drive for 2¾ miles to Waterman and the public pier.

Beach Drive East, paralleling the water along the south side from Rich Passage to the town of Port Orchard, is an ideal bicycle or Sunday-drive route with plenty of places to stop and picnic, birdwatch, fish, or photograph. Monster ferries lumber by, sailboats blow in the breeze, the naval shipyards

look like some enormous Erector Set construction, and above it all rise the crystal peaks of the Olympics.

At minus tides the baring shoreline shows interesting lines of parallel rock strata extending diagonally outward from the beach. These are the edges of tilted layers of hard rock that were ground off by an ancient glacier.

Annapolis • The community of Annapolis, on the east side of Port Orchard is home to many of the workers at the Bremerton Naval Shipyard. Kitsap Transit operates a commuter ferry between Annapolis and Bremerton from a long dock on the south shore of Sinclair Inlet. A parking area east of the dock offers access to a DFW hand-carry launch site into the inlet at high tides. The 300-foot-long dock has a float that can be used for fishing when the ferry is not in.

Inspired by the prospects of the naval shipyards about to be built on Sinclair Inlet, the founders of Annapolis named their town after the site of the U.S. Naval Academy in Maryland and gave the streets names of naval heroes such as Farragut and Perry.

The current Waterman Pier is located on the site of a former Mosquito Fleet dock.

Waterman Pier (Port of Bremerton) • In the late 1800s steamers of the Mosquito Fleet stopped regularly at Waterman, on the south shore of Port Orchard, to load bricks from the local brickyard and pick up and discharge passengers. The brickyard closed in 1889; in time the steamers ceased calling here and the old piers of the brickyard rotted away. Today the only reminder of the once-busy town is a pier rebuilt on the pilings of the former ferry dock.

The 200-foot-long pier, maintained by the Port of Bremerton, has a fishing platform at its end. At the head of the dock, a wooden deck with a pair of benches and a toilet fronts a paved narrow parking area. Next to the shore, wooden stairs give access to the beach; however, the beach is public only immediately under the pier.

Port Orchard   Map 20

Port Orchard (the town) is frequently the prime destination for people boating in Port Orchard (the waterway). The town is the antithesis of industrial Bremerton, facing it across the inlet—here life is slow-paced, except briefly during shift change at the navy shipyards, when commuter traffic pours through. The town caters to tourists; its main street, with wooden-canopied walkways reminiscent of the Old West, has an assortment of interesting shops to browse and eateries to try.

Port Orchard began its history in 1866 as Sidney, named after the father of town founder Frederick Stevens. In 1903, after ten years of political arm wrestling with the town fathers of Charleston, on the opposite side of the inlet, who decided they wanted the name Port Orchard too, Sidney was re-named Port Orchard. At that time the shipyard mail was addressed to Port Orchard (the waterway), and everyone was trying to capitalize on it.

Port Orchard Log Cabin Museum • Three blocks straight up the hill on Sidney Avenue at the intersection of Dekalb Street is the town's Log Cabin Museum—a case where the building is every bit as fascinating and historic as its contents. The two-story log structure, which dates from 1913 to 1914, houses a collection of memorabilia and authentic furnishings. Hours are Saturday 1:00 PM to 4:00 PM, May through December, and by arrangement at other times.

Port Orchard Passenger Ferry • From the beginning, Mosquito Fleet boats were vital to the existence of businesses in Sidney (Port Orchard), but once the shipyards became active the steamers also served to transport workers from their homes on the south side of the bay. The historic Mosquito Fleet is now just a fond memory, but it is possible to recapture some of the feeling of that era by hopping the little passenger ferry still running to Bremerton.

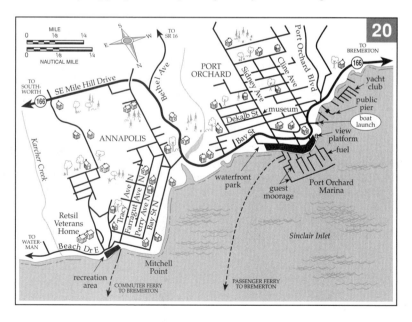

The boat departs from the terminal immediately east of the marina about every half hour; crossing time is about fifteen minutes. Take advantage of the trip and linger to walk around Bremerton, avoiding parking or mooring woes. A second passenger ferry leaves from Annapolis, on the east side of town, but that boat is primarily used by shipyard workers and operates only during commuting hours.

Port Orchard Marina and Waterfront Park (Port of Bremerton)
Map 20

Boating • Paddling • Picnicking • Views

Facilities: Guest moorage with power and water, diesel, gas, restrooms, showers, laundry, marine pumpout station, picnic tables, picnic shelter, viewing platform. Nearby: Restaurants, marine supplies, passenger ferry to Bremerton

From Bremerton follow SR 304 west until it joins SR 3 southwest of the city, and then continue on SR 3 to its junction with SR 16. Follow SR 16 and then SR 160 to Port Orchard. The marina is north of Bay Street in the heart of the town.

The marina is on the south side of Sinclair Inlet. Guest moorage is along the breakwater float and the easternmost of floats within the breakwater. The marina entrance is on the west end of the breakwater.

A waterfront promanade overlooks the Port Orchard Marina, with Olympic peaks in the distance.

Centerpiece of the town of Port Orchard is the large modern marina operated by the Port of Bremerton. More than fifty slips and 1500 feet of dock space in the marina are allocated for guest moorage—which soundly attests to the popularity of the town and its facilities as a cruising destination. A long, concrete float cups around the moorage area; the entrance is at the west end. The fuel dock and a short guest moorage dock are at Gate 1, immediately inside the marina. The main guest area is along the breakwater and at its western end, adjoining Gate 4. In summer, late-arriving boaters might have to tie up on the outside of the breakwater, where waves and wakes can make for an uncomfortable stay.

Near the west end of the marina parking lot is a unique, cylindrical concrete viewing platform that provides a great overlook of the mothballed navy fleet across the inlet. Grocery stores, restaurants, marine supplies, and other shopping are only a block's walk away.

Immediately east of the marina is a three-block-long promenade with benches that overlook nautical activities. A waterfront park has a small pavilion that serves as a picnic shelter when not used by entertainment playing to the bleachers. Concrete steps lead down to the sand and gravel beach. Take along a sandwich and make use of the park's picnic tables or shelter.

Port Orchard Boat Launch and Public Pier (City of Port Orchard)
Map 20

Boating • Paddling • Fishing

Facilities: Surfaced launch ramps, restrooms, fishing pier

🚗 From the west side of Port Orchard (SR 166) continue east along Bay Street to find the city's public launch ramp, immediately across the street from the white concrete block Port Orchard municipal building.

The two launch ramps at the intersection of Bay and Kitsap Streets are separated by a 50-foot finger pier for loading. A commercial boathouse lies to the west of the launch ramps, and beyond that, at the intersection of Bay Street and Port Orchard Boulevard, the City of Port Orchard Pedestrian Pier juts into Rich Passage. The 150-foot-long float, reached by a ramp, nearly rests on the bottom at low tide. Take advantage of the pier and float for fishing or just dawdling.

Sinclair Inlet Wildlife Viewing Area   Map 11

Wildlife • Paddling

Facilities: Hand-carried boat launch

🚗 The preserve is immediately west of the interchange where SR 160 joins SR 16. A large dirt parking lot on the north side of the road has a log-framed sign at the edge of the wooded shoreline, but there are no signs along the highway to identify the lot, so you must watch carefully for it. The preserve lies immediately west of a large garden nursery on the north side of the road. A concrete median in the highway blocks access to the lot by eastbound traffic, but there is a turn-around loop just after SR 160 E leaves SR 16.

Migrating waterfowl are often seen at the end of Sinclair Inlet.

Paddlecraft can be put in at the parking lot at high tide.

A variety of waterfowl gather at the head of Sinclair Inlet—cormorants perch on old pilings and scan the water's surface for an unwary fish, migratory ducks paddle in flocks along the protected shoreline, resting and refueling here before continuing on their journey. On the south shore of the inlet 24 acres of tidelands have been set aside by Kitsap County and the U.S. Fish and Wildlife Service as a fish and waterfowl refuge.

The shoreline is soggy and densely overgrown—not much for walking—and the offshore tideflat is a wide, mucky mess at minus tides. However, the area was meant as a habitat for wildlife, not people, and it serves that function nicely. The best way to appreciate the extensive wetlands and possibly view some of the waterfowl is at eye level from a kayak or canoe.

BREMERTON AND THE PORT WASHINGTON NARROWS
Map 21

Bremerton is a one-industry town, and life here revolves around its blue-collar job of maintaining navy ships. The town waterfront has some allure from a distance, with the latticework of the enormous hammerhead crane silhouetted against the pale outline of the Olympic Mountains and the moth-balled ships lying in the harbor like snoozing dinosaurs. Up close, however, the oppressive barrier of cyclone fencing and the gritty industrialism of the shipyard sink in.

The local residents are pretty defensive about the shipyard, though—they know that either directly or indirectly it puts food on the table for nearly everyone in town. In fact, if it weren't for the shipyard, Bremerton might not exist. There were several other well-established towns in the vicinity when Lt. Ambrose Barkley Wyckoff selected a site on the north shore of Sinclair Inlet as the best possible location for a new navy shipyard. In 1891 he purchased 190 acres of land from several property owners, including 86 acres owned by William Bremer. The Bremer property was part of a 168-acre parcel he had previously acquired from his brother-in-law, Henry Hensel. Bremer sold the land to the navy for less than he had paid for it, feeling the presence of the shipyard would increase the value of his remaining holdings. He built

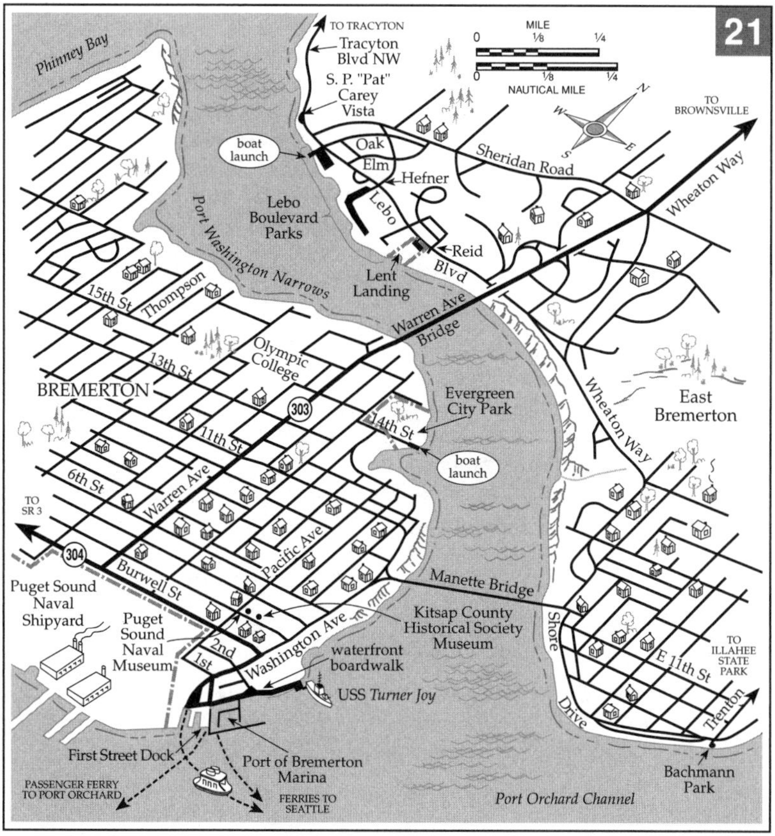

a wharf on the water near the shipyard, cleared and platted 40 acres, and named it Bremerton. A town was born.

Currently, the nearby town of Keyport has an expanded role as the Naval Undersea Warfare Center; torpedo testing areas were expanded from the Port Orchard Channel to include most of Dabob Bay on Hood Canal. The Bangor facility went through several cycles of activity, with highs during the conflicts in Korea and Vietnam and lulls in intervening periods. The conversion of Bangor to a home port for Trident submarines brought this area to its present-day mission and condition.

The city of Bremerton straddles the 1/4-mile-wide trough of the Port Washington Narrows. Two bridges span the channel: near the mouth, SR 304 crosses on the Manette Bridge; midway up the channel the Warren Avenue Bridge carries SR 303. The 3½-mile-long Port Washington Narrows runs between 80-foot bluffs that gentle out midway up the channel. ❈The channel has no navigational hazards; however, tidal currents, which can run in excess of 4 knots, might noticeably affect boat speed and can cause problems for paddle-powered craft. The east side of the channel is quite shoal, boats of any draft should favor the west side.

Aside from the yacht club on the west shore of Phinney Bay, the only commercial marine facility on the Port Washington Narrows or in Dyes Inlet is the Port Washington Marina, on the south shore of the narrows, west of the Warren Avenue Bridge.

Bremerton Marina (Port of Bremerton)   Map 21

Facilities: Guest moorage with power and water, restrooms, showers, laundry, portable marine pumpout station

North of the ferry terminal is the First Street Dock, a pretty waterfront facility with a distinctive clock tower and park benches under a broad-roofed pavilion. A breakwater that runs north from the end of the dock serves both as a loading platform for passenger ferries to Seattle and Annapolis and as protection for the waterfront moorage basin. Behind the breakwater are floats with room for more than 50 guest boats. Access to all but the breakwater floats is secured by a keypad gate; the code is provided by the harbormaster upon payment of moorage fees.

Bremerton Waterfront   Map 21

Museum • Ship tour • Picnicking • Viewpoint

Facilities: Restrooms, picnic tables, museum, destroyer

🚗 Exiting the ferry leaves visitors on the Bremerton waterfront. Kitsap County's SR 303 and SR 304 pass through the city, intersecting at the shipyards.

⛴ The marina on the waterfront is midway down Port Orchard Bay, on the north shore, 13 n.m. from Seattle's Duwamish Head.

Today many downtown Bremerton stores are linked to the needs and tastes of shipyard workers and the navy. Scattered among the blue-collar taverns, bars, and cafes are such navy-specific enterprises as a uniform supply. The downtown shopping district lies along Pacific Avenue, two blocks from the ferry terminal. For years this business area gradually deteriorated; to rejuvenate it, the city began sprucing up it and the waterfront; some has been accomplished, more is in the works. As well as new businesses lured here and streets gussied up with fountains and flowers, there are plans to create a maritime park and naval museum. The fusty old girl of a city is finally getting a face-lift.

Bremerton Waterfront Boardwalk • Pilings support an over-water concrete boardwalk that runs along the waterfront between First and Burwell Streets. Benches, tables, and planters create a pleasant park and provide places for a picnic lunch or to watch seagulls supervising waterfront activities. A huge, bronze, shaft-mounted propeller (approximately the size of those that drove the nearby destroyer) has been etched with a montage of historical photos of the navy shipyard.

At the foot of 2nd Street a small, one-story building has a circular staircase winding up its side to an observation platform topped by a tall flagpole. Views are south and east across the marina and the boardwalk to Dyes and Sinclair Inlets.

USS **Turner Joy** • The revitalized waterfront features the 418-foot destroyer DD-951, the USS *Turner Joy*, which is open for self-guided tours—in itself well worth the trip to Bremerton. Kids (and/or accompanying adults) will quickly get lost in the rabbit warren of companionways on the ship's five decks. The narrow corridors lead past wardrooms and elbow-tight berthing areas, with peeks into various rooms. A memorial replica of a POW prison cell in Vietnam is a sobering note.

Everyone will want to command the ship from the bridge and pilot house, and the more agile will revel in climbing into the gunner's position in one of the aft 5-inch-gun mounts. Tickets for self-guided tours can be purchased at a gift shop on 4th Street at the end of the boardwalk. The ship is open for tours daily from Memorial Day through Labor Day from 10:00 AM to dusk. Winter hours might vary from year to year. A tour ticket is good for all day, so you can make a quick pass through, go ashore for lunch, and return for more exploration.

The USS Turner Joy *is open for tours. The bridge is pictured above.*

The Naval Memorial Museum of the Pacific has ship models and many other fascinating displays.

Naval Memorial Museum of the Pacific (Bremerton Naval Museum) •
This outstanding museum currently is in a building at the corner of 4th and Pacific, next door to the County Historical Museum. A move is planned for 2006 when a building housing the museum will be part of the waterfront redevelopment just west of the ferry terminal. The museum is open Monday through Saturday, 10:00 AM to 4:00 PM, and Sunday, 1:00 PM to 4:00 PM No admission is charged, but donations are gratefully accepted.

The museum focuses on the history of the navy yard and the ships built there, but it also has displays of ship memorabilia, swords, cutlasses, armaments, mines, and other interesting nautical paraphernalia. There are numerous minutely detailed 15-foot-long replicas of battleships, cruisers, destroyers, and aircraft carriers, and some plastic see-through builder's models that reveal all the interiors. Other attractions include maps of Pearl Harbor showing locations of ships and military facilities before and after the Japanese Navy attack in 1941.

Kitsap County Historical Society Museum •
The early history of Kitsap County was centered on logging and farming but eventually was influenced by the local military installations in Bremerton, Keyport, and Bangor. The historical museum, in a remodeled bank building at 280 4th Street, does an exceptionally nice job of depicting the growth of the county by the use of an illustrated time line. It covers time from its original pioneer days, through its agricultural period, on through the build-up of the navy yard, and finally ending with the development of the Naval Undersea Warfare Center at Keyport and the Naval Submarine Base at Bangor. In addition to the main time-line displays, the museum has rotating displays of various other facets of the county's history. The museum is open Tuesday through Saturday, 9:00 AM to 5:00 PM

Evergreen City Park (City of Bremerton)   Map 21

Boating • Paddling • Picnicking • Fishing

Facilities: 2-lane paved launch ramp with boarding float, restrooms, picnic tables, picnic shelters, fireplaces, children's play equipment, basketball half-courts, volleyball court

Area: 10 acres; 1900 feet of shoreline on Port Washington Narrows

🚐 From the ferry terminal head north on Washington Avenue for nine blocks to 11th Street. Head west on 11th to Park Avenue, and then north on it for three blocks to the park at 14th Street and Park Avenue.

🛥 The park is on the west side of the Port Washington Narrows halfway between the Manette and Warren Avenue Bridges.

The level, grassy park has numerous picnic shelters for family picnics. Play equipment is available for energetic youngsters, and a pair of World War II–vintage 3-inch rapid-fire guns sit astride at the head of the launch ramp. A large parking lot adjoins the two-lane, concrete launch ramp with a boarding float. The gravelly beach is not inviting for swimming but is a good spot to try your hand at shore fishing.

Bachmann Park (City of Bremerton)   Map 21

Picnicking • Viewpoint • Paddling

Facilities: Picnic tables, gazebo

Area: 0.5 acre; 110 feet of shoreline on Sinclair Inlet

🚐 From the ferry terminal, head north on Washington Avenue seven blocks and cross the Manette Bridge. On the east side of the bridge take E 11th Street east for eight blocks to Trenton Avenue; the park is at the south end of Trenton in two blocks.

🛥 The park is 500 yards north of the tip of Point Herron, at the entrance to the Port Washington Narrows

On the east side of the entrance to the Port Washington Narrows, a tiny park offers an excellent view of traffic shuttling to and fro in the bay and entering the narrows. The park's small wooden gazebo sits on pilings over the water; another bench and a pair of picnic tables are in grass patches onshore. A breach in the concrete bulkhead allows visitors to reach the water and walk the cobblestone beach or launch hand-carried boats.

Lebo Boulevard Parks (City of Bremerton)   Map 21

Bicycling • Picnicking • Paddling • Fishing • Boating • Swimming • Team sports • Beach walking • Views

Facilities: Fishing pier, 3-lane paved launch ramp with boarding float, picnic tables, fireplaces, children's play equipment, concession stand, baseball diamonds, restrooms, tennis courts, view gazebos

🚐 From the ferry terminal, head north on Washington Avenue seven blocks and cross the Manette Bridge. On the east side of the bridge take Wheaton Way northwest for 1 mile, and turn northwest on Lebo Boulevard and follow it.

The launch ramp is at the west end of the park, on the north side of the Port Washington Narrows, 1 n.m. west of the Warren Avenue Bridge

Lebo Boulevard follows the north shore of the Point Washington Narrows, west of the Warren Avenue Bridge. This scenic road is edged by pretty little parks at three points. The level, blacktop road, marked as a bicycle route, is ideal for cycle touring, but use care as it is narrow and has no shoulder.

Lent Landing Park • At Lebo Boulevard and Reid Avenue, a 1.5-acre, broad lawn with a paved path along one side tapers down the beach at a tiny cove on the Port Washington Narrows. A gazebo and benches on the bank above the beach invite a leisurely survey of the boat traffic on the narrows. A short staircase drops down the medium bank to a gravel and cobble beach. It would be feasible to launch a hand-carried boat here.

Lions Park • Two blocks beyond Lent Landing Park, the city of Bremerton and the local Lions Club have put a 15-acre, five-block-long stretch of waterfront to its best possible use—a multipurpose recreation complex, appealing to interests ranging from tennis to baseball to boating. Beach walks west from here can continue past the park along the shore below Tracyton Beach Road for a distance of 3 miles. The central section of the park fronts on a shallow sandy beach, perfect for sunbathing or courageously swimming in the chilly waters of the narrows.

Boating facilities at the west end of the park by the Oak Street entrance include a three-lane, surfaced launch ramp with a short concrete float (aground at low tide). A long fishing pier parallels the shore. Benches in a pretty wooden gazebo at the head of the boarding float provide a spot to relax and enjoy the stunning view up Dyes Inlet to the rugged Olympic peaks.

S. P. "Pat" Carey Vista • A few blocks north from the Lebo Boulevard Recreation Area is a tiny Bremerton city park with a picnic table overlooking the stretch of the narrows between Phinney Bay and the Warren Avenue Bridge. Pause for a leisurely snack and watch boats headed to and from Phinney Bay and Dyes Inlet.

DYES INLET
Map 22

Dyes Inlet is a cruising delight, with fascinating little bays and coves, scenic shorelines, and quiet anchorages. Once past the Port Washington Narrows, the waterway suddenly opens to the 1½-mile-wide inlet, resembling a large protected lake rather than the open reaches boaters are accustomed to on Puget Sound. The sheltered waters are ideal for kayak and small boat exploration, as well as cruising in bigger boats. Several deep bays penetrate the south shore of the inlet. Phinney Bay, at the northern end of the narrows, hosts moorages of the Bremerton Yacht Club. The next cove to the west, slender Mud Bay, is well named—it is a tideflat, navigable only at high tide by kayaks or dinghies.

Ostrich Bay, the largest cove on Dyes Inlet, is on the southwest corner. Adventuresome boaters will want to follow the narrow slot on the east shore of Ostrich Bay leading into the tiny pocket of Oyster Bay; at extreme low tide there is 6 feet of water midchannel. Good anchorage can be found in either bay. ✿ A large rock lies near the west shore of Ostrich Bay, about 250 yards north of the large abandoned navy wharf. A ¼-mile section of shore along the southwest side of Ostrich Bay is a Bremerton city park. All other

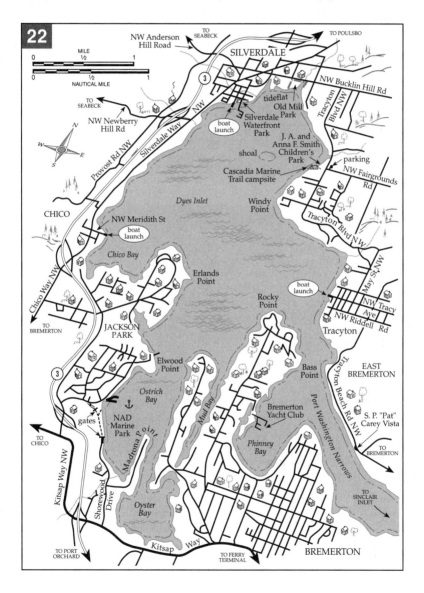

shoreland is either private or part of the Naval Ammunition Depot and the Jackson Park housing for navy families.

We readily decided there are no ostriches on Ostrich Bay, but oysters on Oyster Bay? Perhaps. Japanese oysters were introduced in the early 1940s by Japanese-American entrepreneurs who established an oyster farm on the east side of Dyes Inlet. The business thrived, but unfortunately, with the outbreak of World War II, the owners were confined in an internment camp, and the operation closed. The oysters remained to fend for themselves in the inlet, wherever they could find a suitable environment. It is believed that ancestors of Manila clams found today in Dyes Inlet hitchhiked here on barges that brought in Japanese oysters. Today, however, the encroaching housing developments along the shoreline have raised pollution levels in the inlet to the point that all shellfish gathering has been declared hazardous by the Department of Health.

Naval Ammunition Depot (NAD) Marine Park (City of Bremerton)   Map 22
Hiking • Picnicking

Facilities: Picnic tables, walking path
Area: 27.5 acres; 1430 feet of shoreline on Ostrich Bay (Dyes Inlet)
🚐 Follow Kitsap Way (SR 310) west out of Bremerton; just before reaching SR 3, turn north onto Shorewood Drive, and follow it to its gated end and a small parking area.

An old road end along the west shore of Ostrich Bay offers a rare treat—public access among the prized waterfront properties. The undeveloped city park lies at the end of Shorewood Drive. The abandoned road can be walked all the way to the Jackson Park navy housing development. Enjoy nice views of the bay through a light screen of trees, or shiver in the reflection of the dense forest above, which reminds one of the haunted forest en route to the castle of the wicked witch in *The Wizard of Oz*. Woodpecker-chopped holes in tree snags and a crescendo of chirping in the woods portend good birdwatching for an observant visitor.

A boot path leads down the 30-foot-high bank near the parking lot to the rocky beach. The beach can be walked to the north end of the park, where a short stub road to a utility building reaches a low rock bank near the beach level.

Chico Launch Ramp (Port of Bremerton)   Map 22
Boating • Paddling

Facilities: 1-lane paved launch ramp
🚐 Take Kitsap Way (SR 310) west from Bremerton to SR 3, then head north on it for 3 miles to the Chico Way NW exit. Continue north on Chico Way NW for ¾ mile to NW Meredith Street. The launch ramp is at the end of Meredith.
🛥 The ramp is on the west shore of Chico Bay (Dyes Inlet), 2½ n.m. south of Silverdale.

In spite of its Spanish-sounding name and the fact that many nearby streets have Spanish names, the community was named for William Chico (or Chaco), a friendly Native American chief who lived nearby.

Chico was a point of commerce for boats of the Mosquito Fleet and settlers who lived inland on the Kitsap Peninsula; one of the first roads in the area led from Chico to Crosby. Many of the early steamers were shallow-draft and could be beached. Passengers disembarked via a gangplank dropped from the deck to shore; cows and horses destined for pioneer farms were simply booted overboard to swim the short distance to the beach. It wasn't until 1905 that a dock (a raft of cedar logs) was built.

The only public facility at Chico today is a surfaced launch ramp just off Chico Way NW at the end of NW Meredith Street operated by the Port of Bremerton. The ramp, whose location is unmarked along Chico Way NW, has only limited roadside parking in the vicinity (take care not to block private driveways). To locate the ramp, watch for a small commercial building on the west side of the road.

Silverdale Waterfront Park (Kitsap County) and Boat Launch (Port of Silverdale)   Map 23

Boating • Paddling • Picnicking • Swimming • Water skiing • Beach walking • Fishing

Facilities: Picnic tables, picnic shelter, fireplaces, restrooms, children's play area, gazebo, fishing pier, guest moorage with power and water, marine pumpout station, portable toilet dump, 2-lane paved launch ramp with boarding float

Area: 2.3 acres; 600 feet of shoreline

🚗 Take SR 3 north from Bremerton for 6 miles, take the Silverdale Way NW exit, and in ½ mile turn east from Silverdale Way NW onto NW Byron Street. In two

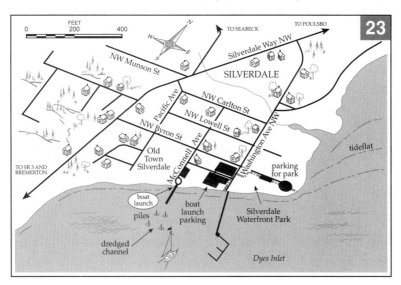

blocks turn south on McConnell Avenue NW to reach the launch ramp. One block farther on Byron, turn south on Washington Avenue NW to reach the park.

The park and launch ramp are at the north end of Dyes Inlet. The water is extremely shoal, so do not stray far from the moorage floats at the park. Follow day-marked pilings for the channel into the launch ramp.

The major boating attraction on Dyes Inlet is the superb little beachfront park at Silverdale at the north end of the waterway. A 300-foot-long fishing pier has floats for forty to fifty boats. Guest moorage is available, with a three-day limit. Although the end of the bay is quite shallow, the dock extends out far enough to provide 35 feet of water under the floats at zero tide. To the north, the extreme head of the bay is a 300-yard-long tideflat.

The remainder of the park is grassy hillocks and a scattering of picnic tables with beachfront views. A low concrete bulkhead, interrupted by staircases, rims the beach; at high tide the water comes right up to the bulkhead. Low tide reveals some cobbles and rocks at the high water level, with a sandy swimming beach below.

A block west of the dock, at the end of McConnell Avenue, is a two-lane concrete launch ramp with a boarding float between lanes, operated by the Silverdale Port District. The ramp extends well out into the bay, so there is no problem launching, even at low tide. A 30-foot-deep channel, marked by offshore pilings, has been dredged in the tideflat outboard from the end of the launch ramp.

Silverdale Waterfront Park has floats for forty or fifty cruising boats.

Old Mill Park (Kitsap County)   Map 22

Walking • Birdwatching • Nature and historic interpretation

Facilities: Restrooms (disabled accessible), paths, interpretive panels
Area: 7 acres; 1150 feet of shoreline on Dyes Inlet

🚐 Take SR 3 north from Bremerton for 6 miles, take the Silverdale Way NW exit, and in 1 mile turn east from Silverdale Way NW onto NW Bucklin Hill Road. The park is on the south side of the road in ½ mile, opposite Silverdale Plaza.

The mill is long since gone, but its memory lives on in this small wetland preserve that celebrates wildlife. The park, at the north end of Dyes Inlet, includes an estuary where the freshwater of Clear Creek mixes with the saltwater of the inlet. Estuaries such as this are unique regions of high biological productivity, and the adjoining wetlands provide habitat for a variety of mammals and birds.

The "old mill" was a sawmill that operated here in the 1950s. The estuary was favored as a log dump because the inflow of freshwater minimized barnacle growth on logs, which could damage saws. The rusting hulk of a large gang saw sits at the edge of the park; an interpretive panel explains how it worked. Other interpretive panels tell of the various species of birds seen here, the Suquamish Indians, and the many types of marine life found in the estuary. Settle in on a bench to watch for waterfowl and songbirds.

J. A. and Anna F. Smith Children's Park (Kitsap County)   Map 22

Picnicking, gardens • Paddling

Facilities: Picnic tables, restrooms, children's garden, Master Gardener demonstration garden, amphitheater, CMT campsite
Area: 6.6 acres; 600 feet of shoreline on Dyes Inlet

🚐 Head east from Silverdale on NW Bucklin Hill Road, and in ¾ mile turn south on Tracyton Boulevard NW. The park is on the west side of the road in 1½ miles, north of its intersection with NW Fairgrounds Road. Parking is in a gravel lot on the northeast side of this intersection. Two disabled-accessible parking spots are off a private road spur about 50 feet north of the park entrance.

🛶 The park is directly southeast across Dyes Inlet from Silverdale Waterfront Park. A battered 4-foot-high concrete bulkhead fronts the park (one of many in the vicinity), so paddlers will need to look sharp for the marine trail campsite sign in the trees at the beach.

About 100 feet north of NW Fairgrounds Road a footpath leads downhill into this small county park on the east side of Dyes Inlet. The focal point of the park is the garden area in the upland portion where a tidy lawn with a few picnic tables edges a cattail-fringed pond. At the south end of the lawn, the twenty-five to thirty little beds of the Master Gardener demonstration garden hold an amazing variety of flowers, fruits, and vegetables.

For an added attraction a trail leads down the high bank, past a tiny

Mom and the kids are out for a stroll at Children's Park.

primitive amphitheater overlooking Dyes Inlet, to a gently sloping gravel and boulder beach. A CMT campsite is at the lower end of the trail where it breaks out at the beach.

Tracyton Launch Ramp (Port of Tracyton)   Map 22

The community of Tracyton on the east shore of the inlet has a small waterfront access at a launch ramp. The single-lane concrete ramp is just off the main road (May Street NW) at the end of NW Tracy Avenue, which is reached from Tracyton Boulevard NW. The upper portion is quite steep, but the ramp is usable at most tide levels. There is parking for about a dozen cars along the side of Tracy Avenue. Boats launched here have ready access to the network of bays at the south end of the inlet. A group of pilings offshore just south of the ramp should help to identify it from the water.

PORT ORCHARD CHANNEL AND LIBERTY BAY
Map 18

Leaving Dyes Inlet, you return to Port Orchard, the long channel flowing north along the west side of Bainbridge Island. Superlative boating country, this wide, unobstructed channel is enclosed by forested shores and graced at its farthest point with the queen of tourist towns, Poulsbo.

❋A torpedo testing area is along the west side of the channel, from Keyport south to Brownsville. Such testing is quite rare, but when it does occur red lights on navy range vessels and on top of one of the buildings at Keyport flash a warning. Boaters should not enter the area at that time. Those remaining nearby should shut off boat engines, depth sounders, or any other equipment generating underwater noise, because some torpedoes are guided by sound.

❋The entrance to Liberty Bay is twisting and becomes narrow as it rounds Lemolo Peninsula, but there are no navigational hazards. Once past Keyport the channel spreads to a 1/2 mile in width and heads north to Poulsbo, at the end of the bay. Excellent anchorages can be found in muddy bottom in several small coves; those near Keyport and Lemolo offer the quiet protection of the beautiful little bay without the summertime bustle of the Poulsbo docks; these snug coves do not have any shore access.

Accesses and anchorages in the Port Orchard channel along the Bainbridge Island shoreline are described in chapter 3.

Illahee State Park   Map 24

Camping • Picnicking • Hiking • Boating • Paddling • Fishing • Shellfish •
Water skiing • Scuba diving • Beach walking • Historic naval guns

Facilities: 25 standard campsites, 2 primitive campsites, group camp, picnic tables, fireplaces, kitchen shelters, 2 group day-use areas, restrooms, showers, RV pumpout, ball field, children's play equipment, horseshoe pit, trails, 1-lane paved launch ramp, dock with float, 5 mooring buoys
Area: 74.5 acres; 1785 feet of shoreline

From the Bremerton ferry terminal take SR 304 (Washington and Burwell Streets) north and west for seven blocks, and turn north on SR 303 (Warren Avenue). 1 mile north of the Warren Avenue Bridge, turn east on NE Sylvan Way, and follow it east for 1½ miles to the park entrance

The park is on the west side of the Port Orchard channel about 1 n.m. due west of Point White.

A 250-foot bluff above the Port Orchard channel might seem an unlikely location for a marine-oriented park, but Illahee State Park manages to blend its wooded uplands nicely with its waterfront attractions. The upland portion of the park—camping and picnic areas—is in timber, with no view of the water. The beauty of the old-growth forest of maple, cedar, and fir more than makes up for the lack of marine vistas. Two 5-inch naval guns mounted on grassy platforms near the park entrance recall the military heritage of the area.

The beach portion of the park is reached via a steeply switchbacking road or a steeply switchbacking trail—take your pick. Trailered boats that have made it down the hairpin turns of the road will find a one-lane launch

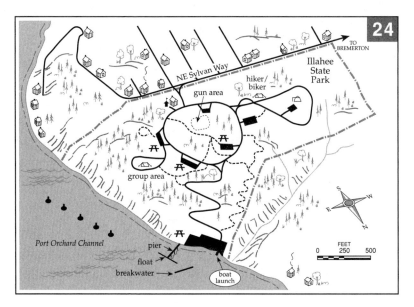

The Illahee State Park dock is a good place to watch boating activity, whether you are a human or a gull.

ramp adjacent to the parking lot. A float at the end of a 380-foot fishing pier provides about 200 feet of tie-up space for cruising boats; a second float to the north serves as a breakwater. Five mooring buoys are strung along the shore to the south.

Tidelands south of the pier flare out gently into sandy beach, delightful for sun-snoozing or wading. A lucky digger might find a clam or two, although the area is heavily harvested. At high tide, water laps the foot of the bluff. The park, lying on the north outskirts of Bremerton, is loved by local residents, who use it heavily.

Illahee (Port of Illahee)   Map 18

Fishing • Boating • Scuba diving

Facilities: Floats, fishing pier, artificial reef. *Nearby:* Groceries, gas, toilets

🚗 From the Bremerton ferry terminal take SR 304 (Washington and Burwell Streets) north and west for seven blocks, and turn north on SR 303 (Warren Avenue). One mile north of the Warren Avenue Bridge, turn east on Sylvan Way NE, follow it east for 1¼ miles, and turn north on Trenton Avenue NE, which shortly becomes Illahee Road NE. In 1½ miles, at Illahee, turn east on the stub of Allview Boulevard NE to pier parking.

⛵ The dock and floats are on the west side of the Port Orchard channel about 1½ n.m. north of Point White.

At the small community of Illahee a pier with two short floats provides a spot for boaters to stop and pick up supplies. ✿ Large boats should approach with care, as the surrounding water is shallow, but small boats should have no problems except during low tides. The dock and floats are closed to the public between 10:00 PM and daylight, and there is a three-day mooring limit. A grocery store, service station, and toilets are a short block up the street. The end of the pier spreads out into a broad platform for fishing.

Pilings of the old dock are coated with a forest of fluffy, pastel-colored sea anemones and purple tube worms—paradise for scuba divers who explore the seawalls south from here to the state park, a mile away. Fishing and diving in the area are greatly enhanced by a 300-foot-long artificial reef, marked by buoys, lying 140 feet off the end of the pier. The old tires forming the reef create a habitat for invertebrates that in turn serve as food for a variety of fish, including cod, flounder, rockfish, and salmon. The fish population in the area has more than doubled since the construction of the reef.

Brownsville Marina (Port of Brownsville)   Map 18

Boating • Paddling • Picnicking • Fishing

Facilities: Guest moorage with power and water, 2-lane launch ramp with boarding float, pumpout station, portable toilet dump, groceries, deli, ice, bait, gas, diesel, propane, wireless broadband, restrooms, showers, laundry, picnic tables, picnic shelter, pavilion, fireplaces, fishing pier (disabled accessible), CMT campsite

From the Bremerton ferry terminal take SR 304 (Washington and Burwell Streets) north and west for seven blocks, and turn north on SR 303 (Warren Avenue). After crossing the Warren Avenue Bridge continue north on SR 303 (which becomes Wheaton Way) for 6½ miles, and turn west on Brownsville Highway NE. Reach the marina in ½ mile at Ogle Road NE.

The marina is on Burke Bay, on the east side of the Port Orchard channel midway between Bremerton and Keyport. Enter the marina from the south side and stay between the floats and the green can buoys, as the rest of the bay is quite shoal.

The narrow slot of Burke Bay, penetrating the Kitsap shoreline for nearly ½ mile, is too shallow to be attractive to boaters; however, the excellent, full-service marina on the north shore at the entrance to the bay makes a nice layover for boaters cruising in the Port Orchard channel. The modern, 335-slip facility, protected by two breakwaters, is a surprise from either

Sun glints off the moorage at Brownsville.

land or water, because the community of Brownsville is just a smattering of homes along the shore.

Visiting boaters can reach the fuel dock by entering the marina float area at the south end of the east breakwater. From here they are directed to available guest slips. An excellent two-lane concrete launch ramp runs steeply into the water north of the fuel dock.

The marina is a pleasant stop, even for nonboaters. The north breakwater serves as both guest moorage and fishing pier and provides nice views up to Agate Passage and across the busy water highway to Bainbridge Island. A Marine Ramp Rider between the pier and the breakwater provides easy disabled access to and from the breakwater float. At the shore end of the pier an open-air pavilion on pilings has picnic tables and displays describing the Brownsville history and ecology. On the high bank above the marina is a small park with a picnic shelter, picnic tables, and fireplaces. This is also the site of the marina CMT campsite.

The 2-mile stretch of tidelands between Brownsville and the Keyport Naval Reservation are public, although the uplands are private. The beach is mostly mud but holds a possibility of shellfish harvesting.

Naval Undersea Museum   Map 25

Maritime exhibits

Facilities: Restrooms, gift shop

🚗 See directions to Brownsville, above. Continue north from the marina on Brownsville Highway NE for 3½ miles to its intersection with SR 308. Head north on SR 308 for 200 yards to the entrance to the Undersea Warfare Center. The museum is uphill on Gannett Way, just outside the center's main gate. *Alternatively:* Take SR 3 north from Bremerton, or Viking Way south from Poulsbo, to their intersection with SR 308, and then follow it east 2½ miles to the museum.

Since 1910, when the navy put Keyport on the map by selecting it as the site for the storage, repair, and testing of torpedoes, most of the activity on this tiny peninsula has been hidden behind chain-link security fences. An impressive new Naval Undersea Museum just outside the security gate of the Naval Undersea Warfare Center gives visitors a chance to share underwater mysteries.

In several galleries, spreading over some 20,000 square feet, exhibits tell of the sea and the undersea technology that helps us explore and better understand it. Some of the exhibits are interactive—great fun for both kids and adults. Dominating the outside displays is the *Trieste II*, a huge submersible that set the world's record when it dove to 35,800 feet off the Guam Trench, and the *Deep Quest*, a four-person research and recovery vessel capable of diving to 8000 feet. A portion of the museum is devoted to undersea weapons and houses collections of various types of mines and torpedoes. The submarine technology gallery has a full-size mockup of the control room of the nuclear attack submarine USS *Greenling*, as well as a full-size submarine rescue chamber.

The submersibles Trieste II *(left) and* Deep Quest *(right) can be seen at the Naval Undersea Museum.*

The museum is open from 10:00 AM to 4:00 PM seven days a week in summer; it is closed on Tuesday October through May, and on Thanksgiving, Christmas, New Year's Day, and Easter.

Keyport Marina (Port of Keyport)   Map 25
Boating • Paddling • Picnicking

Facilities: Guest moorage, 1-lane launch ramp, toilet, picnic tables. *Nearby:* Groceries and ice

See directions to the Naval Undersea Museum, above. Continue north on SR 308 past the museum gate, and in ¼ mile arrive at Keyport. A block from the navy station fence turn west on Washington Avenue and reach the marina in another two blocks.

The marina is on the southeast side of Liberty Bay, just inside and south of the narrow entrance to the bay.

The acres of stern gray buildings and warning signs visible from the water at Keyport's Undersea Warfare Center are a rather intimidating introduction to Liberty Bay. By land, a sign at the outskirts of town announces, "Welcome to Keyport, Torpedo Town USA," and visitors have the feeling they should step ver-r-ry carefully.

Up until the time that the town became the site of the navy facility, it had been just another of the struggling little villages along the Kitsap shoreline. When early settlers gave the town its name, they expected it to become the key port on Liberty Bay. They certainly could never have envisioned its future.

A small marina offering some limited boating facilities lies just west of

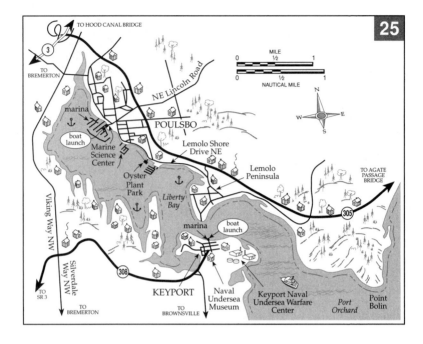

the navy installation at Keyport. About 40 feet of short-term guest moorage space is available on the outside of the most northerly float, with the stay limited to six hours. All the remaining slips are private. A single-lane surfaced launch ramp is tucked behind the floats—its location makes it difficult to spot from the water.

POULSBO
Map 26

Walking • Viewpoints • Paddling • Picnicking • Bicycling • Shopping

Facilities: *Marina:* Guest moorage with power and water, wireless broadband, gasoline and diesel, 1-lane launch ramp with boarding float, kayak rentals, restrooms, showers, laundry, marine pumpout station, portable toilet dump, tidal grid. *City of Poulsbo Parks:* Picnic tables, fire rings, restrooms, pavilion, children's play area, trail, overwater causeway, pier

🚙 The town can be reached either by taking the Winslow ferry to Bainbridge Island and following SR 305 across the island and the Agate Passage Bridge to Poulsbo or by driving SR 3 north from Bremerton and turning south onto SR 305 to reach Poulsbo. *Oyster Plant Park:* On Fjord Drive NE, ¾ mile south of the center of Poulsbo.

🛥 Poulsbo lies 13 n.m. from Shilshole Bay in Seattle, via Agate Passage, or 12 n.m. from the Bremerton or Port Orchard waterfront. *Oyster Plant Park:* In the middle of the north side of Liberty Bay, between the Liberty Bay Marina and the Poulsbo Yacht Club. It is approachable only by paddlecraft.

Even that shrewd old Norseman, Lief Eriksson, would think he had set foot on his native country rather than on some foreign shore if he had landed his ship in Poulsbo. Streets above the waterfront are named King Olaf V Vei and Queen Sonja Vei, "Velkommen til Poulsbo" a sign proclaims, and storefronts decorated with peasant designs echo the greeting. The historic town is not ersatz Scandinavian—it has a deeply rooted Nordic heritage, from the graceful spire of the First Lutheran Church overlooking the town to the fishing fleet moored in its harbor.

For pleasure boat crews the supreme attraction of the town is the opportunity to browse the shops and haul off bags full of mouthwatering booty from the Scandinavian bakeries. Several fine restaurants offer a welcome break to galley slaves.

Poulsbo townsfolk love their celebrations and have plenty of them—Viking Fest, celebrating Norwegian Independence Day, is in mid-May; in summer, Trawler Fest, Midsommer Fest, the Fourth of July (celebrated with nautical events), and a Boat Rendezvous are scheduled; for the strong-of-stomach there's the Lutefisk Dinner in November, and for Christmas, it's Julefest

The Little Town on Dog Fish Bay

Poulsbo was settled in the 1880s by Norwegians from the Midwest, who were drawn here by tales of thickly forested hills and fish-filled bays, so much like their homeland. The first postmaster named the town Paulsbo or "Pauls Place," after his home village in Norway, but the U.S. Postal Service, whose early errors have had a hand in changing a number of Washington names, misspelled it as Poulsbo, and thus it has remained.

These first settlers were tough farmers and fishermen, well prepared to deal with the rigors of pioneer life. Before the advent of the Mosquito Fleet, it was necessary to row 20 miles to Seattle, the growing metropolis on Elliott Bay, in order to get provisions. After such a round-trip, an oarsman's hands were frequently so cramped he could not uncurl his fingers for several days. It is claimed that one sturdy pioneer, after crossing the roadless wilderness of the Cascade Mountains with a covered wagon and horses, loaded wagon and team onto a boat in Seattle and rowed them to Poulsbo. (Oh, for an Evinrude!)

One of the earliest waterfront industries gave the bay its name—a dogfish rendering plant produced the odoriferous oil that was used to grease logging skid roads, and the waterway was officially known as Dog Fish Bay. In the 1890s townsfolk petitioned that the name be changed to the more attractive Liberty Bay. When the legislature refused, stubborn Norwegians used their preferred name anyway, and common usage finally won out. Today, only a small cove near Keyport bears the original name.

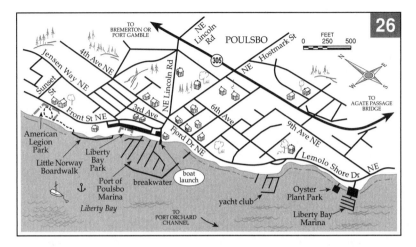

and Julelog. All of these festivals attract huge numbers of visitors, both by land and by water. Scandinavian and Northwest food, crafts, and art are offered for sale, and ethnic musicians and dancers entertain. At such times boating facilities usually are filled, and boats are anchored hull-to-hull at the head of Liberty Bay.

Poulsbo Marina (Port of Poulsbo) • Among boaters, Poulsbo's reputation lies in its fine waterfront facilities. The marina, operated by the Port of Poulsbo, provides 130 guest moorage slips at the downtown docks, half of which are

Although pastries aren't usually thought of as a tourist attraction, in Poulsbo they certainly qualify.

Rental kayaks form a colorful pattern at the Port of Poulsbo Marina.

reservable for groups of 15 boats or more. A plank and piling breakwater shelters the yacht basin. The south side of the moorage is filled with boats of the commercial fishing fleet, and beyond that, next to the harbormaster's office, is a single-lane surfaced launch ramp with a boarding float.

Liberty Bay Park and American Legion Park (City of Poulsbo) • If trolls indeed live under bridges (as claimed in old nursery tales), this is certainly the place to find one. Two waterfront parks are linked by the Little Norway Boardwalk, an 800-foot-long wooden walkway elevated on piers above the shore. Stairs at its north end provide beach access. Look quickly over the edge and you might catch a glimpse of a grizzled troll scurrying out of sight.

Liberty Bay Park is on the downtown waterfront, by the marina. The beautifully groomed and landscaped park has restrooms, picnic tables, fire rings, and large rock erratics for small children to play king-of-the-mountain on. This is the favorite stop (aside from the bakeries) for bicycle tourers, who rest on the manicured grass and soak in the atmosphere. Centerpiece of the park is the Rangvald Kvelstad Pavilion, which provides a nice view of bay activity and is also used for concerts, folk dances, and social functions. A statue of a Viking (Leif Eriksson himself, perhaps?) stands guard over it all.

From the north end of the park, the wooden boardwalk rounds a bluff above the tide and below hillside homes, eventually joining an asphalt path continuing along the bank. Side trails lead down to the mud and rock beach. Shortly, the children's play apparatus and picnic tables of American

Legion Park are reached. Here the path turns uphill to a concrete platform (restrooms) overlooking the bay. Return via the beach if the tide is out, or via the road; round-trip walk is about ½ mile.

Oyster Plant Park (City of Poulsbo) • A joint effort of the city of Poulsbo and the North Kitsap Rotary, this short section of beach on Liberty Bay, the site of a former oyster plant, has been transformed into a small eco-sensitive park. The old plant property was acquired by the state DFW, which leased it to the city. Volunteers from the local Rotary pitched in to construct the park. A grass mound around a flagpole sits at the head of a broad wooden pier with benches and picnic tables.

An interesting highlight of the pier is a series of glass prisms imbedded in the deck every 6 feet or so, which funnel light below the pier to promote growth of near-shore eel grass to augment the intertidal environment. A short gravel path to the beach permits launching of hand-carried craft.

AGATE PASSAGE AND PORT MADISON BAY
Map 18

Agate Passage, with its lofty bridge linking Bainbridge Island and the Kitsap Peninsula, marks the north entrance to the Port Orchard channel. ❀The tidal current here can reach a velocity of 6 knots where the channel is squeezed between the rocky walls to a mere 300 yards wide. A shoal near the middle of the north end is marked by a buoy. Kelp covers rocks lying near the shore. The passage is frequently used by skilled scuba divers who "drift" dive here—floating and tumbling along the channel as the current provides an exhilarating roller-coaster ride. Inner Port Madison is described in chapter 3, Bainbridge Island.

Although agates can be found along the shore, the corridor was named, not for the rockhound's prize, but for Alfred T. Agate, the artist who accompanied Lt. Charles Wilkes on his surveying expedition of 1841.

The north end of Agate Passage opens into the lovely round bay of Port Madison, rimmed by bluffs and a scattering of homes. All of the Kitsap shoreline facing on Agate Passage and Port Madison, with the exception of a portion of Miller Bay, was part of the Port Madison Indian Reservation, assigned to the Suquamish and Duwamish Tribes in the 1855 Treaty of Point Elliot. Over the years much of the land, especially the waterfront, was sold off, sometimes by federal agents who were empowered to act for the individuals they considered "incompetent." Suquamish holdings are now about half of the original reservation and are largely inland.

Suquamish Museum (Suquamish Tribe)   Map 18
Museum • Picnicking • Nature trail

Facilities: Museum, restrooms, gift shop, picnic tables, nature trail
Area: 10 acres; 1000 feet of shoreline
🚐 From SR 305, 1 mile east of Poulsbo, or ½ mile west of the Agate Passage Bridge,

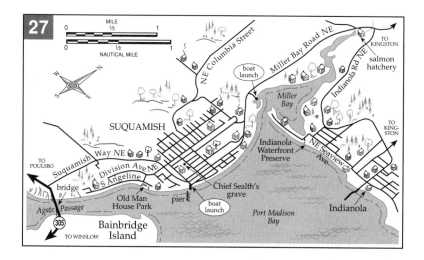

turn south on Sandy Hook Road, signed to the Suquamish Tribal Center. In ¼ mile at 15838 Sandy Hook Road is the road to the tribal center and the museum.

Photos, recorded words, and artifacts tell the story of the Suquamish Indians from the time of the arrival of European explorers through pioneer days. In its major exhibit, The Eyes of Chief Seattle, the Suquamish Museum uses the words of tribal elders to eloquently evoke not only a time gone by, but a culture nearly lost.

The museum was built by the Suquamish Tribe to house and display artifacts discovered by a 1975 archeological excavation at Old Man House. The exhibits also include items on loan from individuals and other museums and more than 2000 historic photos that have been copied for tribal archives. Hours are 10:00 AM to 5:00 PM daily, May through September, and 11:00 AM to 4:00 PM Friday through Sunday, for the rest of the year. It is closed holidays and during tribal center funerals.

The museum is on the top floor of the tribal center, on a timbered hillside overlooking Agate Passage. A short nature trail departs from near the museum, looping south in the cedar-scented forest for ¼ mile. A few picnic tables on a grassy platform below the building have nice water views.

Old Man House Park (Suquamish Tribe)   Map 27

Historical displays • Picnicking • Scuba diving • Swimming

Facilities: Fireplaces, picnic tables, toilet, interpretive displays, hand-carry boat launch

Area: 0.7 acre; 210 feet of shoreline

From the north end the Agate Passage Bridge between Bainbridge Island and the Kitsap Peninsula, turn north from SR 305 onto Suquamish Way NE. In ¼ mile

head west on Division Avenue NE, and then south on NE McKinstry Street. This
Ts into S Angeline Avenue NE and the park.

The park is on the west side of Agate Passage, ¾ n.m. northeast of the Agate
Passage Bridge. Look for the "cable crossing" sign.

Enrich a visit to the Suquamish Museum with a stop at the site of Old Man
House. It is believed that Chief Sealth, who befriended the white settlers, was
born in the longhouse that stretched along the shore, although Blake Island
also claims that distinction. An informational display at the park tells the
history of the longhouse, said to be the largest such structure ever to have
been built, and shows methods used in its construction. Exact dimensions
of the building are uncertain, but it is known to have been at least 500 feet
long, and possibly close to 900 feet. It extended far beyond the boundaries
of the present-day park, onto what is now private property.

The longhouse was burned sometime after 1870 by federal agents who
wanted to discourage communal living and force the Indians to lead a
"civilized" life. Some of the large framing posts remained standing for many
years; the last is reported to have fallen in 1906. Archeological digs show
that Indians lived on the site even before the longhouse was built.

The park previously was operated by Washington State Parks but now is
under the mantle of the Suquamish Tribe. It faces on a beautiful beach with
sand at the high tide level and gravel below (no wonder the Native Americans

*Cedar poles representing trees and canoes surround Chief Sealth's grave. They
are representational of the traditional Suquamish burial method.*

chose this spot). A broad grassy expanse provides plenty of spots to spread a picnic cloth. Scuba divers frequently use the park as a put-in for dives along Agate Passage. Boats can easily be beached or hand-carried on the sloping beach, as the Native Americans did for several centuries.

Suquamish (Suquamish Tribe)   Map 27

Boating • Paddling • Historic site

Facilities: 1-lane launch ramp. *Nearby:* Groceries, gas, shopping, historic Native American cemetery

🚐 From the north end of the Agate Passage Bridge between Bainbridge Island and the Kitsap Peninsula, turn north from SR 305 onto Suquamish Way NE. In ½ mile enter the town of Suquamish.

A 450-foot-long fishing pier on the Suquamish waterfront once offered incredible views down the throat of Agate Passage, across Port Madison, and up to Indianola. In recent years the unmaintained pier has slowly disintegrated and now is missing a vital section connecting it to the beach. The path to the pier site is adjacent to the launch ramp and is marked with a sign quoting Chief Sealth's admonition to "love this beautiful land." The parking area is across the street from the town's two taverns; the narrow single-lane surfaced ramp drops down steeply from the parking lot (a real challenge to back a boat trailer down).

Just 1½ blocks uphill on South Street is St. Peter's Catholic Church and Cemetery, where Chief Sealth is buried. The structure surrounding the grave site—four cedar poles topped by canoelike carvings—is representational of

You Say Suquamish, Ole Said Silverstrand

Suquamish has had a checkered past with regard to the community name. The tiny hamlet was originally named Bartow, for an early Indian agent. This name didn't last, however, and it was renamed to its original Native American *Suk-wa-bish*. Real estate entrepreneur Ole Hansen purchased the Suquamish waterfront in 1909 from its Native owner. Hansen renamed the area Silverstrand, subdivided it, and hyped his lots to Seattlites looking to invest in view property. Locals objected to the new name, and one day, as he was arriving with a boatload of prospective buyers, Hansen was startled to find his new, neatly lettered town sign floating in the bay. Suquamish it has been ever since.

The difficulties of early transportation slowed growth of the area, so Hansen did not realize the fortune he had hoped for from the property. He went on to fame as a flamboyant mayor of Seattle, and even hoped to run for president on his ability to see a Bolshevik behind every bush in those Socialist-paranoid times.

the traditional Native American burial method of putting the deceased in a canoe tied high in a tree. A number of interesting old gravestones in the cemetery give insight into life on the reservation. A remarkable number of graves are marked with simple flat stones marked "Unknown." John Kettle, whose grave is here, is the Native from whom Ole Hansen purchased Suquamish.

Miller Bay and Indianola   Map 27

Boating • Paddling • Fishing pier • Viewpoint

Facilities: *Miller Bay:* Marina, 1-lane paved launch ramp with boarding float, fishing tackle, marine repair. *Indianola:* Dock

🚗 Take Miller Bay Road NE north from Suquamish for ³/₄ mile to reach the marina. *Alternatively:* From SR 104, 3 miles west of Kingston, turn south on Miller Bay Road NE to reach the marina in 4³/₄ miles. *Waterfront Preserve:* Take Miller Bay Road north from Suquamish for 3 miles and turn east on Indianola Road NE. In 2 miles turn south on Geraldcliff Road NE, and in ¹/₄ mile turn west on NE Seaview Avenue, which enters the Miller Bay community. Turn south on Chief Sealth Drive NE and at a corner junction with NE William Rodgers Road find limited roadside parking The path to the preserve is on the east. *Indianola:* Remain on Miller Bay Road, and in 3 miles from Suquamish turn east on Indianola Road NE. Reach the tiny community of Indianola in 3¹/₄ miles.

🛥 The marina is on the west side of Miller Bay, just inside its entrance from Port Madison. Indianola is on the north side of Port Madison, 1¹/₄ n.m. northeast of Suquamish.

A whimsical bench created from driftwood graces the beach at Indianola.

Miller Bay • The only marine facility on Port Madison is north of Suquamish in Miller Bay. A small marina on the west shore, just off Miller Bay Road NE, has a single-lane concrete launch ramp and boating facilities. ⚜ A long sand spit extends from the east side of the bay, nearly blocking the entrance. Do not enter at low tide, as the channel and much of the bay hold a foot of water or less at low tide. A good anchorage in 6 feet of water can be found just north of the second buoy.

Boaters who enjoy exploring out-of-the-way corners will delight in the quiet little bay ringed by homes. All shoreland is private. A Suquamish Tribe salmon hatchery is on Grovers Creek at the north end of the bay. Visitors are welcome; displays answer several frequently asked questions about salmon and hatchery activity.

Indianola • The community of Indianola was developed in 1916 as a summer and weekend getaway, but because it was only an hour's steamer ride to Seattle, soon property owners who wanted to live here year-round and commute to Seattle demanded regular ferry service. Boats were soon shuttling back and forth on regular passenger runs, and in 1938 the dock was widened and an auto ferry was put in service. Landing or loading could be a real adventure when winter storms whipped the long pier. The ferry service was discontinued in 1951 after the bridge across Agate Passage was built.

The 300-yard-long dock used by the ferries was rebuilt in 1972 and refurbished in 2004 by the Indianola community and the Interagency for Outdoor Recreation. It serves as a fishing pier and view platform, with views down Agate Passage and across to Seattle. Pause to imagine a doughty little ferry chugging up to the dock to transport a waiting flapper-era crowd.

In summer a short float at the end of the pier serves for boat loading or unloading, but overnight moorage is not permitted. The beach at the head of the pier is only for use of residents. A small grocery store and the post office are on shore nearby. The dock is at the end of Indianola Road NE.

Indianola Waterfront Preserve (Greater Peninsula Conservancy) • A section of beach on the northeast shore of Port Madison and a strip of uplands were acquired by the neighboring Greater Peninsula Conservancy with funds from the Washington Wildlife and Recreation Program. The property is designated as open space with public access permitted during daylight hours. The entrance path from the Miller Bay community heads through 10-foot-high blackberry bushes to reach the beach in about 50 feet. The broad shallow beach dries well out into Port Madison at low tide. Uplands are a dense brushy jungle, a preserve indeed! Just a quiet spot to watch for birds and catch a suntan snooze.

chapter five

East Passage

THE BROAD, BUSY CHANNEL OF EAST PASSAGE serves as the main entrance to South Puget Sound. It runs between the mainland and Vashon and Maury Islands, beginning (loosely) at Seattle's Alki Point, flowing south past cities and subdivisions, and then ending at Browns Point, on the edge of Tacoma's Commencement Bay.

East Passage is the major water thoroughfare for commercial ocean traffic bound for Tacoma or Olympia. ☸More than 3 miles wide throughout most of its length, the spacious waterway is free of any natural navigational hazards, and tidal currents are generally weak. Morning fog is common,

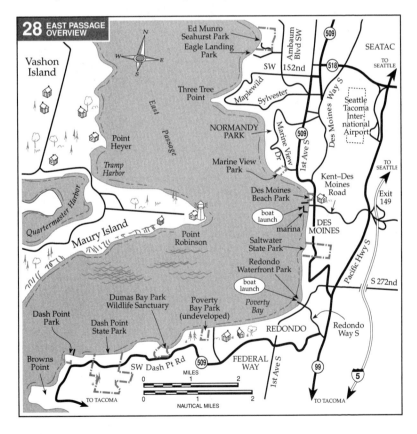

The beach at Dash Point State Park enjoys steady winds off East Passage.

especially during fall and winter, but it generally dissipates by noon. The winds that sweep up and down the length of Puget Sound accompanying storm fronts do, on occasion, kick up fairly sizable waves, especially when the wind direction opposes that of the tidal current.

Bays along the passage are for the most part broad and exposed, offering scant protection except at marinas, buoys, and private floats. The sand and gravel beaches extend only about 100 yards offshore before sinking below the 5-fathom level; beyond, the bottom drops more steeply to the 100-fathom depths of the center of the passage. Clams, crabs, and other sea life that would normally thrive on such beaches, however, have suffered from the overharvesting and pollution that come with dense population.

Steep underwater cliffs that support thick growths of life are marine pastures for a variety of fish; boat and pier fishing and scuba diving are popular pastimes here. Divers, and possibly even beachcombers, might also discover antique bottles and other historic treasures from the days of Native American villages and pioneer settlements.

SEATTLE SOUTH TO DES MOINES
Map 28

Although heavily rimmed with homes, East Passage has more than a dozen public access areas scattered along its east side. Here are viewpoints where bicyclists can pause for a scenic rest, beaches where frazzled families can exhaust children's energy in sun and salt spray, and parks where city dwellers seeking respite from the lung and ear pollutants of civilization can escape to earth-scented forests and choirs of birds.

Ed Munro Seahurst Park (City of Burien)   Map 29
Beach walking • Swimming • Picnicking • Scuba diving • Fishing • Hiking

Facilities: Picnic tables, picnic shelters, fire braziers, restrooms, outside showers, playground, fish ladder, Marine Technology Center, artificial reef, nature trail, disabled accessible
Area: 185 acres; 4000 feet of shoreline

From I-5 take Exit 154B (SR 518W, Burien, SeaTac Airport) and head west on SR 518 for 3½ miles to its end at 1st Avenue S. The road continues west as SW 148th Street, and in ½ mile intersects Ambaum Boulevard SW. Turn north on Ambaum Boulevard and in four blocks, west on SW 144th Street. In ¼ mile turn north on 13th Avenue SW, which drops downhill to the park entrance in another ¼ mile.

First-time visitors to Ed Munro Seahurst Park are usually quizzical about the huge metal "doughnut" mounted between a pair of posts near the beach. This abstract sculpture is a product of legislation that decreed mandatory

The marine technology center at Ed Monro Seahurst Park has twenty viewing slots so visitors can peek into the fish tanks.

art for public areas. To some, the sculpture might seem redundant because the most remarkable work of art is the park itself.

The name honors Ed Munro, a former county commissioner. This show-piece saltwater park is an outstanding example of how creative design can shape a beautiful natural setting to meet human needs. Earth mounds, landscaping, and a pair of parallel bulkheads divide the beach into intimate pockets, each just right for a family picnic or a private rendezvous with a beach blanket and a novel. The upper bulkhead is a prettily undulating concrete seawall. At the mid-tide level is a lower gabion bulkhead—a unique construction of riprap and wire mesh.

From the park entrance gate, the steep road passes a large parking area halfway down the hill on the south side. The small parking area immediately above the beach has disabled parking and a passenger drop-off and pickup loop for visitors who park in the lot above. At the lower parking lot the beachfront divides both in function and in character. To the south the path crosses a bridge, passes a picnic shelter, and then continues for 700 yards along the edge of a steep, wooded bank past clusters of picnic sites just above the beach.

North from the lower parking area, the curves of the concrete bulkhead separate the large grassy plots from the beach. The grassy expanse offers benches, picnic areas, a playground, a picnic shelter, and restrooms. A miniature fish ladder next to the caretaker's residence leads to an adjoining fish pond.

At the far north end of the park is the two-story Marine Technology Occupational Skills Center. Wooden beams, carved with stylized fish heads, extend outward between the two stories. The building is not open to the

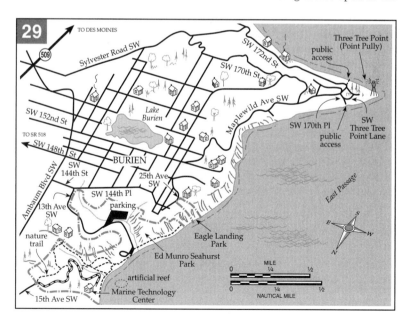

public; however, twenty viewing slots in an outside wall look into tanks containing local fish and marine life.

Shallow-draft boats can easily be beached on the gradually sloping shore. Boaters approaching Seahurst Park should be watchful for scuba divers who frequent a barge sunk just offshore. The sunken barge, placed here for the benefit of scuba divers and local fish, attracts a wide variety of sea life to an area that otherwise, because of the smoothness of the bottom, would be fairly barren.

Near the center of the park a nature trail wends uphill through the woodlands on the north end of the park. The trail heads north on a flat below the steep bluffs and then leads to a bridge crossing the main creek draining through the park. Paths lead downhill to the west alongside this drainage to emerge at the beach near the play area and uphill to the east along the steep drainage wall to the park boundary. The main trail, which can be slick and muddy in spots, continues relentlessly uphill to the northeast and finally reaches the top of the bluff at the end of 15th Avenue SW.

Eagle Landing Park (City of Burien)   Map 29

Beach walking • Views

Facilities: Staircase to beach
Area: 6 acres; 250 feet of shoreline on East Passage

See directions to Seahurst Park, above. At the intersection of SW 148th Street and Ambaum Boulevard SW go south one block then west on SW 149th Street, which bends northwest at 22nd Avenue SW, and then heads north as 25th Avenue SW. A paved parking lot is at the junction of 149th and 22nd.

The high bluffs along this section of East Passage make park development a challenge. Here, a 257-step metal stairway connects the top to the bottom. If you are willing to tackle the climb back up, you'll be rewarded with a pristine beach and eagle viewing area where you might spot the birds that nest in the vicinity.

Three Tree Point (City of Burien)   Map 29

From I-5, take Exit 154B (SR 518W, Burien, SeaTac Airport) west to Ambaum Boulevard SW. Drive south four blocks to SW 152nd Street, and then west twelve blocks to where the road name changes to Maplewild Avenue SW as it twists downhill. Turn west from Maplewild onto SW 170th Place, just short of the end of Three Tree Point. In one block, where 170th deadends, there is space for two or three cars west of the intersection of SW Three Tree Point Lane.

The name Three Tree Point was given to this area by early settlers who preferred that visually descriptive name over Point Pully, the one now shown on nautical charts. That name was given to the bluffy prominence in 1841 by the Wilkes Expedition in honor of Robert Pully, the ship's quartermaster for that expedition.

The bit of public beach at the end of SW 170th Place provides access for hand-carried boats and is a popular spot for scuba diving. All adjoining beaches are private. Parking in the vicinity is limited.

A second put-in for hand-carried boats is at a City of Burien public access at the bend of Maplewild Avenue SW just beyond 170th, where it turns south and becomes SW 172nd Street. Little to no parking is available, however.

DES MOINES TO DASH POINT
Map 28

Continuing south, the heavily residential shoreline gives way to forested uplands. Two large state parks offer a bit of the backcountry among the suburbs. The city of Des Moines is a major nautical destination, with one of the best marinas to be found on the South Sound. Land access is primarily from roads that branch from SR 509 and twist down steep ravines to reach parks and communities tucked along the shore.

Marine View Park (City of Normandy Park)   Map 30
Beach walking • Hiking

Facilities: Toilets, picnic table, trail, nature information panels

🚗 At Exit 151 (SeaTac, S 200th Street) from I-5, head west on S 200th Street, which jogs north to S 199th Street; in 3 miles turn south on 1st Avenue S (SR 509), and in one block again head west on S 200th Street for ¼ mile to Marine View Drive SW. Just south of SW 208th Street the park is on the west side of the road.

🛶 The beach is 1 n.m. northwest of Des Moines, where boats can be launched. Beachable boats can be landed on the shore.

The fabulous panoramic view the upper level of Marine View Park once offered has now largely been overgrown with trees; however the view can be seen from the head of the stairs that descend to the beach. The trail to the beach—actually a paved service road—switchbacks very steeply downhill; several benches along the way provide a welcome respite during the climb back uphill. The path ends at the top of a 50-foot, near-vertical clay bank. Here a three-story staircase with a view platform descends the high bluff. The limits of the 1000-foot-long rock and cobble beach are marked by pairs of poles in the beach at either end of the park. At a minus tide the cobble blends out into a pleasant sand beach.

A three-story-high staircase makes the final descent to the beach at Marine View Park.

Des Moines Marina (City of Des Moines)   Map 30

Boating • Paddling • Fishing • Picnicking

Facilities: Marina, boat launch slings, fishing pier, picnic tables, restrooms, artificial reef, gas and diesel, marine supplies, guest moorage with power and water, boat rental, marine repair. *Nearby:* Groceries, restaurants

🚗 From I-5 Exit 149 (SR 516, Kent, Des Moines) take Kent–Des Moines Road (SR 516) west for 2¼ miles to Marine View Drive (SR 509). A block to the north head west on S 227th Street, which leads to the marina complex.

🚢 Des Moines Marina is on the east side of East Passage, southeast of Point Robinson, and 4 n.m. south of Three Tree Point. The entrance to the marina is at the north end of the rock breakwater, just south of the fishing pier.

The city of Des Moines might sound as if it were a transplant from the middle of Iowa, but its waterfront park dedicated to maritime pursuits makes it quite clear that its heart belongs to Puget Sound. The extensive city-operated marina and launch facilities are combined with a 670-foot-long public fishing pier. Come to fish or just to stroll the docks and enjoy the bustle of others fishing and boating.

At the marina a pair of sling lifts (capable of handling boats up to 36 feet) provide the first public launch facility south of Seattle. A utility pier just inside the marina is reserved for touch-and-go moorage and dinghy launch.

A small store with marine supplies, bait, ice, and some groceries is near the launching lifts. For those needing more in the way of ships' stores, a shopping center about five blocks from the visitors' floats provides a full line of groceries, liquor, and other necessary provisions.

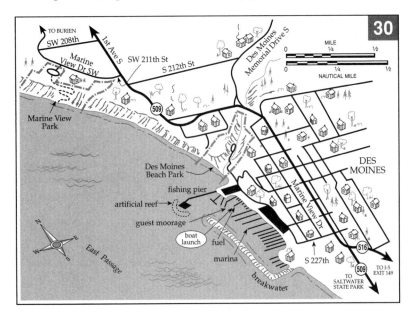

The public fishing pier at Des Moines extends far out into East Passage.

At the entrance to the yacht basin, a 670-foot-long concrete fishing pier extending far out into the sound has fillet boards, rod holders, overhead lights for night fishing, and maps of reef locations. The reef provides homes for various links in the food chain, culminating in such table fare as shrimp, crab, squid, cod, flounder, cabezon, rockfish, perch, and (rumors have it) an occasional salmon. Sunny weekends find the pier crowded with anglers of all ages, from Huck Finns to seasoned fishermen expertly landing and filleting their evening meal. The reef is closed to all spear fishing; scuba diving is allowed only by special permit.

Des Moines Beach Park (City of Des Moines)   Map 30

Picnicking • Beach walking • Hiking

Facilities: Picnic tables, restrooms, rental facilities, children's playground, trails
Area: 19.6 acres; 500 feet of shoreline on East Channel
🚗 See directions to Des Moines Marina, above. The park is just north of the marina at the end of Cliff Avenue S.

Tiny Des Moines Beach Park is especially interesting historically, as the site and its remaining cabins were once a church camp typical of many such camps found along Puget Sound in the 1930s and '40s. The buildings are still used for youth group camps. A newer building addition is an activity center for groups.

Des Moines Creek, which trickles down a deep ravine and reaches the shore at the park has been severely impacted by surrounding urban areas.

Efforts are being made to improve the water quality of the creek in order to restore wildlife habitat and runs of salmon, cutthroat, and steelhead. Squirrels, raccoons, and mountain beaver live in the forested ravine, and towhees, jays, and robins nest there. Mallards, coots, and great blue herons feed in the stream and along the saltwater shore.

The grassy beach strip at the entrance to the park has picnic tables; views are south past the marina fishing pier to Vashon Island. A narrow beach offers chances for some beachcombing, or at least the opportunity to play among a noisy horde of gulls.

Saltwater State Park   Map 31

Hiking • Beach walking • Swimming • Picnicking • Camping • Scuba diving • Fishing • Boating • Paddling

Facilities: 50 standard campsites, 3 primitive campsites, group camp, 4 group day-use areas, picnic shelters, picnic tables, restrooms, outside shower, trails, artificial reef, concession stand, 3 mooring buoys, trailer dump station, volleyball stanchions, horseshoe pits, children's play equipment, swimming beach.
Area: 88 acres; 1445 feet of shoreline

🚗 Take Exit 149 (SR 516, Kent, Des Moines) west from I-5. At the first traffic light, turn south on Pacific Highway S, and in ½ mile turn west on S 240th Street. After 1½ miles turn south on Marine View Drive (SR 509), and in ¾ mile turn west on S 251st Street for 50 feet, and then south on 8th Place S to reach the park in two blocks.

🛥 The park lies 2 n.m. south of the Des Moines Marina, the nearest launch site.

Saltwater State Park seems to inspire sandy bottoms.

Right in the urban heart of metropolitan Puget Sound lies a marvelously green swale with beaches, trails, and a forest campground. No carefully groomed lawns here—just rugged, utilitarian facilities. Here is the place for the office to hold its salmon bake, the Cub Scouts to camp out, or toddlers to squish sand between their toes and romp in the water on a hot summer day. Here is *not* the place for solitude, however. The park annually attracts (and withstands the use of) over 750,000 day users and some 17,000 campers. In winter, when the crowds are gone, the park still has charms for those who enjoy the invigorating sting of wind-driven salt spray and the woodsy smell of damp forest trails.

Immediately inside the park is a large parking area adjoining a group camp area with a picnic shelter and a lawn

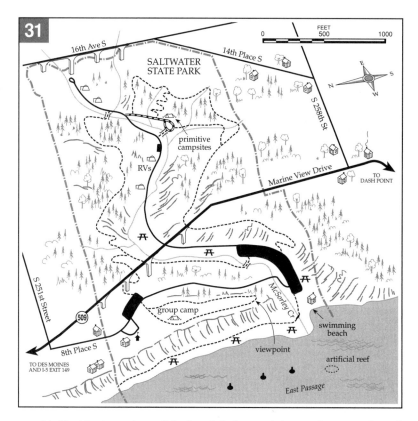

on a bluff with viewpoints of the beach below and the southern reaches of East Passage. The entrance road drops steeply downhill to parking lots near the beach and along the ravine floor. The overnight camping area begins beyond the foot of the Marine View Drive bridge, which spans the park. Farther east, trailer sites give way to tent spots as the steep hills close in and the road ends.

The waters of Puget Sound flow over the shallow, sandy tideflat at the south end of the beach and in summer warm to temperatures pleasant enough for wading and splashing. What sea life once existed here has, sadly, long since been carted away from this heavily used beach. A boulder seawall defines a broad, man-made spit north of the beach and supports a wide pathway that heads north to the park boundary.

Three mooring buoys offshore are available for marine visitors. The protruding spit offers the best landing for small boats and put-in for kayaks; the beach to the south is so shallow that a wade ashore is usually necessary. A white can buoy with a diagonal red stripe about 150 yards offshore marks a reef created by tires and the remains of a sunken barge, placed there by the state in 1971 to provide a home for undersea life. The wreck, lying at

A rock bulkhead stabilizes the beach and walkway at Saltwater State Park.

the 50-foot depth, attracts scuba divers who come to observe the array of marine invertebrates, fish, and even octopus that find shelter here.

Saltwater State Park not only offers picnicking, camping, and a beach, but it also boasts nearly 2 miles of trails with a seclusion unexpected for such an urban area. Paths pass knotted old bigleaf maple trees, moss-covered logs, and spring blooms of trillium and skunk cabbage. Jays and crows call in the green canopy overhead, while wrens and sparrows rustle in trail-side shrubs. Here even slugs have their charms, as their silvery trails leave a delicate tracery on fallen leaves.

Redondo Waterfront Park (City of Des Moines) Map 32

Fishing • Boating • Swimming • Picnicking • Scuba diving

Facilities: 2-lane paved launch ramp with boarding floats, fishing pier, restrooms, boardwalk, stairs to the beach

Area: 2.79 acres; 2200 feet of shoreline on East Passage

From I-5 Exit 147 (SR99, S 272nd Street) take S 272nd Street west for 1¼ miles, crossing both SR 99 and 16th Avenue S. At a T intersection head south on 12th Avenue S, which becomes Marine View Drive S, then 10th Avenue S, and in 1 mile Ts into Redondo Beach Drive S at the park

The park launch ramp is at the southeast side of Poverty Bay, 4 n.m. south of the Des Moines Marina

A seaside hamlet often overlooked by motorists and boaters, Redondo has some salty elbow-to-elbow cottages along the shore drive and an outcrop

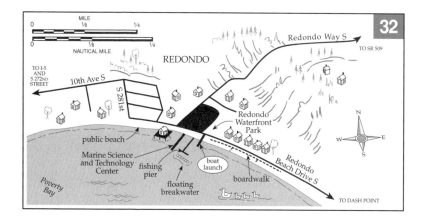

of condominiums abutting a narrow road above the beach. A public boardwalk atop the concrete seawall has a few informational displays; a couple of staircases lead down to the beach.

The major attractions of the Redondo waterfront are its fishing pier and launch ramp. Take along a picnic lunch to enjoy while soaking up the nautical atmosphere, or indulge in fish and chips from the nearby restaurant.

The long, T-shaped pier features a fish cleaning station, park benches, overhead lights for night fishing, and lowered sections of railing for the convenience of disabled and pint-sized anglers. Stairs at the head of the pier permit beach access. The concrete launch ramps have adjacent floats for securing small craft when boarding and loading. A strong northerly wind can stack up some fairly bouncy waves at the launch ramp, so a floating

Condominiums press against the waterfront at Redondo.

breakwater has been installed offshore from the ramps; the boarding floats can still buck a bit in weather.

The pier north of the fishing pier houses the Highline Community College Marine Science and Technology Center. Its aquarium is open to the public on Saturdays from 10:00 AM to 2:00 PM

At the north end of the waterfront, a pleasant, sandy, two-block-long beach is open to the public for swimming, sunbathing, or just plain lolling about. Scuba divers often use the beach as a start point for offshore dives.

Dumas Bay Park Wildlife Sanctuary (City of Federal Way)   Map 33

Birdwatching • Beach walking

Facilities: Parking, trail to beach

Area: 19.3 acres; 500 feet of shoreline on Dumas Bay

From I-5 take Exit 143 (Federal Way, SW 320th Street) and head west on SW 320th Street to 21st Avenue SW. Here turn north on 21st, and in ¼ mile west on SW Dash Point Road. Follow Dash Point Road north and west for 2 miles, and turn north on 44th Avenue SW. Reach the park in ½ mile, just beyond SW 310th Street.

Paddlecraft can land at the park, on the southwest side of Dumas Bay, 2 n.m. east of Dash Point.

While some parks suffer from lack of public facilities, this one thrives on it—any elaborate development or heavy public use would surely destroy this delicate tideland environment. Fortunately, the Federal Way Parks Department plans to leave this nature refuge basically undisturbed.

A wide, flat gravel trail leaves the parking area and wanders for 300 yards through woods and a small clearing before arriving at the beach. A creek threads through the maple and alder thicket, seeping into a cattail

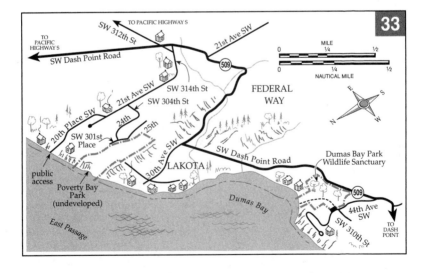

marsh and finally entering the bay. This environmental combination serves as a haven for a wide variety of land birds, waterfowl, and small wild animals. The park has one of the largest heron rookeries on Puget Sound; an information display tells of heron breeding and nesting habits. A quiet approach through the woods might be rewarded with sightings of wildlife. Watch, photograph, and enjoy, but do not litter or destroy.

✸ Dumas Bay is quite shallow, drying well out into the sound at low tide. Even inflatables and flat-bottomed boats should use caution approaching the park from the water.

Dash Point State Park Map 34

Hiking • Beach walking • Swimming • Picnicking • Camping • Kite flying • Fishing • Scuba diving • Marine life study • Paddling

Nesting boxes at Dumas Bay Park Wildlife Sanctuary

Facilities: 110 standard campsites, 28 RV sites, group camp, group day-use area, restrooms, showers, outside shower, picnic tables, picnic shelter, 7.4 miles of trails, amphitheater.

Area: 419.56 acres; 3301 feet of shoreline

🚐 *From I-5 headed south:* take Exit 143 (Federal Way, S 320th Street) and turn west on S 320th Street. In 4³/₄ miles turn north on 47th Avenue SW. After three blocks head west on SW Dash Point Road (SR 509) and follow it to the park entrance in 1 mile.

From I-5 headed north: take Exit 137 (Fife, Milton) and head north on 54th Avenue E for 1 mile, and take Marine View Drive (SR 509) to the northeast. Follow Marine View Drive for another 5¹/₂ miles, where it becomes Eastside Drive NE to reach the park in another 4 miles.

As does Saltwater State Park, its northern counterpart, Dash Point offers a forest campground, a beachfront, and trails just a hop from the city. Although it is less heavily used than Saltwater, Dash Point has twice the shoreline and four times the land area. Some parts of the forested inland remain undeveloped except for trails, which adds to the feeling of a wilderness in the heart of the subdivisions.

Southwest Dash Point Road splits the park, with the day-use area lying to the north, fronting on the water, and the overnight camping area to the south. Campsites on two loop roads, one for trailers and one for tenting, are tucked away in timber and shrubbery.

More than 7 miles of trails wander through the forest of second-growth alder, fir, and maple. One leads through timber along the west side of the campground and down the ravine beneath the highway overpass to the lower

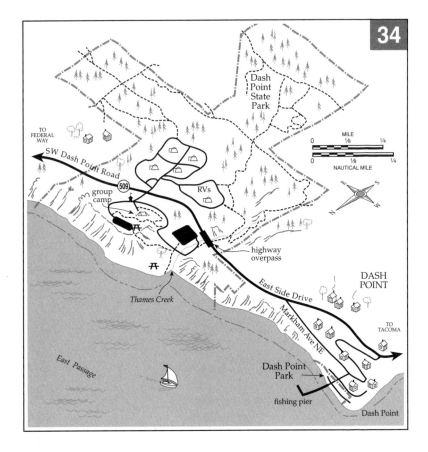

level of the park and the beach. Other longer trails leave the camping area and skirt the south and east boundaries of the park.

The section of the park north of the highway is divided into three separate day-use areas. A picnic area is in a timbered flat atop the steep, 200-foot bluff rising from the beach. A ravine separates it from a large group campsite to the south. Trails wind down through the woods to connect both areas to the third day-use area, the beach.

Dash Point State Park is one of the few places in the sound where saltwater bathing can be enjoyable. The sandy beach extends outward over 2000 feet at a minus tide, giving the sun an opportunity to influence the normally frigid water, which can run 10 to 15 degrees warmer here than in deeper water. *Caution:* Lifeguards are not on duty—solo swimming can be dangerous.

The sandy expanse invites exploration and study of intertidal marine life, but pollution makes shellfish unsafe for human consumption. Picnic tables are scattered about the park. A picnic shelter between the entry road and the parking lot has a bridge and an easy path for disabled access.

At Dash Point, a mucky tideflat is always irresistible.

Dash Point Park (Metro Parks Tacoma) Map 34

Fishing • Picnicking • Swimming • Paddling • Scuba diving

Facilities: Picnic shelter, picnic tables, fishing pier, children's play area, basketball court, hand-carry boat launch, toilets

See directions to Dash Point State Park, above. Marine View Drive (SR 509) heads north and becomes Eastside Drive NE in 1¾ miles; turn west on Markham Avenue NE, and in ¼ mile head north on Soundview Drive NE to reach the park in one block.

The park is on East Passage on the northeast side of Dash Point.

This day-use city park in the town of Dash Point is quite different in character from nearby Dash Point State Park. The park's focal point is a 200-foot-long fishing pier that juts into East Passage. The pier is a favorite spot for throngs of anglers, but even nonanglers can enjoy a stroll along the dock to admire the catch of others and to take in views downsound to Point Robinson and upsound to Dalco Passage and Point Defiance.

There are no docking or launching areas, but hand-carry boats can be launched and landed on the sloping beach. Two shipwrecks, one just off Dash Point and the other about ¼ mile farther south, are popular exploration sites for scuba divers.

Onshore, a children's play area, picnic shelters, and park benches are interspersed on a narrow, grassy strip that separates the beachfront from the parking lot. Below the low concrete bulkhead, a block-long sandy beach that tapers gradually into the sound is ideal for swimming when the water warms enough to be tolerable.

chapter six

Vashon and Maury Islands and Colvos Passage

BOUNDING THE WESTERN EDGE OF EAST PASSAGE are a pair of large islands: Vashon and Maury. In reality they are physically one, joined by a narrow isthmus that is crossed by a road at the community of Portage. Colvos Passage, which is nearly a mile wide throughout most of its length, separates Vashon Island from the Kitsap Peninsula.

In May 1792 the members of the Vancouver Expedition became the first Europeans to sight Vashon Island and Colvos Passage. Captain Vancouver, still hoping to find the elusive Northwest Passage, cautiously anchored his expedition flagship, the *Discovery*, north of Blake Island and sent a launch and cutter commanded by Lt. Peter Puget to explore the waterways farther south. This small band of adventurers made their way up the sound via the passage and returned by the same route.

Vashon Island was named after one of Peter Puget's first commanding officers, James Vashon, but it was not until the Wilkes Expedition of 1838–42 that Maury Island and Colvos Passage received their names. The name Maury is for expedition member Lt. William Maury. As for Colvos Passage, perhaps Wilkes thought the name of his Greek midshipman, George Colvocoresses, was as long as the channel. He evidently gave up in his attempt to spell it, however, for he abbreviated it to Colvos on his charts and it has remained thus ever since. Be grateful.

VASHON AND MAURY ISLANDS
Map 35

Vashon and Maury Islands serve as a bedroom community for the cities of Seattle, Tacoma, and Bremerton and also as a semi-isolated sanctuary for a number of people who wish only to "do their own thing." Large ships of the Washington State Ferry System run between Seattle's Fauntleroy landing to the north end of Vashon Island, and then continue on to Southworth on the Kitsap Peninsula, while a small ferry operates between Tacoma and Tahlequah, on the south end of Vashon. The ferry ride from Seattle takes about twenty minutes, from Southworth about ten minutes, and from Tahlequah fifteen minutes.

The ferry for Point Defiance leaves from Tahlequah at the south end of

Opposite: *The popular boat moorage area at Blake Island State Park is often jam-packed in summer.*

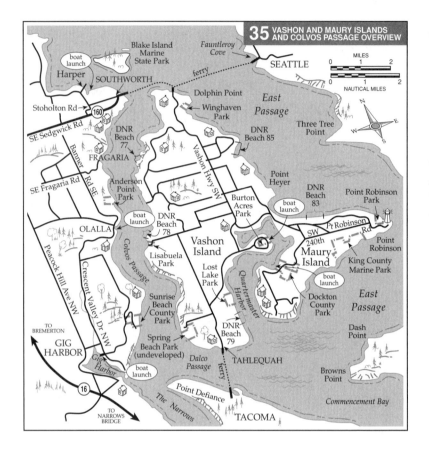

the island. The crossing takes only fifteen minutes, but, because of usually light traffic, the boat has long pauses at the terminals instead of shuttling back and forth continuously. Consult a current ferry schedule to avoid a long wait.

The two islands are a bicycling delight; roads are lightly traveled, and the main thoroughfare, Vashon Highway SW, has a wide shoulder. Most roads on the islands are inland, with a few high vistas of Colvos Passage, Quartermaster Harbor, and Point Defiance. The roads encircling Quartermaster Harbor frequently border the water, with several spots appropriate for picnicking. There are no camping facilities, so unless you are staying at one of the few motels or bed-and-breakfast inns, you must leave by the evening ferry; however, all of the islands' 50-plus miles of highway are easily explored in a day.

East Passage DNR Beaches ●
The DNR manages two beaches fronting on East Passage, one on Vashon Island and one on Maury. They are accessible only by boat, as both have private uplands. The first, Beach 85, a very narrow cobble beach, 1500 feet long, is ½ mile south of Point Beales on the east

Washington's state ferries, such as this one arriving at Vashon Island, are the successors to the Mosquito Fleet.

The Mosquito Fleet

Today, Vashon and Maury Islands are connected to the mainland by Washington state ferries. In early days the islands were served by a collection of private boats, dubbed the Mosquito Fleet, that carried passengers back and forth, brought goods to the islands, and took away marketable products. The individual enterprise of the boats of the Mosquito Fleet eventually gave way to the more organized efforts of commercial shipping. By the 1920s the islands were served primarily by the Black Ball Line, a privately operated fleet that carried both people and cargo, landing at a long wharf on the north end of Vashon Island near Dolphin Point.

Over the years the rising rates of the private ferries caused irate islanders to pressure the state into taking over the line. In 1951 a large portion of the Black Ball fleet was purchased by the state of Washington, which then went into the ferry business; however, the state was never able to operate the boats any more cheaply or efficiently than private industry had.

Ever since the islands were settled there has been talk of building a bridge—or two bridges—across the channel to the Kitsap Peninsula (as was done with Bainbridge Island to the north), or east across East Passage to the mainland proper. The project has never proceeded past the talk stage, and rising construction costs, environmental concerns, and the islanders' growing appreciation of isolation make it unlikely that such a bridge will ever be built.

side of Vashon Island, facing Three Tree Point. Backed by a steep bluff, it extends south to where a number of residences are grouped around a pair of creeks that empty into a slight cove. There is little marine harvest here, except for sea cucumbers and rock crab.

DNR Beach 83 is at the south end of Tramp Harbor on the north side of Maury Island. The 2000-foot-long, sand and cobble beach begins a mile east of Portage, the isthmus between Vashon and Maury Islands. Little harvestable marine life is found on the tide-swept shore.

North End Beach Access • The Washington state ferries dock at the ferry terminal near Dolphin Point at the north end of Vashon Island. A surfaced public boat-launch ramp immediately east of the ferry landing provides water access for hand-carried boats—it is not suitable for launching trailered boats. While paddlers are exploring, cars can be left at the ferry terminal parking lot, one block straight uphill from the ferry dock between 103rd and 104th Avenue SW.

Old pilings near the ferry terminal, as well as the steep walls of the headland all the way from Point Vashon to Dolphin Point, are frequently explored by scuba divers. Gain access to the shore at the launch ramp, but do not dive among the pilings of the ferry wharf; it is unlawful to dive within 100 feet of a state ferry terminal. The beach below the ramp is privately owned. Beach access is permitted, but do not remove any marine life. West Seattle's Fauntleroy Cove is 3 n.m. to the northeast.

Winghaven Park (Vashon Island Parks)   Map 36

Paddling • Beach walking • Clamming

Facilities: Picnic table, toilet, CMT campsite
Area: 12 acres; 400 feet of shoreline

🚗 From the ferry landing, head uphill on Vashon Highway SW for ¾ mile and

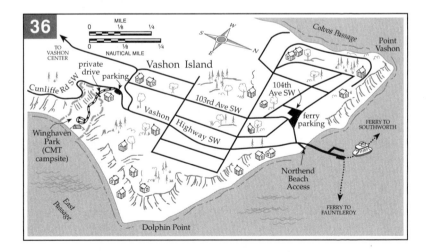

turn southeast on Cunliffe Road SW. In ⅛ mile a signed parking area on the east side of the road has room for a few cars.

🚣 The park is on the west side of East Passage (east side of Vashon Island) ¾ n.m. south of Dolphin Point. The park is easy to identify from the water by two old wooden pilings just offshore and the remains of the ornate brick and concrete balustrade that can be seen on top of the bulkhead onshore.

Just a short distance south of the Vashon ferry landing is a small, undeveloped property. To reach the beach from Cunliffe Road, walk the gravel road as it descends a steep narrow ravine for ¼ mile through dense woods, passes a small dam-created pond, and arrives at a marshy area above a grassy flat.

The park is an abandoned estate that was deeded to the county. The home that once was here has been removed, and now only a picnic table graces the lawn where it stood. A deteriorating bulkhead

A mouldering balustrade and concrete steps are reminders of the fine estate that once occupied the shore and uplands at Winghaven Park.

with ornate concrete balusters stretches along the bank above the beach. Engulfed in blackberries and weeds, the remains of an elaborate fountain sit at one end of the bulkhead, a reminder of prouder days.

Below the remnants of the garden a 400-foot-long sandy beach looks across East Passage to West Seattle. Empty shells give evidence that clamming is worth a try. See comments in the introduction regarding harvesting shellfish. Private residences mark the park boundaries on both sides. Shallow-draft boats can easily land on the gentle beach, and CMT camping is permitted.

Point Heyer (KVI Beach) Map 37

Scuba diving • Birdwatching

Facilities: None

🚗 From Vashon Highway SW, turn east on SW 204th Street, which becomes SW Ellisport Road in ½ mile, and winds downhill to intersect with Dockton Road SW and Chautauqua Beach Road SW. Go north on Chautauqua Beach Road SW for ½ mile to SW 204th Street, turn east on it, and in a few blocks, at 78th Place SW, reach the property gate.

🚣 Des Moines is 4½ n.m. to the east

At the north end of Tramp Harbor the broad, flat expanse of Vashon Island's Point Heyer pushes into East Passage. An artificial reef, marked by red-and-white-striped buoys, lies 1000 feet southeast of the point, in 45 to 100 feet of

Sandy KVI Beach is one of the nicest places to play on Vashon Island.

water. The massive rocks and chunks of scrap concrete that form the reef provide habitat for such popular food fish as rockfish, perch, lingcod, and cabezon. The state DFW has placed a string of these reefs at approximately 10-mile intervals along Puget Sound to enhance local saltwater fishing.

The gently sloping beach at Point Heyer, known locally as KVI Beach, is open to the public, subject to revocation of the privilege by that radio station, which owns the point and has a large transmission tower on the property. Parking near the access path at the intersection of SW 204th Street and 78th Place SW is limited to one or two roadside spaces. Be aware that neighbors are quick to have illegally parked cars ticketed and towed.

A saltwater lagoon, serving as home and hotel for shorebirds and waterfowl, lies between the bluff and the beach grass and sand of the point. The thick collection of silvered driftwood at high tide levels indicates that this would be an exciting place to visit during stormy weather.

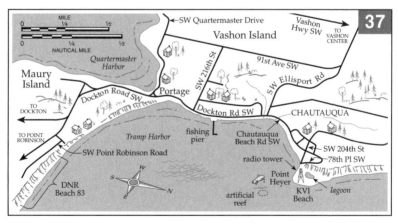

Tramp Harbor Fishing Pier (King County)   Map 37

Beach walking • Picnicking • Fishing • Scuba diving

Facilities: Fishing pier, picnic table, toilet

See directions to Point Heyer, above. At the intersection of SW Ellisport Road and Dockton Road SW, head south on Dockton Road SW for ¼ mile to the parking area at the head of the pier

What once was an old, decaying commercial pier on Tramp Harbor has been nicely refurbished by King County into a public fishing pier. The 300-foot-long dock ends in a square platform with a few sturdy benches and a picnic table. A pair of holes in the deck surrounded by pipe railings give anglers a chance to drop a line in the midst of the pilings. Stairs leading down to the rock- and boulder-strewn beach offer scuba divers access to the gradually sloping shore. The old pilings that support the pier carry a thick coating of anemones and other marine life. Mooring of boats to the dock is prohibited.

Point Robinson Park and Lighthouse (Vashon Island Parks)   Map 38

Picnicking • Beach walking • Views • Lighthouse • Fishing • Scuba diving

Facilities: Picnic tables, toilets, rental house, CMT campsite
Area: 10 acres; 600 feet of saltwater shoreline on East Passage

From the Vashon ferry landing take Vashon Highway SW south for 8 miles, and turn east on SW Quartermaster Drive. At a T intersection in 1½ miles, turn south on Dockton Road SW, and in ½ mile bear southeast on SW Point Robinson Road. Reach the park in another 3 miles.

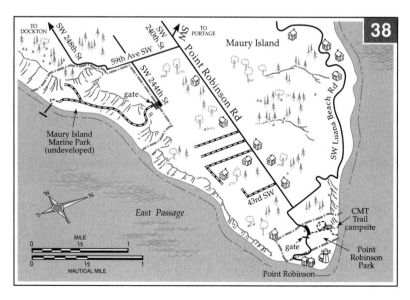

The lighthouse shares Point Robinson with a tower for the Vessel Tracking System.

Point Robinson is on Maury Island on the west side of East Passage, due west of Des Moines. The CMT site is on the north side of the point about 200 yards west of the lighthouse.

Maury Island reaches out to the mainland, constricting East Passage to less than 2 miles across at Point Robinson. The point is known primarily to boaters as the site of a lighthouse and Coast Guard station, a spot where storm warnings are posted, a weather reporting station, and (incidentally) a fine place to go salmon fishing. Less well known is the pretty little park that perches on the hill above the lighthouse.

The day-use park, which is primarily a picnic area, has parking for a few cars. Tables are tucked in the woods beside the parking lot and along a short trail that loops through the trees on the north side of the park. One of the latter is the CMT campsite. Between these two wooded sections a narrow swath of grassland sports a field of aesthetically placed boulders and cast concrete slabs.

A Light on the Island

The first navigational light placed on Point Robinson in 1887 consisted of a lantern attached to a wooden arm. In 1894 a wooden tower was built housing a lantern augmented by a mirrored lens. A high-powered Fresnel lens made in Paris was installed in the present lighthouse when it was constructed in 1915. This modern light is visible for 15 miles in clear weather. The foghorn, too, has had a succession of improvements, beginning as a hand-operated steam whistle and culminating in today's electronic horn. In marked contrast to the old lighthouse is the 100-foot-high metal tower that has been erected next to it to support a high powered radar antenna, part of the Puget Sound Vessel Tracking System.

The light station was one of the last in the state to be manned but is now automated. The Coast Guard Auxiliary offers tours of the light station by appointment. Contact Capt. Joe Wubbold at (206) 463-6672. One of the two lightkeeper houses is occupied by the park manager, but the other is available as a weekly vacation rental. Contact the Vashon Park District for information.

A poorly maintained trail leads down through the grassy meadow to the beach. Stairs reach the beach at a wooden kayak rack in the trees above the high tide level. All of the broad sandy beach below the park and clear around the point by the lighthouse is open for public use—beachcombing, picnicking, sunning, sand castle building, what have you.

Maury Island Marine Park (Undeveloped, King County Parks)
Map 38

Hiking • Fishing • Clamming • Paddling • Beach walking
Facilities: Fishing pier, toilet
Area: 320.55 acres; 1¼ miles of saltwater shoreline on East Passage
🚐 See directions to Point Robinson Park, above, 1½ miles west of Point Robinson (1½ miles south of Dockton Road SW) head south on 59th Avenue SW, and in ¼ mile turn east on SW 244th Street, which deadends at the parking area in ¼ mile. Access to the beach is via a hike down a steep ½-mile-long gravel road.
🛥 The park's beach is 4 n.m. west of Redondo, where boats can be put in. Beachable boats are easily landed on the shore.

What might someday be one of the finest marine parks on the South Sound lies southwest of the tip of Point Robinson. It is here that King County purchased 320 acres of spectacular waterfront property on Maury Island. For more than fifty years the property had been used as a gravel quarry, shipping bargeloads of gravel throughout the area. Some of the old quarry is already so overgrown that it appears nearly natural; vegetation will soon reclaim the rest. The large 200-foot-long dock that was once used to load the barges still remains and has been converted into a fishing pier. A barge mooring pier was once across the outer end of the main pier, but only pilings and dolphins remain.

The real gem of the park is the 1¼-mile-long, gradually sloping, gravel and cobble beach facing on East Passage—one of the best to be found hereabouts. The beach is backed by a madrona-clad, 400-foot-high bluff. Park property that extends as much as ½ mile inland holds the promise of future trails. Views extend south across the channel to the bluffs of the mainland and beyond to icy Mount Rainier.

Quartermaster Harbor   Map 39

Clamming • Fishing • Paddling

Facilities: Marina (private), supplies, restrooms
🛥 The entrance to Quartermaster Harbor is off Dalco Passage, 2¼ n.m. northwest of Browns Point.

Separating Vashon and Maury Islands, Quartermaster Harbor is a tranquil 5-mile-long haven for boaters, probably the best such place in South Puget Sound. It might be that Lieutenant Wilkes, who surveyed this region, had run out of individual names of crewmen by the time he reached this bay, so he named it generically after his officers as a group. Another story is that he thought the harbor was so beautiful that he named it as a suitable resting place for the spirits of his crew.

❋ Aside from a buoy-marked shoal, extending 300 yards offshore west of Piner Point, the harbor is a comfortable 4 to 6 fathoms deep all the way to the Burton Peninsula. Excellent anchorages can be found near Dockton and on the southwest side of the Burton Peninsula. At the end of the harbor, where it hooks to the south behind the peninsula, is a private marina that has no guest facilities. Parks at Burton and Dockton provide land access to the harbor. Large heron rookeries are at Judd Creek and on Melita Creek, at the head of the bay directly across from the Burton Peninsula.

At the head of the bay, a low isthmus, scarcely 200 yards wide, ties Vashon to Maury Island. Indians using Quartermaster Harbor as a shortcut between East Passage and Dalco Passage portaged their dugout canoes across this neck of land. The small community now located here thus is named Portage.

Here, also, the resident Shomamish Natives, part of the Suquamish Tribe,

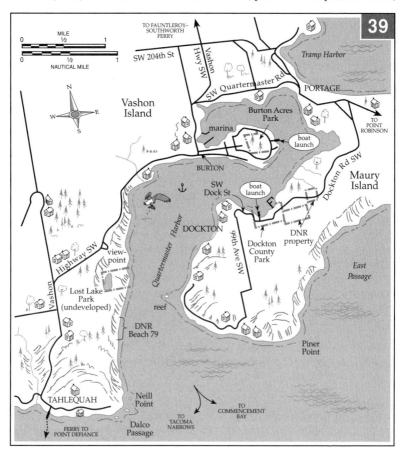

The view to the northeast, looking up Quartermaster Harbor to Portage.

raised nets on poles to snare low-flying waterfowl as they landed or departed from the harbor. The nets, fashioned from thin, braided strips of bark and plant fibers, are reported to have been over 300 feet in length. This hunting technique thoroughly puzzled early European explorers, who were unable to visualize a use for the tall poles they saw standing in areas such as this.

Quartermaster Harbor Public Beaches • Quartermaster Harbor is ideal for paddle exploration of nooks and crannies. In addition to the county parks, two short strips of public beach on the Vashon side of the harbor are good stops for lunch breaks. DNR Beach 79 is 1 mile north of Neill Point at the entrance to the harbor. The 627-foot beach, which is rocky above, with a wide stretch of sand at low tide, is said to hold some clams. It is accessible only by boat, because the uplands are private.

A second beach farther north along this same shore belongs to Lost Lake Park, an undeveloped Vashon Island Parks holding. The property, ½ mile north of the DNR beach, has about 1500 feet of waterfront. Extending inland for ¼ mile to the base of a steep cliff, the unimproved park encompasses a swampy bog, the source of its name. Again, no land access is available; boats can land on the gradually sloping shore.

Burton Acres Park (Vashon Island Parks)   Map 40

Fishing • Hiking • Paddling • Swimming

Facilities: 1-lane paved launch ramp, boathouse, paddlecraft rentals, picnic tables, trails, restrooms, nature trail

Area: 68 acres; 250 feet of saltwater shoreline on Quartermaster Harbor

🚗 From the Vashon ferry landing head south on Vashon Highway SW for 9 miles to the small community of Burton. Turn east on SW Burton Drive, which in ½ mile Ts into SW Harbor Drive, to the north, and SW Bayview Drive, to the south. Either road follows its respective shore of the peninsula, and they meet again at the east side of the peninsula near Jensen Point.

🛥 The Jensen Point launch ramp is on the east tip of the Burton Peninsula on the west side of Quartermaster Harbor.

A madrona at Burton Acres Park overhangs Quartermaster Harbor.

The blunt thumb of the Burton Peninsula projects into the north end of Quartermaster Harbor, creating a harbor within a harbor. A park lies in the wooded heart of the small peninsula. The Jensen Point Small Craft Center, a part of the park, offers canoe and kayak rentals. The adjacent long, paved launch ramp is usable even at minus tides.

The bulk of the park lying west of the launch ramp is densely wooded and at a glance seems impervious; a closer look reveals a series of old trails weaving their way through the overgrown former campground. A Tacoma Eagle Scout troop recently brushed out the trails and installed numbered posts

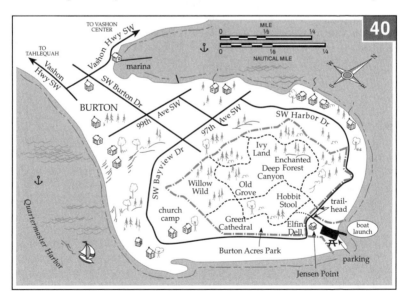

that identify flora found along the major north–south path. An information board near the launch ramp trailhead has a map identifying the trails.

A rustic sign at the southern park boundary, near a church camp, has a map of the trails and tells the fanciful names of the forest areas through which they wend—Elfin Dell, Willow Wild, Enchanted Forest, Deep Canyon, Old Grove, Hobbit Stool, and Green Cathedral. Look sharp for leprechauns!

Dockton County Park (King County Parks) Map 41
Swimming • Fishing • Picnicking • Boating • Paddling • Hiking

Facilities: Swimming beach, dock with floats, 1-lane paved launch ramp with boarding float, marine pumpout station, portable toilet dump, picnic shelter, picnic tables, fire pits, children's play area, restrooms, showers, trails

Area: 20.52 acres; 1000 feet of saltwater shoreline on Quartermaster Harbor

From the Vashon ferry landing take Vashon Highway SW south for 8 miles, and turn east on SW Quartermaster Drive. At a T intersection in 1½ miles turn south on Dockton Road SW and follow it for 3½ miles to the park.

The park is on the east side of Quartermaster Harbor, about 4 n.m. from its entrance.

Today it is difficult to envision Dockton as it looked in the 1890s when it was the site of a thriving shipyard. Huge vessels were built here, as well as many of the boats of the Mosquito Fleet—a flotilla of small craft that ferried goods and people to all points of Puget Sound. In 1892 a 315-foot-long floating dry dock was installed at Dockton. The only such facility on the sound, it provided a place where large steamships coming in from foreign ports could make repairs. At that time more than 400 workers were employed in the Dockton shipyards. Despite having one of the finest harbors on South Puget Sound, Dockton had one failing—it was on an island. Originally all

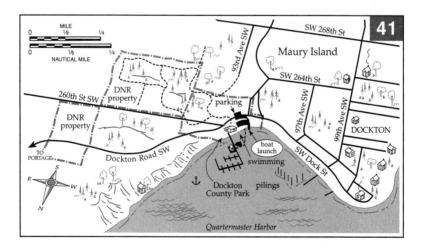

Spacious floats at Dockton County Park offer moorage for the day or for longer stays.

of the communities on the sound relied on water traffic to supply materials and labor for their industries, but with the arrival of the railroad in December 1873, mainland industries gained a major advantage. Suddenly Dockton seemed remote by comparison. Unable to compete, it became a ghost town in a few short years. Today all that remains of the shipyards are a few deteriorating pilings in the cove. The onshore property is now a pleasant, water-oriented King County park.

At the south end of the park beach is a public boat launch ramp, marked by pilings and a boarding float alongside its water end. In the middle of the beach is a shallow, roped-off swimming area; a lifeguard is usually on duty during the summer. A long pier leads to floats for fishing, swimming, and boat moorage. The floats accommodate about seventy-five boats; there is a three-day moorage limit.

For land visitors and boaters ready to stretch their legs, the inland portion of the park and a quarter-section of adjoining DNR property have a pair of trail loops, totaling over 2 miles, through a second-growth forest of alder, bigleaf maple, and madrona. The park trailhead is at the northwest corner of the overflow parking lot; trails are open to hikers and equestrians.

West Side Shore Accesses   Map 35

Paddling • Picnicking • Beach walking • Clamming

Facilities: *Lisabuela Park:* Picnic tables, toilet, CMT campsite

🚗 *Lisabuela Park:* From the Vashon ferry landing head south on Vashon Highway SW for 7 miles, and turn west on SW 216th Street. In ¾ mile head south on 11th Avenue SW, which in ¼ mile turns sharply west to become SW 220th Street. At a corner in 2 miles SW Lisabuela Road winds downhill south to the park in another ¼ mile.

🚤 *Lisabuella Park:* On the east side of Colvos Passage across the water from and a little south of Olalla. It can be identified by a conspicuous "Cable Crossing" sign at the beach. *Spring Beach Park:* On the east side of Colvos Passage about 1¼ n.m. north of Point Dalco.

DNR Beaches • Two stretches of DNR beach on Colvos Passage, on the west side of Vashon Island, are public but are accessible only by boat because their uplands are bordered by private property. Each offers a brief respite to boaters in small craft who want to stop for a while and watch traffic go by in busy Colvos Passage.

Both beaches are cobblestone covered at their upper reaches; sand at low tide provides some opportunity for clamming. See comments in the introduction regarding harvesting shellfish. The more northerly, Beach 77, only 760 feet in length, is 500 feet north of the green navigational light located between Cove and Point Peter, directly across Colvos Passage from Fragaria. The second, Beach 78, is longer, 1780 feet, and is across Colvos Passage from Olalla, just south of where Green Valley Creek empties into saltwater.

Lisabuela Park (Vashon Island Parks) • This tiny beach haven on the shores of Vashon Island, southeast across Colvos Passage from Olalla, has a lawn for picnicking and a secluded little wooded pocket where CMT paddlers are permitted to camp. The gentle gravel and cobble beach has only sparse driftwood at the high tide level and might offer opportunities to dig for clams at a minus tide.

Graceful firs offer some shade at Lisabuela Park.

Spring Beach Park (Undeveloped, Vashon Island Parks) • Another Vashon Island public area on Colvos Passage is at Spring Beach. The park begins just south of the small residential enclave of Spring Beach and runs south along 1400 feet of sandy beach. The property extends uphill and includes a stream flowing down one of the steep, wooded ravines. ❋ The waters offshore in Colvos Passage are subject to tide rips, so use caution approaching in a small boat. At present there is no public access by land; the road dropping down to the beach from the end of SW 280th Street is private.

COLVOS PASSAGE
Map 35

This 13-mile-long, straight channel is a busy saltwater highway, providing a more direct route down Puget Sound than East Passage. Weekends find hundreds of cruisers and sailboats in the passage, making their way to their favorite recreation destinations, or merely enjoying the pleasure of being out. In midweek the channel is frequently used by commercial craft—tugs, barges, fishing boats—plying north and south with their cargoes.

Colvos Passage is especially favored by northbound traffic because the tidal current continually ebbs to the north. It even maintains a weak ebb tide during the major south-flowing flood tide in East Passage. Tide rips might be encountered near the north entrance, especially when a strong flood tide meets opposing strong south winds. Less severe tide rips also occur at the south end of the channel.

Public areas along Colvos Passage are skimpy: only a few DNR beaches, two small county parks, a Vashon Island park, and an undeveloped county park property. This is more than compensated for by Blake Island Marine State Park, one of the state's favorite marine recreation areas, at the north entrance to the channel. Marking the south end is Gig Harbor, a former fishing village on a well-protected harbor, which proudly displays its historic and ethnic origins.

The heavily wooded shores of Colvos Passage are occasionally dotted by private homes, but there is no significant commercial development along its length on either the Vashon Island or Kitsap Peninsula side. Beaches are narrow and drop off steeply to a depth of 60 fathoms. Cyclists will find the dips and rises of the roads to be a leg-killing challenge, especially near Olalla.

Blake Island Marine State Park Map 42

Picnicking • Boating • Camping • Hiking • Clamming • Beach walking • Swimming • Fishing • Scuba diving • Paddling • Birdwatching • Native American dances

Facilities: 48 campsites, 3 CMT campsites, group camp, adirondack shelter, picnic tables, 2 picnic shelters, group day-use areas, fire rings, mooring floats, 20 mooring buoys, 200-foot-long lineal moorage system, horseshoe pits, volleyball court, 14.75 miles of trails, nature trail, restrooms, showers, marine pumpout station, portable toilet dumps, artificial reef, restaurant, Native American dances, tour boat service from the Seattle waterfront

Area: 475.5 acres; 17,307 feet of shoreline

Blake Island lies off the east side of the Kitsap Peninsula, south of Bainbridge Island. It is 6 n.m. from Seattle's Elliott Bay, 9 n.m. from Shilshole Bay, and 1 n.m. from Harper or Southworth. The nearest launch facilities are at Don Armeni Park in West Seattle, and at Manchester and Des Moines. It can be reached from the Seattle waterfront Pier 55 via a Tillicum Tours boat.

Captain Vancouver's ship's log reports that Indians brought a deer they had killed on nearby Blake Island to the *Discovery*. The crewmen, enjoying the fresh meat, also went ashore to try their hand at hunting. Thus they became the first "tourist" visitors to the island—millions have since followed. One of the most heavily used of Washington's marine state parks, Blake Island now receives some 300,000 visitors annually. Deer are still to be seen—but not hunted.

❄ Boat approaches to the east, west, and south sides of the island are clear. A shoal extends from the north side of the island for about ½ mile. At the northeast corner of the island, a narrow, dredged channel, with markers on pilings, leads to a small harbor protected by a rock breakwater. Here a series of floats have space for about fifty boats to tie up, and several times that many to raft alongside during busy weekends.

The first two floats at the entrance to the harbor are for tour ferries and park boats. The outside of the first visitor float is limited to thirty-minute loading and unloading. When the visitor floats overflow, or when boaters desire more privacy, numerous buoys west of the breakwater and on the east, south, and west sides of the island give additional moorages. Good anchorages can also be found near any of these sites, depending on the wind direction.

A word here about courtesy. It is sometimes the practice to raft off other boats on the floats; however, no boat is required to permit others to tie alongside, and many people resent the intrusion of pounding feet and sand-covered children crossing their boats. Ask permission before tying onto another boat. If refused, leave, and do not feel too resentful. For those who do allow rafting, it is often a nice opportunity to make new friends and exchange sea stories. Those rafting off should be considerate of their host's privacy and boat. Friends who rendezvous at the park should consider tying up together, leaving dock space for others.

A replica of a Native American longhouse, Tillicum Village, operated by a private concessionaire near the boat moorage area is a major tourist attraction. Tour boats ferry visitors year-round from Seattle's Pier 55 to the island for a catered salmon buffet, traditional Native American dances, and a quick view of the island. Boats run two or three times daily during the summer, less frequently from October to May. Visitors who arrive by private boat can take part in the dinner or just view the dances. In either case there is a fee, but it is well worth it.

Hikers or campers who lack boat transportation can avail themselves of the tour boat by making reservations with Tillicum Village and Tours in Seattle. It is possible to arrive on one boat and leave on a later one, permitting a longer visit to the park. Check with the tour service.

But what is there to see and do on the island? For those who enjoy the out-of-doors with a large dash of marine atmosphere, the list is long. The region around the boat harbor and campground is often crowded,

Glorious beaches are one of the many attractions at Blake Island State Park.

but with a general air of laid-back conviviality. Cruising friends rendezvous in the boat moorage; families play Frisbee on the lawn; lovers stroll the beach. For those seeking solitude there are shadowed forest trails and distant pocket beaches on the outskirts of the island. Because of its popularity the park can be enjoyed at a more leisurely pace and with more solitude if a visit can be scheduled midweek or off-season rather than on crowded summer weekends and holidays.

A grassy play area, picnic tables, shelters, fire rings, campsites, restrooms, and park ranger headquarters fill the area above the moorage. The west and south points of the triangular island have two more camping areas with fire rings, picnic tables, and a number of mooring buoys offshore. A group camp, available by advance arrangement with the park ranger, is in the timber near the south end of the island. CMT campsites can be found at the northwest tip of the island.

The island's western point and the beach south of the campground have sloping, sandy beaches that are wonderful for swimming and wading. At low tide lucky diggers might find a few clams, although heavy use has seriously depleted their numbers. The south and southwest beaches are mainly cobbles beneath steep embankments of clay, while the north side is rimmed by steep cliffs that drop off to rocky slabs above low-tide sand.

Off the south end of the island, an artificial reef attracts fish and fishermen. The old tires and broken concrete of the reef provide nooks and

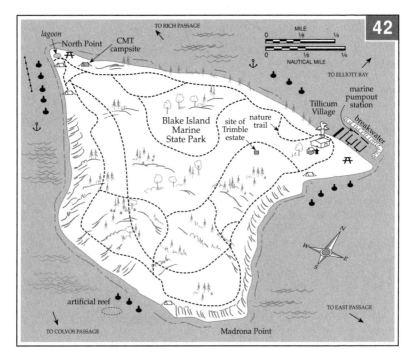

crannies where rockfish can hide to protect themselves, their eggs, and their young. Anemones, tube worms, and hydroids are part of the food chain. Such reefs have been found to be especially effective in providing spawning grounds for lingcod; there is hope that technology might be able to rebuild the Puget Sound population of this once-abundant species. Scuba diving is permitted, but check local regulations before diving. *Strong tidal currents make this a dive only for the experienced.*

An extensive trail system leads around the island's perimeter and cuts across the middle. Because most of the trails are old service roads, they are wide, with relatively gentle grades. The 4-mile-long perimeter trail starts immediately beyond the longhouse. During moderate to low tides hikers can alternate between trail and beach walks for variety. Shorter trails lead to the site of the Trimble estate, 300 feet or so inland from the main campground. A nature trail, broad and flat through open timber, identifies the local florae and tells how they were used by the Natives. Remnants of logging operations that took place during the 1850s can also be spotted by sharp eyes.

The nighttime view of Seattle from Blake Island is breathtaking. The lights of the city stretch from north to south, their glow reflecting in the water, but still far enough away not to obscure the brilliance of a star-filled sky. The Space Needle is visible, as well as the lights of airplane traffic at Sea-Tac and the blaze of ferries shuttling back and forth across the sound.

Southworth and Harper Public Access   Map 43

Boating • Paddling • Beach walking • Fishing • Scuba diving

Facilities: *Boat Launch:* 1-lane packed sand launch ramp. *Fishing Pier:* Fishing pier, toilet, small store with kayak rentals

🚗 *Boat Launch:* From the Southworth ferry landing head west on SE Southworth Drive, which bends north in 1/4 mile, and in 3/4 mile turn east on SE Olympiad Drive. The ramp is on the north side of the road just beyond this junction. *Fishing Pier:* Continue north on SE Southworth Drive for a few short blocks to where the road makes a sharp turn to the west at the fishing pier.

🛥 The launch ramp is on the southeast side of Yukon Harbor 1 n.m. west of Southworth

Southworth Beach Access • The Fauntleroy ferry serves the Kitsap Peninsula via Southworth, sometimes with an intermediate stop at Vashon Island. The ferry dock is at the easternmost protrusion of the Kitsap Peninsula, Point Southworth. Immediately north, separated from the ferry landing by a wire fence, a short stretch of beach provides a public access that can be used to put in canoes, kayaks, and other hand-carried boats.

To reach the beach access, turn north on the first side road after leaving the ferry and follow the road that parallels the ferry landing (Sebring Drive) back to the water. The street deadends into a sandy stretch of beach at a break in the fence. There is no parking here, and only limited turn-around space, but boats can be launched after being carried across the beach. Adjacent property is private.

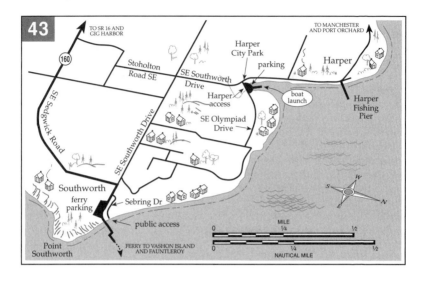

The fishing pier at Harper is popular with both anglers and scuba divers.

Harper Boat Launch (Kitsap County) • At Harper, the gravel beach serves as a primitive launch ramp, usable only at high tide. Pause to explore this interesting mudflat at low tide for clams and other sea creatures before going on to Harper. Parking is immediately east of the intersection of SE Southworth Drive and SE Olympiad Drive.

Harper Fishing Pier (Port of Bremerton) • Harper, 1½ miles west of Southworth, was the original site of the ferry terminal. After the terminal's relocation to Southworth, the abandoned wharf at Harper was acquired by the Port of Bremerton and made available to the public as a fishing pier.

Parking is limited to space for two or three cars along one side of a short stub road just north of the bend in the highway.

The old pilings of the ferry landing support a thick growth of anemones, barnacles, mussels, and other marine creatures. Starfish, crabs, and a multitude of fish come to feed on the abundant life. The water is only 30 feet deep at its maximum; the bottom is sandy and gently sloping, making it an excellent spot for anglers, novice snorkelers, and scuba divers.

Anderson Point Park (Kitsap County)   Map 44

Hiking • Picnicking • Beach walking • Fishing • Paddling • Views

Facilities: Toilet

Area: 66 acres; 1000 feet of shoreline on Colvos Passage

🚙 From SR 160 (SE Sedgwick Road), 3 miles west of the Southworth ferry landing, or 5 miles east of SR 16, turn south on Banner Road SE. In 4¾ miles head east on single-lane gravel SE Millihanna Road to reach the park in ¼ mile.

🛥 Anderson Point is on the west side of Colvos Passage, 1½ n.m. north of Olalla and 5 n.m. south of Point Southworth.

There are no amenities here other than a toilet—but who needs more than the fine natural setting, loll-in-the-sun sandy beach, and nifty views up and down Colvos Passage. From a large gravel parking area inside the park entrance, walk a gated gravel road that winds steeply down the high forested bluff for about ¾ mile. The trail ends at a broad, flat, grass-covered point extending out into Colvos Passage. The sandy beach tapers to gravel at low tide. Waste an afternoon burnishing a tan while watching traffic in Colvos Passage, but save some energy for the grueling haul back uphill to the parking lot.

Olalla   Map 44

Boating • Paddling • Fishing

Facilities: 1-lane launch ramp, groceries, fishing supplies, fuel (service station)

🚙 From SR 160 (SE Sedgwick Road), 3 miles west of the Southworth ferry landing, or 5 miles east of SR 16, turn south on Banner Road SE. After 5 miles of ups and downs the road twists down to Olalla Bay.

🛥 Olalla is on the west side of Colvos Passage, 6½ n.m. south of Point Southworth.

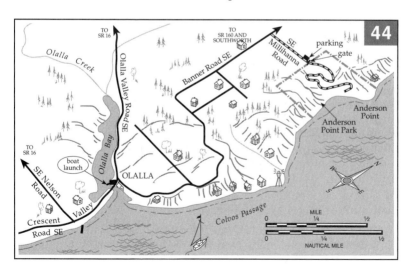

A great blue heron hunts for a seafood snack in the water off Olalla.

Very few public access points are found along the west shore of Colvos Passage. The only small boat launch on this side is at Olalla, midway down the 13-mile channel. The settlement consists of a combination grocery store/gas station/post office; the latter has been in operation since the late 1800s. A small paved parking area at the northeast end of the bridge over Olalla Bay sits just above a surfaced launch ramp. ✳The entrance to the bay is quite shallow, suitable only for small boats—in fact, it becomes a mudflat at minus tides. A rock lying outside the entrance on the north side dries at half tide.

During the 1880s the shores of the bay were the site of a Native American village. *Olalla* is Chinook for "berries" and undoubtedly referred to the abundance of that staple food to be found in the vicinity. At one time the community was larger, with a wharf for fishing boats and a large store offering merchandise to both fishermen and settlers. The remains of the old Olalla Trading Company is south of the bay. An elegant mansion on the hill above Olalla—further evidence of the community's former prosperity—was built in 1914.

Sunrise Beach County Park (Pierce County)   Map 35

Beach walking • Fishing • Picnicking • Scuba diving

Facilities: Picnic tables, toilet, beach access
Area: 82 acres; 2400 feet of shoreline on Colvos Passage

🚗 Take Harborview Drive northwest, and then N Harborview Drive northeast along the shore of Gig Harbor. Turn east on Vernhardson Street, which Ts into Crescent Valley Road NW in ¼ mile. Here go north for a couple blocks and then head east on Dana Drive NW, which progressively becomes 24th Avenue NW, then 94th Street NW, then Moller Drive NW. 1½ miles from Crescent Valley Road NW, turn east on Sunrise Beach Drive NW, a narrow road that winds down to the park in ½ mile.

🚤 For beachable craft, the park is on the west side of Colvos Passage, 2¼ n.m. north of Gig Harbor.

About 2 miles north of Gig Harbor, Pierce County holds property with 2400 feet of beachfront on Colvos Passage. The park, dedicated to the homesteaders of the property, Rudolph and Matilde Moller, is only modestly developed, with a few picnic tables on a small grassy knoll above the beach.

A dirt road leads east from the park gate to a field flanked by sheds and the residence of the park caretaker. A gated dirt service road drops another 100 yards downhill to the small picnic area above the beach; a short trail on the right leads to the beach. The cobble beach, scattered with boulders, runs below a 40- to 50-foot-high jungle-like embankment. Houses and bulkheads define the north and south boundaries of the public beach. Small boats can easily be beached here, and scuba divers often explore offshore. Buoys in the area are private.

GIG HARBOR
Map 45

Fishing • Boating • Shopping • Sightseeing • Paddling • Picnicking

Facilities: Groceries, fuel, marine repair, boat launch (ramp, slings, hoists), boat rental, guest moorage, lodging, restaurants, museum, viewpoints, stores. *Skansie Brothers Park and Jerish Dock:* Picnic tables, open air pavilion, public dock, marine pumpout station, restrooms (disabled accessible), historic displays

🚗 From I-5 Exit 132 (SR 16W, S 38th Street, Gig Harbor, Bremerton) take SR 16 west for 5½ miles to the Tacoma Narrows Bridge. In 4½ miles take the exit (Wollochett Drive NW, City Center, Kopachuck State Park). Head northeast on NW Pioneer Way to reach Harborview Drive, the main street through town, in ¾ mile.

🚤 Gig Harbor is on the west shore at the confluence of Colvos Passage, Dalco Passage, and the Narrows. The public dock is on the southwest side of Gig Harbor about 400 yards from its entrance. Look for the large conspicuous flagpole at the head of the dock.

If ever there was a classic boating town, Gig Harbor must surely be it. It is the home port of the South Puget Sound commercial fishing fleet, and the beautiful, protected harbor at the confluence of Colvos and Dalco Passages is the destination of thousands of pleasure boats annually. The town is a tourist's delight. Fascinating shops sell an array of goods, including arts and handicrafts (heavy on the nautical influence); taverns and restaurants range from casual to elegant; a museum displays pioneer history. Summer is a brightly colored kaleidoscope of people and boats.

❄The water entrance to Gig Harbor off the southern end of Colvos

Passage is neither conspicuous nor generous. A 250-yard-long sand spit constricts the entrance to less than 200 feet wide. Its tip is marked by a small lighthouse. The narrow entrance channel is only 10 feet deep at its center at mean low tide and sometimes has strong currents as the tides change. Heavy traffic through the channel can cause navigational gray hairs for skippers of deep-draft boats when high-powered cruisers challenge for the right to the middle of the channel. The center of the harbor has excellent anchorages in 3 to 7 fathoms of water.

Skansie Brothers Park and Jerish Dock (City of Gig Harbor) • A small public park in the heart of Gig Harbor commemorates the site of the first cabin on

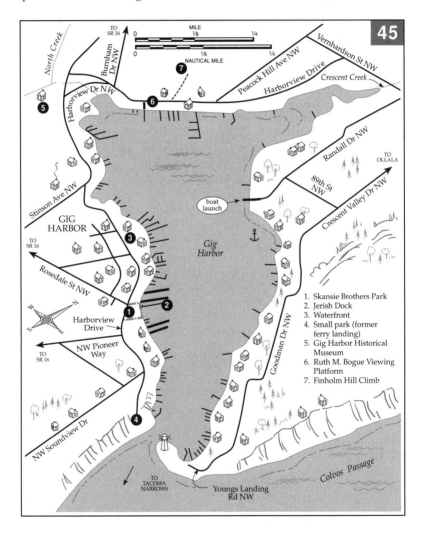

Generous facilites for tourists make Gig Harbor a prime cruising destination.

this side of the harbor, built by Andrew and Bertha Skansie in 1900. The dock is named for Samuel Jerish, Gig Harbor's first settler. The park and dock are on the southeast side of the harbor. Historic displays tell the stories of the Skansies and Jerish; a monument to fishermen lost at sea and a public float for visiting boaters are also located here.

⚜ The area surrounding the 450-foot-long public float and for a distance of about 20 feet to the southeast has been dredged to a depth of 5 feet at mean low water. The bottom beyond that has not been dredged and is much shallower; use care entering and leaving at low tide. The channel on the northwest side of the float next to the covered moorages is about 4 feet deeper. The square concrete float at the end of the dock is reserved for loading and unloading; unattended boats are not permitted to tie up here.

The Gig Harbor Waterfront • Several marinas are along the south side of the harbor, as well as at its extreme west end; some provide guest moorage. Grocery stores, restaurants, and interesting shops are within easy walking distance of all moorages. Some restaurants have moorage floats for diners.

The mile-long bay was discovered by men of the Wilkes Expedition. Several small boats—gigs, as they were commonly referred to in those days—had been dispatched from the mother ship for purposes of exploration. A sudden storm forced them to seek refuge within the harbor, which thus received its name.

A tiny park at the south end of Harborview Drive has benches, a few small picnic tables, and a historic plaque. The site, on a steep high bluff overlooking the entrance to the harbor, was once the landing for the ferries that served Gig Harbor between 1928 and the completion of the Tacoma Narrows Bridge in 1940.

The Gig Harbor Historical Museum is just west of the intersection of Harborview Drive and N Harborview Drive. Its displays include Native American artifacts and historical memorabilia from the early fishing and logging industries. Pictures and posters show early-day Puget Sound steamboats. It is open Tuesday through Saturday from 10:00 AM to 4:00 PM, or by appointment.

Ruth M. Bogue Viewing Platform and Finholm Hill Climb (City of Gig Harbor) • The classic view of Gig Harbor, with a tranquil, boat-filled bay and Mount Rainier rising above, can be seen from a viewing platform just

Fishing Days on Puget Sound

One of the earliest settlements on the sound was begun on the west side of Gig Harbor by Samuel Jerish, a Yugoslavian immigrant. Jerish and two partners, Peter Goldsmith and John Farragut, arrived at Gig Harbor in 1867, after rowing a flat-bottomed skiff all the way south from British Columbia. Although his partners decided to return north, Jerisch stayed. He and his wife, a fifteen-year-old Canadian Indian woman, were the only settlers in the area until others began arriving in 1883. Jerisch started the local fishing industry by selling smoked fish and dogfish oil to pioneers in Steilacoom and Olympia. The foul-smelling oil, rendered from livers of the abundant dogfish, was used for burning in lamps.

By the end of the century a large commercial fleet of Slavonian, German, and Scandinavian fishermen was based in Gig Harbor. These men developed the purse-seining method of netting large schools of salmon. Two teams of four-man, flat-bottomed skiffs would row to the fishing grounds; while one boat remained in position at one end of the large net, men in the other would row around a school of fish and trap it. The filled nets were then hauled in by hand. There are accounts of salmon runs so large in those days that the laden nets could not be lifted into the boats. At times the men from Gig Harbor would follow the salmon runs as far north as the San Juan Islands, living in camps onshore until the season was over.

The catch was marketed locally to be served as fresh table fare and to canneries and salteries in Seattle, Tacoma, Everett, Anacortes, and numerous other cities along the sound, where it was processed for distant markets. Often the fish were sold to passing steamers or to cannery tender boats, which then delivered them to the canneries, permitting the fishermen to return to the salmon banks to reset their nets.

The summer of 1903 saw the introduction of the first gasoline-powered purse seiner and also an automatic fish-processing machine that cleaned salmon more quickly and more cheaply than hand labor. It was the beginning of a new era.

Unloading a day's catch of scallops at a Gig Harbor dock

south of the small business strip along N Harborview Drive. A series of planked wooden decks with benches and colorful flower boxes extends over the beach. Shore access is via a staircase from one of the decks. The scene is especially beautiful in late afternoon and evening, when the setting sun sets the icy mountain aglow.

A block east, on the opposite side of the street, is a wooden staircase that climbs the 100-foot-high bank and links several viewing platforms overlooking the harbor. The top platform is disabled accessible at Franklin Avenue and Fuller Street.

Gig Harbor Public Boat Launch (Pierce County) • Launching for trailered and hand-carried boats is available at a ramp on the north shore of Gig Harbor. The ramp can be reached by driving northeast on N Harborview Drive along the northwest end of the bay. Where Harborview intersects Vernhardson Street NW turn east, cross Crescent Creek, and turn south on Randall Drive NW. In ½ mile this road deadends into the single-lane concrete launch ramp. The launch, which extends well out into the water, is usable at all tide levels. Parking is available alongside the road on Randall Drive and also adjacent to 89th Street NW. The north end of the harbor is a shallow tideflat—nice for investigating with canoe or dinghy.

chapter seven

Tacoma

THE CITY OF TACOMA is the metropolitan focal point of South Puget Sound, attracting visitors by both land and water. Within walking distance of the waterfront are neighborhoods of interesting Victorian homes dating from the 1800s, excellent examples of public architecture (both old and new), and an outstanding state historical museum. Recreation-minded visitors will find a wide spectrum of parks to enjoy, including huge Point Defiance Park, which boasts impressive historical displays.

COMMENCEMENT BAY
Map 46

The Puyallup River drains into South Puget Sound at Tacoma's Commencement Bay. The broad alluvial fan formed here by centuries of river deposits serves as a vast staging area for the industries that are the city's trademark.

Marinas are within a paper-clip-toss of Tacoma's business district.

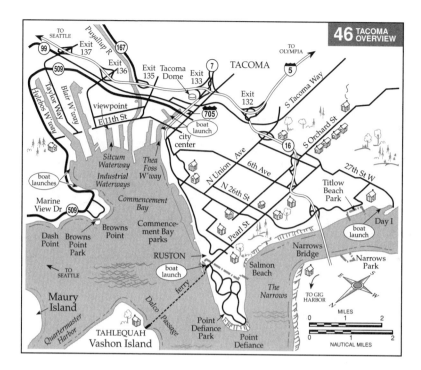

First noted on the charts by the Vancouver expedition, Commencement Bay was named by the 1841 Wilkes expedition, which used it as a base of operations and dispatched several small boats from here. Cartography efforts commenced from this point, and thus it was named "Commencement Bay" on the charts.

Browns Point Park (Metro Parks Tacoma)   Map 46

Picnicking • Wading • Swimming • Kite flying

Facilities: Picnic tables, barbecue grills, restrooms, museum

🚗 The community of Browns Point can be reached from either the north by Eastside Drive NE or the south via Marine View Drive.

🚤 The park is on the tip of Browns Point. The nearest launch ramp is 1¼ n.m. away on the north shore of Commencement Bay. The gated launch ramp immediately south of the park is private. Shallow-draft boats can be landed on the beach.

The northeast perimeter of Commencement Bay terminates at Browns Point, a former coast guard facility that today is a small park. The day-use park's large lawn holds scattered picnic tables and a few graceful old trees. The grass gives way to a gravel beach rimmed with driftwood at its high-water mark. At the extreme tip of the point a white concrete lighthouse still serves

The navigational light at Browns Point is modest, but the sweeping vista is outstanding.

as a navigational aid. The beach that wraps around the point offers ideal sunbathing and pleasant wading in its shallow waters, and the frequent stiff breezes across the point lure kite aficionados.

A one-room building north of the old Coast Guard quarters (now the caretaker's residence), houses the Points Northeast Historical Society. The tiny museum, which contains a collection of historical photos and prints, is open on Saturday from 1:00 PM to 4:00 PM, except December and January, or by appointment.

Tacoma Waterways Industrial Area   Map 46

Boating • Paddling • View point

Facilities: Marinas, boat launches (ramps, slings), restaurants, fuel, guest moorage, supplies, restrooms, walkways, viewing tower

To reach the view tower, from I-5 Exit 136, take Port of Tacoma Road north to 11th Street and go west on it. Turn right off E 11th Street onto Sitcum Way, and then north onto Milwaukee Way just northeast of where the 11th Street Bridge crosses railroad tracks; follow signs that indicate a public access point.

When approaching the waterways by boat, refer to current navigation charts for waterway bridge clearances and the location of fog and visual signals.

Dredging and landfill have converted the once-swampy Puyallup River delta and neighboring tideflats into a many-fingered industrial complex that hosts such diverse enterprises as grain elevators, pulp mills, electrochemical plants, boat building, commercial fishing, and pleasure-boat marinas. The sensory impact of the area is overwhelming—batteries of smokestacks spew steam, behemoth ships lie offshore waiting to load or offload their cargoes, chains of railroad cars whump and bump as they are coupled and uncoupled, and everywhere is the roar and clang and buzz of Tacoma earning its living.

❃A 5-knot speed limit is enforced in all the waterways and within 200 yards of Commencement Bay shorelines. Pleasure boating should be done cautiously, with an eye for the movement of commercial ships. Boats under sail in the bay might legally have the right-of-way but should not argue the point with a freighter. Paddlers in canoes or kayaks should use care not to endanger themselves, nor to impede the movements of commercial boats.

For boats in need of services, several marinas provide all necessary supplies and repairs; some have guest moorage. Two of these facilities are on the northeast side of Commencement Bay on Marine View Drive, between Browns Point and the entrance to the Hylebos Waterway. Ole and Charlie's Marina offers sling launching. Chinook Landing Marina, a relatively new marina on the northeast side of the Hylebos Waterway west of 11th Street has both tenant and guest moorage, showers, restrooms, and a limited selection of groceries and supplies. Additional marinas within Hylebos Waterway on the northeast shore have marine repairs, and tenant floats. Other large marinas on the southwest shore of Commencement Bay provide full services for boaters, including guest moorage and launching for trailered boats.

For visitors there is little within the waterways except an opportunity to gape at the penultimate industrial uses of marine resources. Fishing and scuba diving are discouraged because of the concentration of chemicals that drain into the water.

A viewing tower adjacent to the Port of Tacoma's administrative buildings provides a close look at the industrial waterfront activities. The two-story tower sits at the end of the Sitcum Waterway, overlooking the huge container cargo cranes at the Sealand Terminal and the twirley cranes and alumina domes at Terminal 7. Displays on the tower's various decks provide detailed explanations of the working waterfront.

Thea Foss Waterway Map 47

Walking • Shopping • Museums • Paddling • Picnicking • Wading

🚗 The walkway begins at E 23rd Street where it bends north to become Dock Street. *Working Waterfront Museum:* At 705 Dock Street. *Thea's Park:* Drive Dock Street north, and at the point it starts to climb up to the Schuster Parkway, turn right into parking for the park.

Thea Foss Waterway has a number of pleasure boat moorages; most are private, with no guest facilities. One marina has two sling launches. Two day-use guest moorage floats face on the channel, one near "The Dock" (a large two-block-long converted warehouse on the west side of the waterway, near its entrance), and a second below a seafood company near the end of the S 15th Street ramp. Both are within easy walking distance of downtown Tacoma.

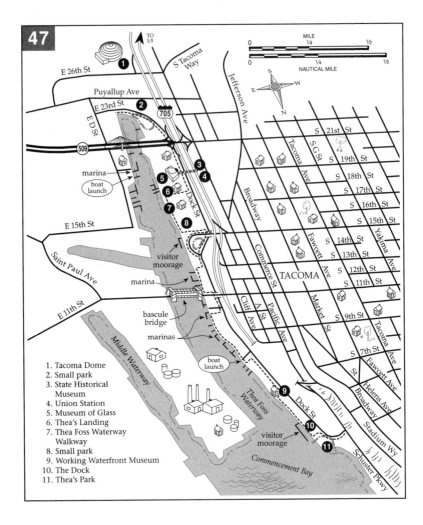

1. Tacoma Dome
2. Small park
3. State Historical Museum
4. Union Station
5. Museum of Glass
6. Thea's Landing
7. Thea Foss Waterway Walkway
8. Small park
9. Working Waterfront Museum
10. The Dock
11. Thea's Park

Thea Foss Waterway Walkway • A fifteen-block-long walkway along the west shore of the Thea Foss Waterway surveys the ever-changing scene of the Tacoma waterways. Anchoring the south end of the promenade is a pretty little park with an overlook and a few benches. The route runs under the graceful SR 509 cable suspension bridge, and then follows the waterfront, climbs up and down staircases, treads a boardwalk, and finally ends at Thea's Park. Along the way waterfront activity is ever-fascinating and ever-different. The west side of the waterway between 16th and 19th Streets includes the multistory leaning pyramid of the Museum of Glass. Next door is Thea's Landing, a multistory condominium building with retail shops at ground level. The promenade on the waterway side has works of art scattered along a three-block-long grass strip.

The Tacoma Dome overlooks the head of the Thea Foss Waterway.

The Working Waterfront Museum • The building housing this museum is nearly as fascinating as its exhibits. The original architecture was maintained when it was converted to a museum. It is one of the last standing of a line of warehouses that once lined the Thea Foss Waterway; it served as a grain warehouse until about 1910. The wooden beams of the ceiling span a length of 95 feet between posts, and the bottom beam of the truss is 150 feet across in some spots.

The displays cover a range of maritime-related subjects: shipwright tools, a video on the construction of the *Lady Washington* replica, and several displays of WW I and WW II shipbuilding at local shipyards. A wing of the building houses a collection of small wooden boats, some working boats, some recreational, and some dating back to the early twentieth century. The museum is open from noon to 5:00 PM daily.

Thea's Park (Metro Parks Tacoma) • At the north terminus of the Thea Foss Waterway Walkway, what was once a debris-laden memory of past Tacoma waterfront commerce has been transformed into a pretty little beachfront park, rimmed by artificial tidepools in the riprap at water's edge. At the north end of the park a large globe of the earth and a tall flagpole stand above a half-moon pocket of cobble that tapers gradually into Commencement Bay. The spot offers easy access for launching kayaks and other hand-carried watercraft.

Ruston Way Waterfront Parks (Metro Parks Tacoma) Map 48

*Fishing • Boating • Picnicking • Beach walking • Sunbathing • Swimming •
Scuba diving • Wading • Jogging • Bicycling • Skating*

Facilities: Fishing piers, artificial reef, guest moorage floats, mooring buoys, picnic
tables, restrooms, children's play areas, historical displays, scenic viewpoints, art
works, concession stands, restaurants, delis, bait.

From I-5 at Exit 133 (SR 7S, I-705N, City Center) take I-705 north for 2¼ miles
to where it becomes Schuster Parkway. In 1½ miles the road splits, with N 30th
Street angling left (west); ahead, at a bridge over the railroad tracks, the road
becomes Ruston Way, which continues northwest along the south side of Commencement Bay for the next 3 miles.

The shore trends northwest along the south side of Commencement Bay
for 4 n.m. Beachable craft can be landed or put in on numerous beaches, and for
larger boats guest floats and buoys are available at Old Town Dock and at several
restaurants. Anchoring is possible in the sand and mud bottom, although there is
no protection from wind or boat wakes.

You must visit Ruston Way, if for no other reason than to marvel at the
many ways Tacoma recreates—strolling, walking, jogging, or being carried
grandly in a backpack. Wheeled recreation runs the gamut from unicycles
to bicycles, tricycles, three-person pedi-cabs, wheelchairs, roller skates, and
in-line skates. The sparkling, marine-oriented parks, fishing piers, and other
recreational attractions are interspersed with several restaurants, concession
stands, shops, and small buildings that house professional offices. Sunny
benches beckon to passersby, and on hot days pockets of sandy beach invite
swimmers and waders. The wide, level sidewalk provides a long, scenic
excursion with great views of Commencement Bay, and above it Mount
Rainier. At several points benches and tables, some covered, encourage
picnicking and lolling.

In the early days of Tacoma the southwest shore of Commencement Bay,
along Ruston Way, was its maritime and industrial heart, lined with wharfs,
warehouses, and factories. As commerce moved to the tideflats at the head

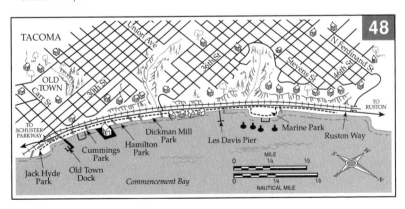

of the bay, many of the old piers and buildings located here fell into disuse. Some burned and were left as moldering hulks—visual and commercial blights. Urban renewal programs have removed rotted pilings and ratty piers and have rebuilt some 2 miles of waterfront along Ruston Way.

Boaters have not been neglected in the restoration. There are guest floats alongside Old Town Dock, and six mooring buoys have been located offshore from Marine Park. The buoys are exposed in heavy weather but offer a nice spot for an overnight stay in the calm weather more typical of the area. Many restaurants that offer waterfront dining, ranging from casual to formal, have floats for visiting boaters.

Jack Hyde Park • The string of waterfront parks begins at the west end of Schuster Parkway with Jack Hyde Park, named for a former Tacoma mayor instrumental in the redevelopment of Ruston Way. At the top of the park's grassy knoll, a huge metal sculpture is sure to pique curiosity: is this some sort of religious monument, possibly part of a Druid ceremony? Not quite, but close—it's a giant ring sundial, a unique center of interest for the park.

The embankment encircling the sundial has an interesting display describing the history and geology of the area. Toddlers can conduct their own geological explorations in the pair of sandboxes tucked along the outer edge of the knoll.

Old Town Dock • Adjoining Jack Hyde Park on its west end, at the intersection of Ruston Way and McCarver Street, is Old Town Dock, which

An interesting sundial is a focal point of Jack Hyde Park.

has forsaken its commercial beginnings and now is a public fishing pier. An artificial reef placed in the vicinity helps increase the fishing odds. For boaters wishing to drop by and stroll uphill to Old Town or tie up for the night, concrete floats off the east side of the pier have moorage space for a half dozen boats.

Three blocks uphill is Old Town (known as Commencement City in early days), where Tacoma was born. A few of the early buildings remain, including the Slavonian Union Hall, a reminder of the fishermen who brought European purse-seining methods to the sound.

Cummings and Hamilton Parks • West of the Old Town Dock a U-shaped view pier, Cummings Park, stretches out on pilings into the bay, framed on the west by a posh waterfront inn on a concrete pier. On the west side of the inn's pier is tiny Hamilton Park—a grassy mound above a rock bulkhead, with a solitary picnic table and benches.

Dickman Mill Park • Once the site of an historic lumber mill that operated continuously on the waterfront from the 1890s to 1974, the last of the "Old Town" mills to shut down caught fire in 1979, and unsightly, dangerous charred pilings and decking were all that remained for many years. With funding from state, city, and private sources, the site was cleaned up, and now is a chain of grassy picnic sites lining the Ruston Way waterfront and boasting sensational views.

An engineering project underway at Marine Park

Les Davis Pier • Northwest from the now inactive fire station is the 300-foot-long Les Davis Pier. The end of the T-shaped fishing pier has a rail drilled to hold fishing rods and mounted with fish-cleaning plates. Puget Sound weather is acknowledged by benches and cleaning stations protected by shelters. Concessions, bait and tackle, and restrooms are at the shore end of the dock.

Marine Park • Marine Park runs northwest along the shoreline from Les Davis Pier. A series of small, sandy pocket beaches is tucked below the rock bulkhead that fronts the narrow park. As it continues along Ruston Way, the grassy ribbon has picnic tables and flower-filled planters, several art works, and a lawn that lures sunbathers and Frisbee tossers. A U-shaped boardwalk extending out above the beach holds benches that offer water views north across the bay, up

Colvos Passage, and west across the waterways to Mount Rainier.

The park (and the waterfront redevelopment) come to an end at N 49th Street and N Ferdinand Street, just southeast of Ruston.

Point Defiance Park (Metro Parks Tacoma)   Map 49

Boating • Paddling • Zoo • Aquarium • Picnic tables • Picnic shelters • Bicycling • Hiking • Sports courts • Museums • Beach walking

Facilities: Zoo, aquarium, botanical gardens, tennis courts, volleyball court, picnic shelters, picnic tables, trails, logging museum, Fort Nisqually historical restoration, children's fantasy land, children's playground, restaurant, shops, marina, 3-lane launch ramp with boarding floats, boat rental and elevator launch, boathouse, scenic viewpoints,

Area: 696 acres; 18,500 feet of shoreline

From SR 16 on the west side of Tacoma, take the 6th Avenue Exit (Ruston, Vashon Ferry) and head west 2 blocks to S Pearl Street (SR 163). Head north on Pearl for 3½ miles to reach the park at N Park Avenue.

The Point Defiance boating facilities are on Dalco Passage on the east side of Point Defiance. The boat launch area is behind the fill peninsula just southeast of the ferry landing, and the fuel dock and boat rental launch are ¼ n.m. to the northwest.

This is without question the greatest park on all of Puget Sound. With nearly 700 acres, it is the largest of Tacoma's parks. In fact, it is the second-largest metropolitan park in the country, surpassed only by New York City's Central Park. But it is not mere size that makes Point Defiance great. The park's diversity provides something for every age and nearly every recreational predilection. It seems incredible that the park can offer so much and still retain much of its wilderness character.

If one were to criticize the park at all (although to some this might seem blasphemous), it would be on the grounds that it does too much, even for its size. On sunny weekends Point Defiance is hard-pressed to accommodate the crowds it attracts. Cruising young people, engaged in modern courtship rituals, take over the pond and lawns near the entrance, and motorcycles and blaring stereos invade Owen Beach. Traffic is heavy, and parking lots and restrooms throughout the park are jammed. As with any well-loved park, to truly savor all it has to offer, visit on an off day, or off-season.

Point Defiance has been in the business of being a park for a long time. Originally the site of a military reservation, 640 acres of the peninsula were set aside for the public in 1888, and a boathouse was built here in 1890. In 1905 the city was given clear title to the land for use as a park. An aquarium opened here in 1936. Developments, improvements, and additions have been made regularly since that time.

Nearly all park roads are one-way loops. The outer drive is a 5-mile scenic route; the end loop is restricted to use by bicycles and foot traffic on Saturdays from 9:00 AM to 1:00 PM All manner of cyclists take advantage of this opportunity, including entire families all the way down to kiddies vigorously pedaling with training wheels.

Inland attractions include a Japanese garden with a large lily-pad pond and formal gardens. The park's zoo is not huge by big-city standards, but it is tastefully done with a strong emphasis on animals native to the Pacific Rim and has a well-displayed collection of the fascinating creatures that inhabit the beaches or find shelter in underwater nooks and crannies.

Beyond the zoo a side road drops down to Owen Beach, and the scenic tour begins, first inland among primeval forest, then skirting the bluff edge to occasional viewpoint pull-outs with dramatic views across South Puget Sound and the Tacoma Narrows. At the very tip of the point a sign relates the origin of the name Point Defiance—it was here in 1841 that Lt. Charles Wilkes looked out across the confluence of the channels and noted that cannons placed here and at Gig Harbor across the way could defy the world. Although the point itself was never armed, the original use of the peninsula as a military reservation was based on that idea.

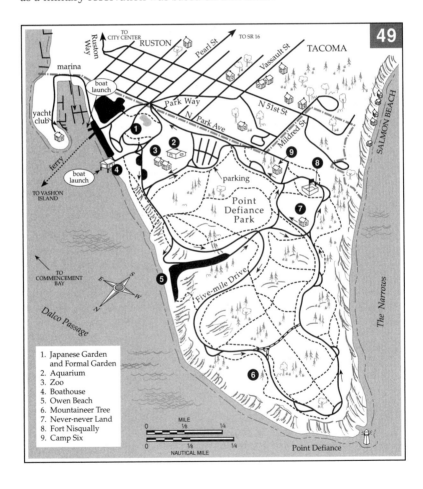

1. Japanese Garden
   and Formal Garden
2. Aquarium
3. Zoo
4. Boathouse
5. Owen Beach
6. Mountaineer Tree
7. Never-never Land
8. Fort Nisqually
9. Camp Six

Miles of hiking paths crisscross the woodland; all eventually intersect the road. A hiking circuit of park uplands, following trails and roads along the outer periphery, covers only about 7 miles but can take forever, with time allowed to stop and explore all there is to see. Because the entire park is on a bluff jutting 200 feet above the sound, beach access from above is quite limited. The only ways to reach the shore are at the boathouse and at Owen Beach.

On the west side of the point, near the end of the 5-mile drive, Never-Never Land has scenes of fairy-tale fantasies, expertly created in wood and concrete in a natural forest setting, that are fun for grown-ups as well as children.

Next door, Fort Nisqually is a replica of a Hudson's Bay trading post circa 1833. Two buildings—the granary and the proctor's house—are original structures, moved here from the actual site of the fort near Dupont, 11 miles to the south. The log palisade wall with its blockhouses as well as several buildings within the walls are authentic re-creations. The proctor's house is now a museum filled with interesting historic artifacts. The Hudson's Bay Company flag flying from the parade ground pole points out that this first settlement on Puget Sound was a British post on then-British soil.

Down the road ¼ mile from Fort Nisqually is yet another museum, but of quite a different sort. Camp Six is an outdoor display of actual machinery and railroad equipment used during the days of steam logging. Steam-powered

Fort Nisqually, at Point Defiance Park, is a re-creation of a stockade used during the Indian War.

train rides around a short section of logging train track through the nearby woods are a popular feature.

So much for the park's inland attractions. Point Defiance also has its share of water-oriented facilities for fishing, boating, and beach play. A road dropping downhill from the park entrance to the shore at the northeast end of the park ends at the loading ramp for the Vashon Island ferry. Immediately east of the ferry ramp is a paved, three-lane, public boat-launch ramp.

The marina east of the launch ramp provides fuel, propane, and ice, plus overnight moorage at four long floats attached to a concrete pier. Beyond the marina the Tacoma Yacht Club has extensive private floats; its distinctive clubhouse is on the end of a long breakwater (built of slag from the Tacoma Smelter) that protects the marina and yacht basin.

West of the ferry terminal is an immense, three-block-long boathouse, a replacement for one that burned down in 1984. The east wall of the boathouse carries a series of permanent posters describing the long and checkered history of the facility. A restaurant on a large deck at the east end of the boathouse has views of the comings and goings of the Tahlequah ferry, as well as other boat traffic in Commencement Bay and Dalco Passage.

The boathouse includes a bait and tackle shop, snack bar, boat rental shop, and fuel float. The interior of the two-story building is a warren of long corridors lined with lockers for small-boat dry storage. Open elevators at the outer edge of the deck are for boats to be launched and hauled out; ramps leading down to several floats permit hand launching of small boats. Whether you are launching a boat or not, it is fascinating to watch

The fishing pier at the Point Defiance boathouse is a busy spot nearly all the time.

the activity. At the end of the pier, adjacent to the boat elevator on the west end, anglers congregate, making one wonder how any fish could possibly escape the minefield of hooks dangling below.

West of the boathouse the shoreline can be walked, with some cooperation from the tide, for 2 miles to the end of the point. An abandoned road below the timbered bank parallels the beach for a ¾-mile stretch to Owen Beach. Any marine life on the tidelands has long since been carried away by beach users, but low-tide excursions offer the rewards of discovering water-washed agates, engineering sand castles, or simply skipping rocks from the sand and gravel expanse.

Owen Beach, which can also be reached by road from above, is a ¼-mile-long band of soft sand edged by driftwood. The break in the high bank caused by a ravine permits the sun to arrive early and linger late. In summer, sunbathing is a major activity, in addition to swimming, wading, picnicking, fishing, and snoozing.

West of Owen Beach the cliffs of sand and clay sweep swiftly upward for 200 feet, and the sandy beach narrows, disappearing entirely at high tide. The only path leading up the steep bluff is a ¾-mile trail from Owen Beach.

A light and foghorn mark the rocks extending from the end of the point, a favorite spot for both shore and boat fishing. South of the point beaches are even narrower, with no upland exits of any sort for tide-trapped beach walkers. Beware.

Immediately south of Point Defiance Park, on the east shore of the narrows, is the small community of Salmon Beach—a string of houses perched on pilings and displaying a spectrum of architectural anachronisms. "Quaint" is definitely an understatement. The houses are also unusual in that their only land approach is by steep (private) trails descending the clay cliffs. The community offers no recreational possibilities, but it is definitely worth seeing for passing boaters.

THE TACOMA NARROWS
Map 50

South of Point Defiance the waters of all the southern reaches of Puget Sound are funneled through a deep, narrow, 4-mile-long underwater canyon. Timid sailors approach the tidal currents of the Tacoma Narrows with trepidation; knowledgeable sailors treat it with respect. Even for boaters who have traveled it many times, the mile-wide channel, with its churning water and spectacular bridge, must cause a quickened heartbeat and a tightening of the hand on the helm. In 2007, the present span will be joined by a companion bridge, running along its south side, which will assist in carrying the more than 90,000 people who now cross the waterway each day.

From any point of view the bridge is awesome, with a central span more than ½ mile long, a vertical clearance of 180 feet at its center, and two giant pylons towering nearly 500 feet above the water of the narrows.

❊The tidal currents in the narrows display the perverse nature of many of the currents in South Puget Sound waterways. An underwater shelf near the east end of the Tacoma Narrows Bridge blocks tidal currents that flow south and tends to make them run in a counterclockwise circle at the north end of the narrows. Consequently, ebb tides are stronger on the east side of the channel, and flood tides stronger on the west side. Boaters will make better headway if they follow the west shore when going south and the east shore when traveling north. Currents in excess of 5 knots can be encountered at the south end of the channel; tidal current charts should be consulted for specific daily predictions.

Narrows Park (Pierce County)   Map 50

Picnicking • Fishing • Paddling • Viewpoint

Facilities: Picnic tables, viewing platform, toilet, CMT campsite
Area: 36 acres; 1000 feet of shoreline on the narrows

From SR 16 at the north end of the Tacoma Narrows Bridge take Exit 8 (24th Street NW, Wollochett, Point Fosdick), then head west on 24th Street NW. At a T intersection in ½ mile, turn south on Jahn Avenue NW, and in three blocks head east on Stone Drive NW. This bends southeast through a bridge construction area, and then heads southwest as Lucille Parkway NW. Reach the park entrance 1 mile from the freeway exit.

The park, accessible by paddlecraft, is on the north side of the narrows ¼ n.m. west of the Tacoma Narrows Bridge.

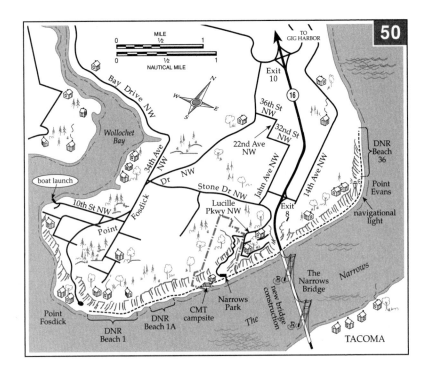

The newest addition to the Pierce County Park system is initially serving as a popular spot to watch the construction of the second Tacoma Narrows Bridge. The road from the entrance winds steeply down a wooded bluff and ravine to a parking area where there are telescopes (courtesy of the bridge contractor) with which to track the activities. A disabled-accessible pathway leads down to a lower viewing platform overlooking the bridges.

The broad sand and gravel beach below sections of chained-down driftwood offers great sunbathing and Frisbee-throwing. The beach is also a popular shore fishing site. The tree-shaded lawn adjacent the manager's residence has been designated a CMT campsite. Drinking water is available, and a toilet is nearby at the parking lot.

War Memorial Park (Metro Parks Tacoma) • This park that once existed beneath the south approach to the Tacoma Narrows Bridge is presently a construction staging area and footings site for the second bridge, whose construction started in 2003. The state Department of Transportation plans to replace the park once bridge construction finishes in 2007.

Tacoma Narrows (DNR Beaches) • Three public DNR beaches are along the west shore of the narrows. All are cobble tapering to gravel at low tide and support some clams and rock crab. Beach 36 (2600 feet long) runs northwest from the navigational light on Point Evans. Beaches 1 and 1A (2300

When this photo was taken, Narrows Park offered front-row-seats to construction of the second bridge span. The second bridge is scheduled for completion in 2007.

Bridging the Tacoma Narrows

During the early part of the century, vehicle traffic across the narrows traveled by ferry from Titlow Beach to the landing at the mouth of Wollochet Bay. As the city grew, and with it demands for residential real estate, the idea was born to build a bridge across the Tacoma Narrows to open up development of the Gig Harbor area.

And so one was built. Economic constraints made it necessary, however, to cut a few corners here and there. When the bridge was open for use in July 1940, it seemed a bit flimsy. In fact, persons driving on it during a crosswind had the interesting (and unnerving) experience of feeling it buck like a horse and seeing cars ahead of them drop down into a valley and reappear at the crest of a hill. By the time winter came the bridge had already been nicknamed Galloping Gertie. On November 7, 1940, as a nice little winter storm brewed up out of the south, winds reached 42 miles per hour. The overstressed span finally snapped, dumping a couple of cars (whose drivers had run for their lives) and an unfortunate dog (that had been left behind) into the channel.

Determined to do it right the second time, engineers took ten years to redesign and rebuild the span, while ferries resumed service between Titlow Beach and Wollochet Bay. In October 1950 the new suspension bridge—Sturdy Gertie—was completed. The old twisted span still lies at the bottom of the narrows, where it makes a nice reef for marine life—not quite the future that had been planned for it.

feet long and 900 feet long, respectively) lie below sandy cliffs northeast of Point Fosdick.

The narrow beaches lie below near-vertical bluffs that range from 100 to 300 feet high with no direct upland access. Once the second Tacoma Narrows bridge is completed, an access to the shore might be built.

Titlow Beach Park (Metro Parks Tacoma)   Map 51

Picnicking • Fishing • Swimming • Beach walking • Jogging • Scuba diving • Field sports • Birdwatching

Facilities: Picnic shelters, picnic tables, kitchens, swimming pool, wading pool, sports fields, fitness trail, children's playgrounds, restrooms, community center, marine preserve, outside shower, information displays

Area: 58 acres; 2800 feet of shoreline

🚗 From SR 16 on the west side of Tacoma, take the 6th Avenue Exit (Ruston, Vashon Ferry) and head west on 6th Avenue for 2 miles to reach the northeast side of the park. Continue on 6th to its end in another ½ mile to reach the beach access.

🚤 The park is on the south side of the narrows, 1½ n.m. southwest of the Tacoma Narrows Bridge. Look for extensive near-shore pilings. Paddlecraft can be launched and landed here. ❋ Use care, as tidal currents can be very strong.

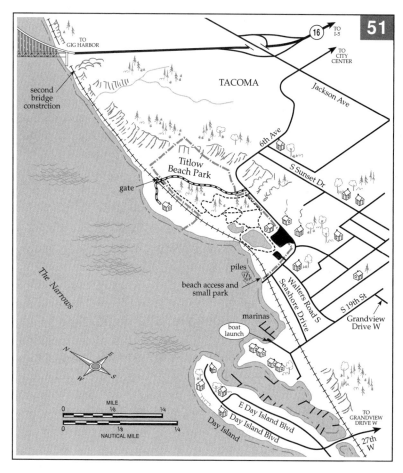

This nice little metropolitan park has many attractions for residents: tennis and volleyball courts, a swimming pool, picnic facilities, and a pair of lagoons filled with ducks clamoring to be fed. But it is just as interesting for tourists, offering a couple of miles of trails, a long beach, and, just offshore, some of the best scuba diving on South Puget Sound.

The park's trail is actually a fitness trail with several loops for different levels of ability and way stations for stretching muscles. It is also a pretty nature walk, skirting the edges of the lagoons and then wandering on through shrubbery and timber. The longest loop trail is 1¼ miles; side trails can make it longer. Enjoy the sights, but slow-paced walkers should yield to joggers.

The main body of the park is separated from the beach by Burlington Northern railroad tracks and a high chain-link fence. The only place where the beach portion of the park can be reached is at the south end of the park where 6th Avenue curves west, crosses the railroad tracks, and deadends just above the water. Here is a tiny spot with benches, picnic tables, an outside

A pavilion with picnic tables, information displays, and great views is one of the features of Titlow Beach Park.

shower for scuba divers, and interpretive displays describing underwater life. Barnacle-encrusted pilings standing in disarray just offshore, many with birdhouses attached, are remnants of the old ferry dock that was used before the Tacoma Narrows Bridge was built. The wooden bird nest boxes attached to the pilings are for purple martins, which migrate from South America in the spring to breed in this area.

The beach is rocky—not inviting for either swimming or sunbathing—but it does offer tideland exploration north for ½ mile to the park boundary. Fishing is good from either beach or boat. The waters offshore are a marine sanctuary—no fauna, flora, or archeological objects may be removed from the area (food fish regulated by the DFW excepted).

Old pilings, such as those offshore at Titlow Beach, harbor different types of underwater life that can tolerate the brighter light and occasional low-tide exposures. Brightly colored hydroids, lacy white sea anemones, and feather-duster worms make the pilings resemble exotic gardens. Red Irish lords, cabezons, and schools of shiny little pile perch graze among the pilings, nibbling on soft-bodied invertebrates. In summer the water near Titlow Beach might have heavy concentrations of red jellyfish, which can give swimmers and scuba divers a nasty sting.

Day Island   Map 51

Fishing • Boating • Paddling

Facilities: Marinas, fuel, ice, marine supplies, boat storage, 2-lane launch ramp with boarding float, sling launch

See directions to Titlow Beach, above. Near the end of 6th Avenue, turn south on Walters Road, and in ¼ mile head west on S 19th Street. Cross the railroad tracks and arrive at the marina area in three blocks.

Days Island is on the south side of the narrows, 2 n.m. southwest of the Tacoma Narrows Bridge.

Several commercial marinas just south of Titlow Beach, near the entrance to the Day Island lagoon, have some marine and fishing supplies for visiting boaters, but all moorages are permanent. A launch ramp operated by one of the marinas provides small-boat access to this side of the narrows.

Day Island, which is joined to the mainland by a marshy spit and a bridge, encloses a long, shallow lagoon. The channel into the lagoon shrivels to a mere 1 foot deep at low tide, and the enclosed bay itself is not much deeper. The slender island is entirely residential, with no public water access.

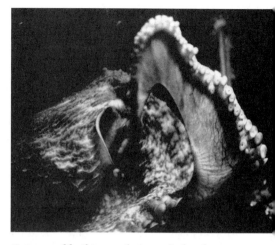

Octopuses like this one photographed at the Seattle Marine Aquarium are often seen by scuba divers in Puget Sound waters.

Octopuses and Others

The dark, subterranean caves of Puget Sound shelter what is believed to be the world's largest concentration of octopuses, as well as the largest individual specimens. While some species measure mere inches, males of the *Octopus dofleini* species commonly grow to a diameter of 7 feet. Individual specimens have been reported that measured in excess of 20 feet and weighed nearly 100 pounds.

Its bizarre appearance is no doubt responsible for its bad reputation, but in fact the octopus is a shy creature with intelligence that is rare for this level of invertebrate. This not-too-distant cousin of the clam is believed capable of curiosity, friendliness, fear, anger, and even a sense of humor. Many scuba divers who once looked on the octopus as a challenging trophy now respect it as a fascinating underwater compatriot. At one time octopus wrestling was considered a worthwhile sport along Puget Sound, but many of the unfortunate creatures that were captured died later. They may now be taken only for food use, and divers are not permitted to use a spear or any device that will mutilate the animal.

Another inhabitant of the murky caves of the sound is the wolf eel, whose ferocious expression and formidable size (up to 8 feet) command instant respect. Although this fish is known to be very timid, divers rarely try to develop a meaningful relationship with a wolf eel, because the eel's strong jaws can inflict a serious injury. However, frequent divers have become familiar with particular "wolfies."

chapter eight

Carr Inlet

ONCE PAST THE TACOMA NARROWS, South Puget Sound spreads out into a jigsaw puzzle of inlets, with shortcut passages running between islands. Carr Inlet, which takes a hard right past Fox Island and heads north, is perhaps the most recreation-oriented of the waterways. There are two large state parks on its shores, as well as an island-based marine state park and a smattering of other public accesses.

The inlet was named for Lt. Overton Carr of the Wilkes Expedition, not (as one might expect) for Job Carr or his brother Anthony, who both played an important part in Tacoma's early history. Peter Puget and his crew were, of course, the first Europeans to see the channel. One can imagine the sense

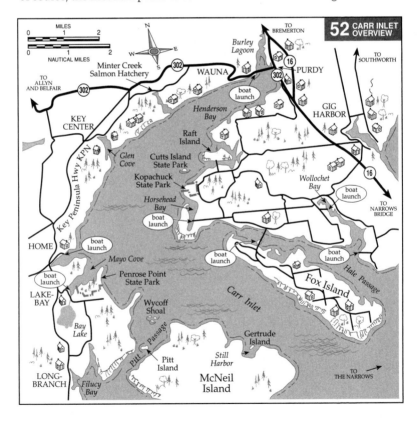

Evening settles over Mount Rainier and the quiet anchorage at Penrose Point State Park.

of wonderment felt by this small band of men after rowing through the stricture of the narrows as an entire inland sea opened up to them.

HALE PASSAGE AND FOX ISLAND
Map 52

Mile-wide Hale Passage separates Fox Island from Wollochet Bay and the Kitsap Peninsula mainland. This favorite fishing area offers chinook salmon year-round in the channel and off both ends of Fox Island. Steep walls around the island support some of the most beautiful seascapes to be found on South Puget Sound and make it a favorite scuba diving ground, but the strong currents on the north and east sides require intermediate to advanced diving ability. Heavy boat traffic in the channel is an additional hazard.

❄ The fixed bridge at the north end of the channel has a restricted clearance of 31 feet, preventing passage of many sailboats. A shoal that bares at low tide lies 350 yards east of the bridge on the south side of the channel and is marked by a buoy on its northeast side.

Wollochet Bay   Map 53

Fishing • Scuba diving • Canoeing • Kayaking
Facilities: Two 1-lane paved launch ramps

🚗 *Ramp on southeast side of bay:* From SR 16 at the north end of the Tacoma Narrows Bridge take Exit 8 (24th Street NW, Wollochett, Point Fosdick) and head west on 24th Street NW. At a T intersection in ½ mile, turn south on Jahn Avenue NW, and in 3 blocks head west on Stone Drive NW. In 1 mile turn south on Point

Fosdick Drive NW, and in ½ mile turn west on 10th Street NW, which becomes Berg Drive NW, and arrive at the ramp in ½ mile. *Ramp on northwest side of bay:* From SR 16, 3¾ miles north of the Tacoma Narrows Bridge, take the exit marked to Wollochett Drive NW, City Center, and Kopachuck State Park. Head southwest on Wollochett Drive NW for 2¼ miles to its intersection with 40th Street NW, and then continue south on Wollochett Drive NW for ¼ mile and turn east on 37th Street NW. The ramp is at the street end in two blocks.

The first ramp is just north of the southwest tip of Wollochett Bay, and the second is on the west shore of the bay, about ½ n.m. from its north end.

While egocentric white men often choose geographic place names to honor friends or patrons or politicians, the more literal-minded Native Americans chose place-names with descriptive significance. Mount Rainier, with its massive glaciers, was known as Tahoma, or "father of the waters." Chilacum (later

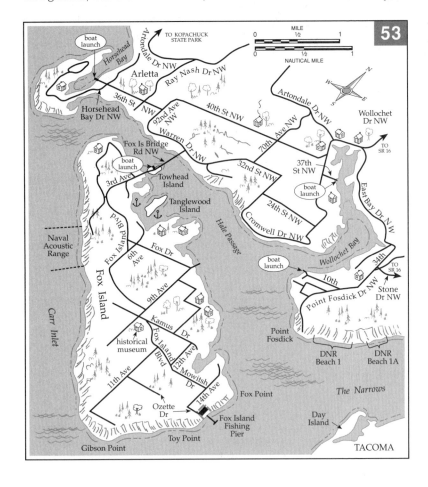

A sailboarder tests the wind on Wollochet Bay.

anglicized to Steilacoom) meant "place with the pink flowers." And Wollochet, literally translated, was the inelegant "bay of the squirting clams."

The few clams and oysters remaining today along the 2½-mile-long bay are on private tidelands. The only public accesses are two boat-launch ramps, one near the entrance to the bay on the southeast side and a second near the much shallower northwest end of the bay. Both are more suitable for launching hand-carried boats than trailered ones. The ramp at the end of Berg Drive NW has no turn-around near the ramp and only limited street-side parking a few blocks uphill. The second public access, on shallower water, leads steeply downhill to a paved launch ramp.

Fox Island   Map 53

Boating • Paddling • Fishing • Scuba diving

Facilities: *Fishing pier:* 1-lane paved launch ramp, hand-carry boat launch, restrooms, fishing pier (disabled accessible)

From SR 16, 3¾ miles north of the Tacoma Narrows Bridge, take the exit marked Wollochett Drive NW, City Center, Kopachuck State Park. Head southwest on Wollochett Drive NW for 2¼ miles then west on 40th Street NW. In ¾ mile turn south on 70th Avenue NW and, at a T intersection in ½ mile, head west on Warren Drive NW. In ¼ mile go southwest on Fox Island Bridge Road NW across Hale Passage. The launch ramp is on Towhead Island at the south end of the bridge. *Fishing pier:* From the bridge, follow the main road, Island Boulevard, through various turns to 14th Avenue, which becomes Ozette Drive and ends at the fishing pier, about 5 miles from the bridge.

The launch ramp is on Towhead Island on the north side of the southwest end of the Fox Island Bridge over Hale Passage. Clearance under the center span of the bridge is 31 feet above mean high water.

Early settlers on Fox Island were farmers and fruit growers, who lived a self-sustained life with little need to visit the mainland. A ferry served Fox Island during its early years, but the construction of the bridge across Hale Passage in 1954 ended the island's isolation, and it became a popular suburban residential area with beachfront homes and acreages for people employed in Tacoma and Gig Harbor. With the exception of a fishing pier on the south end of the island, there are no public recreation areas, either inland or along the shores; the few public beach accesses are used primarily by anglers and scuba divers.

The south bridge abutment actually touches down not on Fox Island but on tiny Towhead Island, which is joined to the larger island by a sandspit. The Pierce County public-access area on Towhead Island has a surfaced launch ramp and parking for a dozen vehicles with trailers. Scuba diving is excellent among the numerous concrete bridge pilings and around the bouldery reef to the east. Sea perch feed on the dense piling growth, while cabezon and lingcod seek the protection of reef crannies.

A second small island, Tanglewood, lies east of the bridge near the Fox Island shoreline. Boaters can find good anchorages on either side of Tanglewood Island in the quiet, protected cove known to early settlers as Sylvan Bay, but all shorelands are private.

At the southeast end of Fox Island a nice wooden fishing pier replaces The Concrete Dock, a failed ferry landing.

A longtime Fox Island landmark was "The Concrete Dock" midway between Fox Point and Gibson Point on the southeast end of the island. The old monster of a dock, built for ferry access to the island, was an instant failure because the location was too exposed to weather and wicked tidal currents. The landing was relocated to the east side of the island. The DFW removed the old dock and in 1997 replaced it with a new, T-shaped fishing pier. Chinook salmon and an abundance of bottomfish are found offshore from Fox Point to Gibson Point and on to Toliva Shoal. For divers, an extravaganza of marine life grows on limestone ledges and canyons down to a depth of 100 feet. The buoy in the channel between here and Steilacoom marks Toliva Shoal. ❋ On the west side of Fox Island, in Carr Inlet, the U.S. Navy maintains an acoustic range. The test area, marked by buoys, is restricted and should be avoided by boaters.

CARR INLET EAST SHORE
Map 52

Because of their easy access from Tacoma via the Narrows Bridge, and from Gig Harbor, recreation areas on the east shore of Carr Inlet are somewhat more heavily used than those farther down the sound. The shoreline is heavily residential, with many homes having docks with boats poised for a quick escape to favorite boating or fishing grounds. SR 16, which rushes quickly from the Tacoma Narrows Bridge to Purdy, at the end of the inlet, provides the major avenue of land access.

Horsehead Bay   Map 53
Boating • Paddling • Fishing

Facilities: 1-lane paved launch ramp

🚗 From SR 16, 3¾ miles north of the Tacoma Narrows Bridge, take the exit marked Wollochett Drive NW, City Center, Kopachuck State Park. Head southwest on Wollochett Drive NW for 2¼ miles then west on 40th Street NW. In ¾ mile turn south on 70th Avenue NW and, at a T intersection in ½ mile, head west on Warren Drive NW. Continue northwest on Warren Drive for 1¼ mile, and turn west on 36th Street NW to arrive at the ramp in 1 more mile.

🛥 The ramp is on the east shore of Horsehead Bay, midway along the bay's shoreline.

Geological tombolos, which are quite common throughout Puget Sound, are sandspits, built up over a long period of time by wave action, that permanently join former islands to nearby islands or to the mainland. The long hook of land enclosing Horsehead Bay at the northwest end of Hale Passage is an example of this phenomenon. It is actually the land formation itself that is shaped like a horse head, but over time the name has been transferred to the slender bay it protects.

Beaches surrounding Horsehead Bay are all private, but a public launch ramp on the east shore provides water access. Roadside parking is available along the west side of Horsehead Bay Drive in the vicinity of the intersection with 36th Street NW.

Kopachuck State Park   Map 54

Camping • Picnicking • Beach walking • Clamming • Wading • Swimming • Scuba diving • Hiking • Paddling

Facilities: 41 standard campsites, group camp, picnic tables, picnic shelters, restrooms, showers, trailer dump station, 2 mooring buoys, artificial reef, CMT campsite, trails

Area: 107.7 acres; 3500 feet of shoreline on Carr Inlet

🚗 From SR 16, 3¾ miles north of the Tacoma Narrows Bridge, take the exit marked Wollochett Drive NW, City Center, Kopachuck State Park. Head southwest on Wollochett Drive NW for ½ mile, turn west on Hunt Street NW, and in three blocks north on Skansie Avenue NW. In ¾ mile head west on Rosedale Street NW to reach Ray Nash Drive in another 2½ miles. Turn southwest on Ray Nash, and then in ¾ mile, west on Kopachuck Drive NW to reach the park in another 2 miles.

🚤 The park is on the east side of Henderson Bay, ½ n.m. north of Horsehead Bay

This park has a cool, forested campground and one of the best public beaches to be found on South Puget Sound—all that and summer eves lovely enough to inspire poetry as the setting sun spreads its glow across Carr Inlet and finally drops behind the black phalanx of Olympic peaks. All campsites sit on an upper road that loops through a timbered flat some 150 feet above the beach. A trail from the west edge of the campground road intersects the lower road and eventually leads down to the beach.

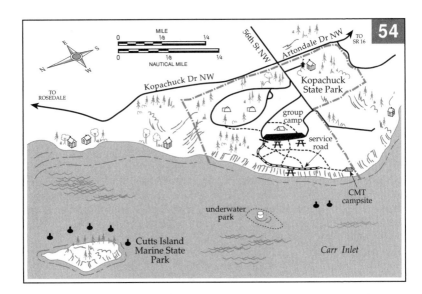

A lower road loops around the group camp area and ends in a huge day-use parking lot. Wooded picnic sites sit just below the parking area, and a gated service road drops steeply down to the beach. At the lower end of the service road are picnic shelters and some picnic tables with views of the beach. A primitive CMT campsite is just above the beach at the south park boundary.

The trail through the uplands that interconnects with the campground road is short, but pleasant. Sun filters through tall fir and alder onto paths lined with salal, false Solomon's seal, and sword fern. Fall brings the promise of some huckleberries—if you get there before the birds.

The long beach is rocky and strewn with driftwood at the high-tide level, but low tide exposes a stretch of gently sloping sand. In summer, water flowing over the shallow tideflat warms enough for wading and swimming. Clam populations are somewhat depleted, but visitors might like to try for a tasty meal. The park is one of several on the sound where geoducks are being reintroduced; the beds are being protected from harvest for several years until the clams reach adequate size and number. Be sure to check regulations and restrictions posted along the service road before heading for the beach with shovel and bucket, and see comments in the introduction regarding harvesting shellfish.

Offshore, two mooring buoys accommodate visiting boaters. Only boats light enough to be carried down from the parking lot can be put in at the park. The nearest ramp for trailered boats is at Horsehead Bay, 1½ n.m. to the south.

Acres of clams (and oysters, too) attract seafood harvesters to the tidelands between Kopachuck and Cutts Island Marine State Parks.

About 200 yards offshore the seabed drops off steeply to the 9-fathom level. This area has been designated as an underwater park for use by scuba divers. An old barge that has been sunk in 50 feet of water increases the opportunities for underwater exploration.

Cutts Island Marine State Park   Map 54

Boating • Paddling • Beach walking • Clamming • Swimming • Scuba diving

Facilities: 10 mooring buoys, artificial reef, no water
Area: 5.5 acres; 2100 feet of shoreline

The park is ½ n.m. north of Horsehead Bay and ½ n.m. offshore to the north of Kopachuck State Park.

By virtue of being accessible only by boat, Cutts Island is designated as a marine state park. However, it lies so close to the mainland that it seems to

A dramatic bluff of compacted glacial till marks the south end of Cutts Island Marine State Park.

be more of an annex to Kopachuck State Park. The 1/2-mile distance between the two parks is an easy paddle, but use a little caution—in a heavily loaded boat it can be farther than it looks.

With its distinctive tuft of scraggly firs above a 40-foot sheer cliff of eroding glacial till, Cutts Island qualifies as the most scenic of South Puget Sound state parks. Wide, level tideflats surrounding the island are rocky on the east, merging into sand on the west. A long sandbar extending from the northeast point of the island reaches nearly to Raft Island at extreme low tide. Clamming might be more productive here than at Kopachuck State Park, but the rocky beaches demand greater effort for the reward.

Ten mooring buoys sit around the south and east sides of the island. Overnight camping is not permitted because the area is without water and restrooms. Cutts Island is shown on some early navigation charts as Deadman's Island, as it was once used as a burial ground by Indians who would place their dead in the trees to mummify—a wonderful tale to relate to wide-eyed kids as evening mists settle over the anchorage.

Henderson Bay and Wauna   Map 55

Boating • Paddling • Fishing • Sailboarding

Facilities: 1-lane paved launch ramp (Pierce County), fuel (service station)

🚐 From SR 16, 3 miles north of Gig Harbor, take the SR 302, Purdy Exit, and then follow Purdy Drive (SR 302) north for 3/4 mile to Purdy. Head west on SR 302, crossing the jetty at the head of Henderson Bay. The launch ramp is on the west side, opposite Goodrich Drive NW.

🚤 The launch ramp is at the north side of Henderson Bay, on the west side of the jetty between the inlet and Burley Lagoon.

The last navigable part of Carr Inlet, Henderson Bay, ends abruptly at a rock jetty crossed by the highway. Beyond here the inlet trickles out into the drying mudflat of Burley Lagoon. These tideflats north of the jetty support commercial oyster production, and the owners are as hostile to visitors' encroachments as were the Native Americans when Lt. Peter Puget and his men visited here. The beach on the south side of the jetty is public, however, and is a popular source of oysters and clams at low tide, as well as a prime spot for sailboarding.

In recent years an added early spring attraction has been a group of gray whales that have appeared for a few days in the bay for a side excursion during their annual coastal migration. News media usually announce when the whales are seen.

A boat-launch ramp at Wauna, at the west end of the jetty, provides ready access to Henderson Bay. Parking is available in the immediate vicinity but is limited to the south side of SR 302.

Two public DNR beaches, accessible only by water, are situated along the north side of Henderson Bay, approximately halfway between Wauna and Minter Bay. Beaches 35 and 35A, which are both private above mean high tide, have some littleneck clams and geoducks at the sandy, low-tide reaches.

CARR INLET WEST SHORE
Map 55

Life slows along the Key Peninsula shoreline of Carr Inlet. Homes are fewer than on the eastern shore, and the ambiance is more rural. Land access is from SR 302 via the Key Peninsula Highway, which runs to its southern tip.

Glen Cove   Map 55
Paddling

Facilities: Inn, hand-carry boat launch

🚗 From SR 16, 3 miles north of Gig Harbor, take the SR 302, Purdy Exit, and then Purdy Drive (SR 302) north for ¾ mile to Purdy. Head west on Key Peninsula Highway KPN (initially SR 302) for 8 miles to Key Center. Here go east on Cramer Road KPN for 1¼ miles to Glen Cove.

🚤 Glen Cove is on the west side of Carr Inlet, 5 n.m. south of the end of Henderson Bay, 4 n.m. north of Von Geldern Cove, and 2½ n.m. northwest of Kopachuck State Park.

Midway along the west shore of Carr Inlet is Glen Cove, a small inlet that has a few protected anchorages in shallow water. The intimate cove makes an ideal destination for canoes and kayaks put in at Kopachuck State Park, directly across the inlet. There are no public launch facilities for trailered boats on the cove, but a break in the bank on the south side of the cove near the Glen Cove Hotel permits launching hand-carried boats at high tide levels.

The Olde Glencove Hotel, on the southwest side of the cove, is a Registered National Historical Landmark, now operated as a bed and breakfast inn. The ornate hotel was built in 1897 and was elegantly furnished. It has been restored to its Victorian prime and is open for paid tours during afternoons on weekends. Better yet, stay for a few days.

Von Geldern Cove

Von Geldern Cove   Map 56
Fishing • Paddling

Facilities: 1-lane concrete launch ramp (Pierce County). *Nearby:* Gas, groceries

🚗 From Purdy head west on SR 302 which becomes Key Peninsula Highway KPN. In 12½ miles reach the community of Home. Just north of the bridge over the end of the cove, turn east on A Street KPN. In ½ mile, at the junction with 8th Avenue KPN, is a pull-out at the launch ramp.

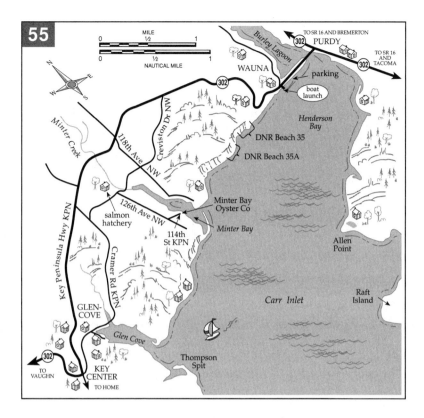

🛥 Von Geldern Cove is on the west shore of Carr Inlet, 3½ n.m. north of McNeil Island.

Farther down the west shore of Carr Inlet is the village of Home, whose quiet, rustic demeanor belies its early history as a nineteenth-century "hippie" colony. Home was founded in 1896 as a Utopian community populated by outspoken exponents of anarchy, free speech, yoga, spiritualism, nudity, and free love. After fourteen years of harassment by less free-thinking politicians and newspaper editors, the colony disbanded, accused of anarchist bombings and victimized by a sanctimonious press.

A concrete launch ramp on the Home waterfront provides public access to Joe Bay and Von Geldern Cove. ❈The bay is extremely shallow west of the launch ramp, drying to a mud flat at minus tides, and a long shoal extends from the north shore into the entrance to the cove.

Mayo Cove   Map 56

Facilities: Marina, 1-lane paved launch ramp, limited groceries, ice, bait, restrooms, guest moorage with power, gas

🚗 See driving directions for Von Geldern Cove, above. From Home continue south on Key Peninsula Highway KPS for 3/4 mile, and turn east on Cornwall Road KPS. At a T-intersection in 1/2 mile go north on Lorenz Road KPS, and immediately east on the stub of Lakebay Dock Road KPS.

🚤 Mayo Cove is on the west side of Carr Inlet, 2 1/2 n.m. north of McNeil Island.

Penrose Point State Park shares Mayo Cove with the village of Lakebay where there are a few residences and a marina that is built on pilings over the water. Lakebay derives its name from Bay Lake, 1 mile to the south, which drains into Mayo Cove.

A boat-launch ramp north of the marina pier is reached from the end of a narrow road near some adjoining houses. The lower portion of the ramp is covered with sand and is only marginally usable unless you are driving a four-wheel-drive vehicle. The marina offers fuel, bait, guest moorage, and a limited selection of groceries.

❄ The water approach to the marina and Penrose Point State Park's floats can be tenuous for deep-draft boats at low tide. A sandspit that projects well into the cove from the northeast must be given adequate berth before turning into the head of the cove itself. The best anchorages are near the northeast shore of the cove.

Penrose Point State Park   Map 56

Camping • Hiking • Fishing • Clamming • Swimming • Beach walking • Paddling • Trail

Facilities: 82 campsites, group camp, CMT campsite, picnic tables, picnic shelters, fire rings, restrooms, showers, nature trail, trails, horseshoe pits, trailer dump station, float, 8 mooring buoys

Area: 160.56 acres; 11,751 feet of shoreline

🚗 See directions to Mayo Cove, above. At the intersection of Cornwall Road KPS and Lorenz Road KPS, turn south on Delano Road KPS, which soon bends east. In 3/4 mile, turn north on 158th Avenue KPS to reach the park in 1/4 mile.

🚤 See directions to Mayo Cove, above. The park mooring floats are on the inner portion of the cove opposite the marina. The mooring buoys are offshore on both sides of Penrose Point.

One might think that Penrose Point had been designed by Mother Nature specifically as a waterfront park, so ideally suited is it to its role. Despite its relatively small size, the park has nearly 2 miles of gentle beaches, along with ample uplands for a forested campground and a couple of miles of trails. Inside the long arm of the point lies Mayo Cove, with the park mooring float and anchorage room for boats, well protected from gusty southerly winds. Low tide reveals the best feature of the park—a 1/2-mile-long sandbar paralleling the point, with clams and seaweed and all sorts of squiggly things to investigate.

Inside the park entrance a branch road to the left leads to the campground, while the main road goes straight ahead. At a T-intersection turn right and pass the group camp to reach the day-use area—a broad lawn with picnic tables, fire rings, and plenty of space to spread picnic cloths or blankets on the ground. Additional tables and a picnic shelter are nearby in the shade of stately firs. The adjacent beach is sandy and shallow—ideal for a summer dip. Just inside the woods to the west is a CMT campsite.

From the T-intersection the left fork of the road heads west to a parking area on the bank above the small harbor with more picnic spots nearby. A service road drops down to beach level where there is a float with space for six to eight boats. Three buoys sited in deeper water offshore from the drying sandspit and five more on the east side of the park give added moorage.

A network of about 2 miles of trails weaves through the timber and brush between the access road and the beach. A nature trail with numbered sites keyed to a brochure loops through the woods. Most paths are broad and well marked; some spurs are more primitive, but most eventually lead somewhere if followed persistently. The main attraction of the trails, however, is not where they lead, but what can be seen along the way—huge Douglas-firs, a trickling creek, nodding trilliums, a marsh blazing with skunk cabbage blossoms, birds, squirrels, and who knows what else.

A nice beach on the east side of the park is headed by a high bank and impenetrable brush but it is accessible by trail from marker A at the picnic

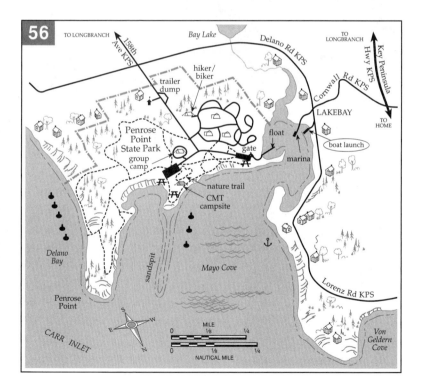

Alders and huge maple and cedar trees tower over picnickers at Penrose Point State Park.

area parking lot. Boaters moored on this side of the park or beach walkers looking for an upland return can locate this trailhead about 200 yards north of the most northerly mooring buoy. There is also a large, white pole marking an underground cable located where the trail breaks onto the beach.

A few oysters, clams, and mussels might be found on beaches on either side of the park, but the best intertidal exploration is on the ½-mile-long sandspit in Mayo Cove that is exposed at a minus tide. Because this is a heavily used clamming beach, the mollusks are somewhat depleted and digging can be a lot of work for a little success. See comments in the introduction regarding harvesting shellfish.

chapter nine

Nisqually Reach

BEYOND THE TACOMA NARROWS are two east–west water thoroughfares, separated by Anderson Island, that lead to the Western Inlets. One route threads between McNeil Island and Anderson Island via Balch Passage, and then doglegs to the left into Drayton Passage between Anderson Island and the Key Peninsula. The second route, somewhat longer but broader, swings south of Anderson Island before heading northwesterly to Johnson Point.

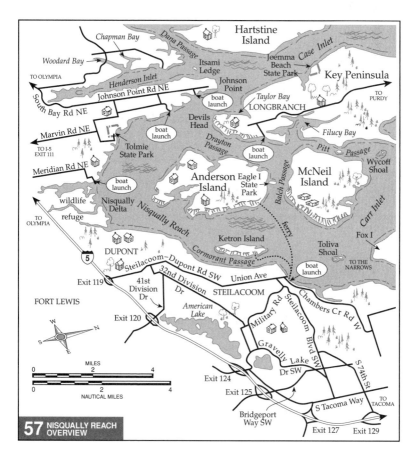

57 NISQUALLY REACH OVERVIEW

207

Filucy Bay is one of the prettiest anchorages on the Nisqually Reach.

Although this chapter describes all of the waterways and abutting lands in this midsection of South Puget Sound, the name Nisqually Reach technically applies only to the portion of the wide southern channel where it curves in a 180-degree arc along the head of the Nisqually Delta. By land, nearly all the area is but a short hop from exits on I-5, which skirts its southern shore.

These channels are noted for outstanding salmon fishing, especially where tidal eddies around points of land and channel entries build feeding grounds. As a result, a number of commercial and public launch facilities are available along adjoining shorelands; some marinas also have boats for rent. In several areas fishing is also excellent from shore or docks.

The four islands located here are wildly diverse: McNeil houses a state penitentiary, Ketron is entirely private, Anderson is mostly private; and tiny Eagle is a marine state park. A second state park, Tolmie, is on the mainland between Nisqually Head and Johnson Point.

On the southern shores of Nisqually Reach, a broad salt-marsh delta, formed where the Nisqually River flows into the sound, is a national wildlife refuge. Here flocks of waterfowl pause to rest and feed in their migratory flights along the Pacific Coast. The refuge is a resource for wildlife education and recreation and the scene of bird hunting during the fall.

THE STEILACOOM REGION
Map 58

This area could certainly be considered the cradle of Puget Sound settlement. In 1824 a contingent of Hudson's Bay Company representatives, scouting the West Coast for possible trading post sites, visited the Nisqually village of Chilacum, at the present location of the town of Steilacoom. On the recommendation of this survey the area's first white settlement, Fort Nisqually, was established near the mouth of the Nisqually River in 1833 by the British-owned business. After that fort was destroyed by Native Americans it was relocated, in 1843, to a site 5 miles south of Chilacum on a hill overlooking Nisqually Reach near Sequalitchew Creek.

Six years later two American ministers and their families built a Methodist mission near the fort. The first white baby on Puget Sound, Francis Richmond, was born here in February 1842.

The Treaty of 1846 settled the American-British jurisdictional dispute, making all of Puget Sound country part of the United States' Oregon Territory. In 1849, in an effort to protect settlers from hostile Indians, a detachment of troops was sent here; they occupied some abandoned buildings on a hillside above Chambers Bay. Fort Steilacoom, which was built on this site, remained a major protective stronghold for white pioneers throughout the Indian War. It was abandoned by the army in 1870 when such protection was no longer necessary.

With shattered dreams of economic importance and residential prominence, Steilacoom looks wistfully back to a time when it was the most important settlement on South Puget Sound. In 1851 Capt. Lafayette Balch first built a wharf and general store on the slight bay near the site of the Native American village of Chilacum. Balch had brought the lumber and goods for the enterprise by ship all the way from his home state of Maine. He named his new settlement Port Steilacoom, but a rival commercial development, Steilacoom City, was established slightly to the west just a few months later

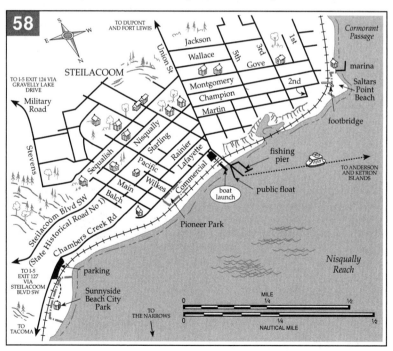

by John B. Chapman. Eventually the competing entrepreneurs joined forces, and in 1854 the town of Steilacoom was the first to be incorporated in the newly formed Washington Territory.

The town, in fact, claims a long string of territorial "firsts": the first Protestant church north of the Columbia (1853), the first jail (1858), and the first public library (1858). By the end of the 1850s it was the fastest growing community on Puget Sound, the home of a busy shipping industry and center of settlement for pioneers who chose to live near the protection of Forts Nisqually and Steilacoom during these times of Native American unrest.

The pin that popped the Steilacoom bubble was its rejection, in 1873, as a terminus for the Northern Pacific Railroad. Businesses fled to the north to become part of the Tacoma boom. In 1895 an electric trolley line from Tacoma to Steilacoom gave the city new hope as it became a popular seaside resort for vacationers from Tacoma and Olympia. When the railroad did finally come to Steilacoom in 1912, it dealt the city a near-death blow, for it located its tracks along the shore and destroyed the waterfront summer homes, resorts, and recreational beaches, effectively separating the town from the beach.

Steilacoom   Maps 57 and 58

Boating • Fishing • Sightseeing • Picnicking • Shopping • Swimming • Scuba diving • Paddling

Facilities: Groceries, stores, fuel, marine repair, 1-lane launch ramp, fishing pier, restaurants, museums, historic buildings, ferry to Anderson and Ketron Islands. *Marina:* Boat rental, fuel, short-term guest moorage, restrooms, portable toilet dump, snacks, bait, tackle. *Sunnyside Beach Park:* Picnic tables, restrooms, outside shower, volleyball courts, children's play area. *Saltars Point Beach:* Picnic shelter, restrooms

🚗 From I-5 Exit 124 (Gravelly Lake Drive) take Gravelly Lake Drive SW north for 1¼ miles then turn west on Washington Boulevard SW. In 1¼ miles the road bends northwest and becomes Military Road SW. In 1½ miles this turns north as Stevens Street, which, in ½ mile, heads west as Sequalish Street, and intersects Union Street in another ¾ mile. Downtown Steilacoom and the Anderson Island ferry terminal are five blocks to the north. *Sunnyside Beach Park:* From downtown Steilacoom head east on Lafayette Street, which becomes Chambers Creek Road and reaches the park in ¾ mile. *Saltars Point Beach:* From Union Street, just above the ferry landing, turn west on Martin Street, in five blocks south on 2nd Street, and in a block west on Champion Street for a block to the parking area at 1st Street. 🚤 Steilacoom is on the south side of the confluence of Carr Inlet, Balch Passage, and the narrows. The launch ramp is on the northeast side of the ferry landing.

Despite its auspicious beginnings, Steilacoom's prime claims to importance today are as the terminal for the ferries to Anderson, Ketron, and McNeil Islands, as a suburb of Tacoma, and as the site of the state mental hospital on the nearby grounds of the old fort. For visitors, Steilacoom's major attractions are the numerous old homes that can be viewed on a walking or bicycle tour of town. Three preserved and restored pioneer buildings are listed on the National Register of Historic Sites. One of these, the Nathaniel Orr Home, at 1811 Rainier Street, dating from 1857, is open for viewing on summer Sundays. Others have signs describing their history.

One of the most fascinating of the historic structures is Bair Drug and Hardware, on the corner of Wilkes and Lafayette, about three blocks up-hill from the ferry landing. Visitors can stroll in to admire a multitude of goods—from mustache cups to patent elixirs—displayed just as they were in Victorian times. A museum that displays pioneer artifacts is in the basement of the town hall at Main and Lafayette. It is open from 1:00 PM to 4:00 PM, in summer from Wednesday through Sunday, and Friday through Sunday in November, December, and February. A second museum at the corner of Lafayette and Pacific features photos, artifacts, and archeological recoveries relating to Native American tribal history.

At the foot of Union Avenue is the landing for the Anderson Island ferry. On the east side a small float is open for loading and unloading small boats. Next to it a narrow passage under the railroad tracks ends in a launch ramp for trailered boats. The Clyde B. Davidson fishing pier extends out along the west side of the ferry dock. The lighted pier is a popular spot for crabbing as well as fishing.

Pioneer Park • This park on a grassy bluff along the north side of Commercial Street between Wilkes and Main Streets provides a pleasant spot to have a picnic lunch or simply to enjoy the splendid view down Carr Inlet and beyond to the high peaks of the Olympic Mountains. A large wood-decked overlook has an interpretive sign identifying the geographic features within

Historic Bair Drug is one of the interesting spots to visit in Steilacoom.

view. This was once the site of a two-story log house that in 1853 was used as the town's first school. A second park nearby links Pioneer Park to the Steilacoom Tribal Center with a pair of decks and a stairway.

Sunnyside Beach Park (Town of Steilacoom) • On the northeastern out-skirts of Steilacoom, at a slight bulge in the shoreline, is Sunnyside Beach. Park in the lot on the west side of the road and cross the railroad tracks to reach the beach. A gravel path permits beach access for disabled persons. A large, grassy area shaded by tall poplar trees forms the heart of the park. The sandy, driftwood-strewn beach is ideal for summer sunbathing and swimming. There arc no boat-launch facilities, but lightweight boats can easily be carried from the parking lot to the beach for put-ins and nearby paddling.

The park is a starting point for scuba divers who explore the steep canyons of the channel and the multitude of old pilings along the shore. Toliva Shoal, a reef 2 miles to the north marked by a red-and-black navigational buoy, is a popular diving and salmon fishing site. ❄Beware of strong currents and tide rips in the vicinity.

Saltars Point Beach (Town of Steilacoom) • Another waterfront park is at Saltars Point, west of the ferry terminal. A wooden footbridge at the corner of 1st and Champion leads over the railroad tracks and down to the small day-use park. The small picnic shelter and single picnic table might seem meager, but the gravel beach provides ample places to spread a portable feast. The quick beach dropoff makes it a fine spot for shore fishing. Immediately west of the park beach is a marina; the bridge over the tracks provides its only land access.

Ketron Island • The 1/2-mile-wide channel of Cormorant Passage separates Ketron Island from the mainland. With steep cliffs bounding most of the beach perimeter and dense timber masking the few homes on top, the island has a decided aura of privacy. A Pierce County ferry makes four daily runs from Steilacoom to Ketron, but all roads are inland and there are no views for sightseers.

Anderson Island   Map 59

Bicycling • Fishing • Boating • Paddling • Swimming • Hiking • Point of interest

Facilities: *Andy's Marine Park:* Trail, picnic tables, toilet, CMT campsite

🚍 Take the twenty-minute ferry ride from Steilacoom to the island. *Andy's Marine Park:* From the ferry landing take Yoman Road west for 3/4 mile, and turn southwest on Eckenstam-Johnson Road. Follow it for 1 1/4 miles, and turn west on Sandberg Road. In 1 mile turn south on Claussen Road, and reach the park in another 1/4 mile.

🚤 The island lies in the curve of the Nisqually Reach, north of the Nisqually Delta. *Andy's Marine Park:* The park is on Nisqually Reach on the west side of Anderson Island 1/4 n.m. south of Treble Point.

Anderson Island is so fiercely private that recreational use is virtually nonexistent; those facilities that do exist are intended primarily for use by residents. Mainland access is via a Pierce County ferry from Steilacoom. Once there you can drive, bicycle, or walk the roads, or take a pleasant hike to one public beach—and then go home, unless you are planning to stay at one of the nice bed-and-breakfast inns. Islanders are friendly folk who wave as they pass on the road, but they clearly do not encourage a large influx of tourists.

Visitors exploring the interior of Anderson Island will find a few interesting tidbits. Lowell Johnson Park, on the north shore of Florence Lake, is an old-style "swimming hole" with space for picnicking and a game or two of volleyball. It's a welcome respite for cyclists on a hot sunny day. Tiny Andy's Park is a boggy wildlife preserve. The interesting, 1900s-era Johnson Farm, operated by the Anderson Island Historical Society, houses artifacts collected from the island.

❋ The only bay of any size that marks the shore of the island is Oro Bay, on the southeast corner—and it is shallow and exposed to the rake of tidal currents and southeasterly weather. The western arm of the bay offers some protection, although it is quite shallow. In good weather, it can be a pleasant

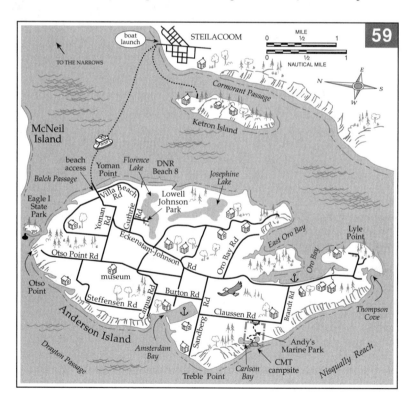

Andy's Marine Park, on Anderson Island, is a nature preserve featuring wetlands and a baymouth bar.

anchorage that offers a knockout view of Mount Rainier. Enter between a pair of red-and-green buoys that mark the entrance along the north side of the bay to avoid a long submerged spit extending from the south side of the entrance. All the shoreline on the bay is private, so it is not possible to go ashore.

Amsterdam Bay, on the northwest side of the island, is a smaller indentation in the shoreline, but it does offer some anchorages well protected from southerly winds. ❃Local knowledge is necessary to attempt the narrow entrance to a larger, shallow inner bay, which is nearly isolated by a long sandbar. The entrance channel dries at minus tides.

DNR Beach • A public DNR beach that has no upland access and must be reached by boat lies along the east side of the island beneath an abrupt cliff, 1/4 mile south of Yoman Point. The combination of a sharp drop-off about 500 feet offshore and strong tidal currents makes this an unattractive anchorage, but shallow-draft boats can be landed when the tide is low enough to expose the 2500-foot-long sand and gravel beach.

Andy's Marine Park (Anderson Island Parks and Recreation) • The only public saltwater beach access on the island is at Andy's Marine Park. The

¾-mile-long trail that weaves through the woods to the west from the parking lot passes signs identifying local flora. The flat, narrow path wends through head-high brush, with damp spots covered with logs. In about ½ mile the trail forks, but both routes join above the beach. A log staircase switchbacks down to the water, where an anchored wooden float connects the trail to a gravel baymouth bar. Beach grass and driftwood line the narrow top of the bar. Here is a CMT campsite; on the far side a wide gravel beach tapers gently into Nisqually Reach. Because the park is a nature preserve, harvesting shellfish is prohibited.

Eagle Island Marine State Park Map 60

Fishing • Beach walking • Swimming • Wading

Facilities: 3 mooring buoys, no water, no toilets, no camping
Area: 10 acres; 2600 feet of shoreline

The small island sits in the middle of already constricted Balch Passage, between Anderson and McNeil Islands. Large boats navigating the passage should stay well in midchannel between McNeil and Eagle Islands. A buoy marks a reef extending from the west side of Eagle Island.

Although the birds were once numerous in the area, Eagle Island was not named for our national symbol, but for Harry Eagle, a member of the Wilkes Expedition. Even though you might not find eagles there today, you are likely to spot a hawk, and the island has the prettiest collection of gnarled madronas to be found anywhere on South Puget Sound. Overhanging the banks are firs with curving, pistol-butted trunks, caused by the tree growing upward as its roots were undermined and the trunk tilted downward.

Beaches are gravel, with little evidence of marine life. The southern point, which reaches toward Anderson Island, has fine-grained sand, worthy of any sand castle and soft enough for a comfortable afternoon of sunbathing. Mooring buoys are set on either side of the sandspit. Anderson Island is invitingly close, but all beaches there are private.

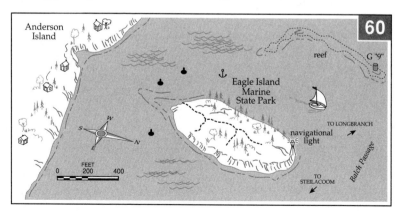

Twisted madronas overhang the beach at Eagle Island.

Trails lace the uplands, some more primitive than others, but all are certain to provide an hour's diversion of brush whacking. The most scenic spot is on the bank on the southeast end of the island, where a break in the trees provides a nice view down Balch Passage and out to Mount Rainier.

PITT AND DRAYTON PASSAGES
Map 61

Boating • Paddling • Fishing

Facilities: *Longbranch:* Guest moorage with water. *Nearby:* Groceries

🚗 *Longbranch:* From SR 16, 3 miles north of Gig Harbor, take the SR 302 (Purdy) Exit, and then Purdy Drive (SR 302) north for ³/₄ mile to Purdy. Head west on Key Peninsula Highway KPN (initially SR 302), then Key Peninsula Highway KPS for 13 miles to Longbranch. *Drayton Passage Launch Ramp:* Continue south from Longbranch on the Key Peninsula Highway KPS for 1½ miles to 72nd Street KPS. Turn east, and in ½ mile a single-lane concrete launch ramp dips into Drayton Passage.

🛥 Filucy Bay is on the east side of the Key Peninsula, opposite the west tip of McNeil Island, at the confluence of Drayton, Balch, and Pitt Passages.

Pitt Passage, separating McNeil Island from the Key Peninsula, is shallow enough that it encouraged early-day prison inmates to occasionally attempt wading across on a minus tide when the narrow portion south of Pitt Island

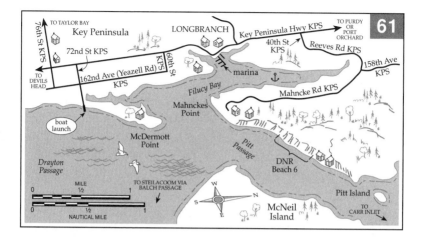

drains to 6 feet deep. A new prison fence now prevents this. ❋Tidal currents run fast through Pitt Passage, however, ranging to more than 2½ knots. For boats attempting the channel, the recommended passage runs east of Pitt Island. Signs on pilings mark shoals north and south of the island. Due to its shallowness, it is not advisable to attempt Pitt Passage at low tide in boats with any draft. Be aware that, contrary to logic, the current ebbs to the north and floods to the south.

The short waterway of Drayton Passage bounds the northwest side of Anderson Island and joins Balch Passage to the west end of Nisqually Reach. It also exhibits some of the illogical tidal flows of the area by always ebbing weakly to the northeast, regardless of the ebb or flood direction in adjacent waters.

DNR Beach 6 • On the west side of Pitt Passage are some 2000 feet of DNR public tidelands. DNR Beach 6 lies beneath a steep, 150-foot-tall clay bluff immediately south of a row of beach cabins, and stretches south to within ¾ mile of Mahnckes Point. The gravel beach changes to sand when low tide exposes the long, shallow tidelands. Beachcombing offers cockles and possibly some clams. All upland approaches are private.

Longbranch and Filucy Bay • Filucy Bay (pronounced "fih-LOO-chee") is every bit as pretty as its name, with tree-lined shores enclosing one of the best anchorages on Puget Sound. A long finger of the bay runs north for 1½ miles, offering ample space for a fleet of boats and solid anchorage in a mud bottom in 2 to 2½ fathoms of water. A small cove at the southern extremity of the bay is protected by McDermott Point. The extreme end of the point, a former lighthouse site, is on an acquisition list of the Trust for Public Lands and Pierce County. The sloping gravel beach is fine for sunbathing and watching passing maritime traffic.

At the center of the bay, on the west side, is the village of Longbranch, which consists of a general store that carries a supply of groceries. A float at the marina here permits access to shore facilities.

Drayton Passage Launch Ramp (Pierce County) • Popular fishing and boating areas in and near Drayton Passage are accessible to trailered boats from a launch ramp on its western edge. There is ample vehicle and trailer parking alongside the road, but all shorelines on either side of the ramp are private.

Wycoff Shoal • Just off the northwest end of McNeil Island, where Pitt Passage joins Carr Inlet, is Wycoff Shoal. Only a hazardous scattering of

McNeil Island

Take a 4400-acre island in the heart of Puget Sound, complete with timber stands, fresh water, sandy beaches, herons, eagles, and seals—and, incidentally, a penitentiary—put it up for grabs to a host of special-interest groups, then stand back and watch the donnybrook. This scenario was played out twenty years ago when the federal government decided to close its penitentiary on McNeil Island.

The island was the site of a territorial jail in 1867 and became a federal penitentiary in 1870 to take advantage of its natural isolation, created by the swift tidal currents and bone-chilling waters of the sound. It was the oldest operating federal penal institution in the country until 1980, when the government closed it down because the facilities were too out of date and too costly for it to operate.

Recreational and conservation forces, as well as the descendants of the former owners, began a battle for the island. Ideas ranged from building a bridge across Pitt Passage for greater public access, to completely vacating the island and leaving it as a wildlife refuge. Washington's own prison requirements finally carried the day, and the buildings were taken over by the state penal system. In 1984 the federal government deeded 3100 acres to the state DFW, which now manages that portion as a wildlife preserve.

The prison complex is on 30 acres on the southeast side of the island, and a large prison garden is near Hogan Point on the southwest; the remainder of the island is largely in its natural state. Signs along the shores warning boaters to maintain a respectful distance because of the prison have helped wildlife to thrive here unmolested. Still Harbor, which deeply indents the northeast shore, is one of the last remaining harbor seal breeding grounds south of Whidbey Island. A colony of some 200 seals haul out to rest and sun themselves on Gertrude Island and the connecting sandspit. A great blue heron rookery is on one of the island creeks, and bald eagles nest nearby. These precious wildlife assets are concentrated on the northern third of the island, away from the penitentiary.

rocks is exposed at high tide, but low tide reveals sand and gravel bars where clams, geoducks, and sea cucumbers can be harvested. All exposed tideland is public. ☸ When it is submerged, the extremities of the shoal are outlined by five red-and-white cone markers.

Access to the tidelands is by boat only. The nearest launch ramps are at Mayo Cove and on Drayton Passage south of Longbranch.

THE NISQUALLY DELTA
Map 62

A bonanza! The Nisqually Delta is a natural cornucopia on the shores of the busy water highway of Nisqually Reach, within eyeshot of the intensely private shores of Anderson Island. Although there are varying accounts of the meaning of the name Nisqually, the favorite one is that the word "squally" imitates the sound of the breeze blowing through the grassland and flowers. The name broadened to become the name of the tribe of Indians living in this region.

Nisqually National Wildlife Refuge (U.S. Fish and Wildlife Service)
Map 62

Fishing • Hiking • Wildlife • Boating • Paddling

Facilities: Education center, visitor center, 7 miles of trails (1 mile disabled accessible), restrooms, photo blinds, observation towers
Area: 3780 acres; 13,200 feet of shoreline on Nisqually Reach
🚐 From I-5 take Exit 114 (Nisqually), and turn north on Nisqually Cutoff Road, which ducks under the freeway and arrives at the Wildlife Refuge boundary.
🚤 Boating is permitted on the Nisqually River and McAllister Creek, however both are quite shoal at minus tides. The nearest launch ramp is at Luhr Beach.

The merging of freshwater and saltwater from river, streams, and the sound, coupled with broad grasslands, deciduous woodlands, and thick conifer forests, creates the uniquely diverse habitat of the Nisqually National Wildlife Refuge. Daily tidal flows through the saltwater marshes bring organic life, an important link in the food chain that includes some 50 species of small mammals, 125 kinds of fish, and 200 species of birds ranging from waterfowl to songbirds to raptors. They are all here to be discovered, enjoyed, and photographed. The gate to the refuge is locked daily at sunset, so plan visits accordingly. Be sure to bring binoculars, a camera, and possibly a bird identification guide. An entrance fee is charged. Persons with an authorized

Canvasback ducks are just one of the many species of waterfowl that can be seen in the Nisqually Delta.

The Nisqually Delta: People or Preservation?

The Nisqually Delta was a favored spot for Indians, who harvested the bounty of the grasslands, marshes, and streams, and who located a major village nearby at Chilacum on the bluff to the east. The Hudson's Bay Company established a post nearby at Fort Nisqually, and its subsidiary, the Puget Sound Agricultural Society, imported livestock. By 1847 some 6000 sheep and 2000 cattle were grazing the lush meadows on the banks of the Nisqually.

James McAllister, an early settler in the region, scratched out a farm on the banks of Medicine Creek, the lower reaches of which now bear his name. He took a place in history when he became one of the first whites killed during the Indian War of 1855–56.

Medicine Creek is best known as the site where the Indians were hornswoggled by Gov. Isaac Stevens when he convinced the chiefs of the tribes living along the shores of South Puget Sound to sign the Medicine Creek Treaty. Leschi, one of the chiefs of the Nisqually, was the lone holdout. The Indians were assigned to meager reservations, one south of the Nisqually River, another on a bluff between Tacoma and Point Defiance, and a third on Harstine Island. A later treaty renegotiation (inspired by the Indian War) gave the tribes somewhat more favorable lands, including the rich prairies and salmon-filled streams south of the delta.

In 1904 Alson Brown purchased the rich delta land and with horse-drawn scoops built dikes to hold back the saltwater. He started a large dairy farm; buildings still stand on the land today. Preserved as farmland, the Nisqually Delta has remained one of the most pristine river deltas in the United States. The threat of industrial encroachment pressed the area in the early 1970s because the Brown farm could no longer compete with modern farming giants. An environmental group, The Nisqually Delta Association, succeeded in their efforts to preserve it with the establishment of the Nisqually National Wildlife Refuge in 1974.

Substantial private holdings now border the refuge, and proposed developments there could have significant impact on its fragile ecology. Major real estate developments are underway on the bluffs immediately east and west of the delta. "Planned communities" will bring over 20,000 residents within a few wing-flaps of the delta, where 1000 people presently live. Although developers, including the Weyerhaeuser Company, assure environmentalists of their sensitivity to the ecology of the delta, concerns for the delta are multiple: the lights and noise from such a concentration of people might affect the sensitive nesting and wintering activities of birds; sewer and storm-water systems could foul the water of the delta or Nisqually Reach; pet dogs and cats from the residential developments could become predators within the wildlife refuge; more residents in the area will likely bring increased recreational use of the delta, making it more of a park than a wildlife refuge.

Golden Passport or duck stamp need not pay.

Several hikes start from the kiosk and visitor center adjoining the parking lot. Some sections of trails might be closed during nesting season. Hunting is permitted in some adjacent sections of the delta managed by the state DFW, and during hunting season some parts of the dike trail might be closed for the safety of hikers.

The longest hike in the refuge is a 5-mile loop atop the dike that surrounded the old farm. The trail, offering a feast of blackberries in season, parallels the banks of the Nisqually River along the east side of the farm, eventually breaking out of the woodland to wend between cattail-filled marshes. Ahead are the Olympic peaks and behind—surprise!—Mount Rainier.

Canada geese nest in marshes of the Nisqually National Wildlife Refuge.

Turning west, the dike separates vast marshes—inside are freshwater

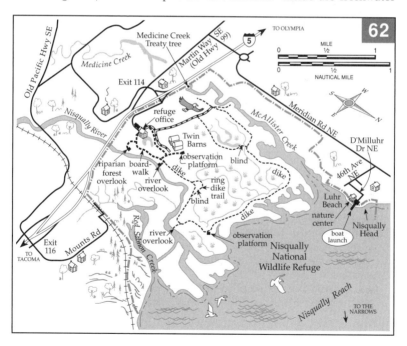

Marshes surround the Twin Barns at Nisqually National Wildlife Refuge.

marshes and outside, saltwater. Both serve as resting and feeding areas for migratory waterfowl and shorebirds. A 20-foot-high viewing platform provides sweeping views over the delta and its bordering islands, Anderson, Ketron, McNeil, and Fox. Heading back south, the dike trail parallels McAllister Creek and passes open freshwater ponds where pintails and mallards raise their broods. Note the nesting boxes on low poles in some of the marshes; these are placed in hopes of attracting wood ducks, which normally nest in hollow trees.

The one-mile Twin Barns Loop Trail from the visitor center is a disabled-accessible boardwalk. Short spurs lead to overlooks of the riparian forest and the Nisqually River; the latter viewpoint has spotting scopes mounted at the railing. Information displays describe the ecology, habitat, and the species of birds that might be seen. A boardwalk branch also reaches an observation tower just north of the Twin Barns. The huge Twin Barns, ½ mile north of the refuge office, once housed dairy herds.

Luhr Beach (DFW)   Map 62

Boating • Paddling • Fishing • Interpretation • Birdwatching

Facilities: 1-lane paved launch ramp, toilet, environmental displays, nature center

From I-5 take Exit 114 (Nisqually) and continue west on Martin Way SE for 1 mile. Turn north on Meridian Road NE; cross over the freeway, and at a roundabout take the Meridian Road NE exit and continue north for 2 miles. Turn east on 46th Avenue NE, and in ¼ mile go north on D'Milluhr Drive NE, which soon heads east to Luhr Beach in ½ mile.

Luhr Beach is on the south side of Nisqually Reach at the mouth of McAllister Creek, on the west side of the Nisqually Wildlife Refuge.

One excellent way to view the Nisqually Wildlife Refuge is by canoe or kayak from the shallow waters of McAllister Creek, the Nisqually River, or the head of the estuary. The only public launch ramp close to the area is at Luhr Beach, where a ramp is maintained by the DFW. Mid- to high-tide is best for exploring the myriad channels of the delta. McAllister Creek and the Nisqually River lead far inland. Red Salmon Creek, near the eastern boundary, connects to the Nisqually. At low tide the exposed riverbeds and tideflats provide an opportunity to examine a wealth of intertidal life—worms, shrimp, jellyfish, clams—all part of the complex web of life in the delta.

South of the ramp parking lot is the Nisqually Reach Nature Center, which offers classes in estuarine environmental ecosystems targeted at school students. In addition, the center conducts research studies sponsored by the Nisqually Tribe, the U.S. Fish and Wildlife Service, and the U.S. Geological Survey. Group beach walks can be scheduled with the center, for a fee. Contact them at 4949 D'Milluhr Drive NE, Olympia, WA 98516, (360) 459-0387.

Tolmie State Park   Map 63

Picnicking • Beach walking • Boating • Clamming • Fishing • Scuba diving • Hiking

Facilities: Picnic shelters, picnic tables, restrooms, outside shower, 5 mooring buoys, 3.5 miles of trails, artificial reef, interpretive displays
Area: 106 acres; 1800 feet of shoreline

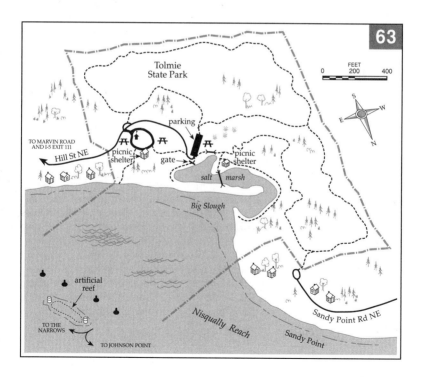

Ferns and moss-covered trees crowd the trail at Tolmie State Park.

🚗 From I-5 Exit 111 (SR 510E, Marvin Road, Yelm) take Marvin Road NE north for 3½ miles, where it Ts into 56th Avenue NE. Head east on 56th, and in ½ mile go north on Hill Street NE, which bends west to reach the park in ¼ mile.

🛥 Tolmie is on the south side of Nisqually Reach at the south end of Drayton Passage. There are five mooring buoys offshore. The nearest launch ramps are at Luhr Beach and Johnson Point.

Although limited to day use, this pretty little state park packs a lot of recreation into its 100-plus acres. The focal point of the park is a saltwater marsh that separates the wooded uplands from the long tideflat facing on Nisqually Reach. Informational plaques explain the natural forces that create such marshes and the unique ecology that makes them important to wildlife.

The park's broad, sandy beach is one of the best in the region for wading, swimming, and clamming. Three wooden barges that were intentionally sunk 500 yards offshore in 40 to 60 feet of water form an underwater park attracting a wealth of marine life, including large rockfish and cabezon. Its location is marked by white can buoys with red stripes. The lack of any significant current makes this an ideal dive site.

Just inside the park entrance, a small loop road with parking pull-outs fronts a grassy picnic area and restroom/picnic shelter. Picnic tables are nicely secluded from each other in cozy pockets among the trees and bushes. Near the lower parking area, just above the beach, are more picnic tables, a kitchen shelter, and adjoining restrooms with an outside shower and inside changing rooms to accommodate scuba divers.

A nearly flat trail that leaves the lower picnic area near the picnic shelter, meanders through woods of alder, cedar, oak, and fir, with a dense understory of ferns and shrubs. The route explores the edges of the park before returning to the end of the lower parking area. The full trail is about 2½ miles long, but for a 1-mile circuit a shortcut leaves the trail halfway along its route and returns to the parking lot. The path is wide and easily followed, but can be muddy. Log benches along the route encourage rest stops for listening to and watching birds, squirrels, and other woods creatures.

Two shorter trails leave from the upper picnic area; the one to the northeast drops steeply down a gully to the beach at the park's east boundary, while the one to the west heads down to the beach area near the lower parking lot.

JOHNSON POINT AND HENDERSON INLET
Map 64

A long finger of land, capped by Johnson Point, marks the confluence of Dana Passage, Nisqually Reach, and Case Inlet. Early Kittitas Indians established a large summer camp on Johnson Point and built fish traps just offshore to harvest the teeming salmon that gathered to feed at the merging channels. Today the region remains one of the most popular in South Puget Sound for sports fishing.

With no public beaches and very limited access, Henderson is one of the less familiar South Puget Sound inlets. ❀ The mouth of the bay is disrupted by Itsami Ledge, a popular salmon fishing site, but a dangerous shoal; it is marked by a light atop the ledge. Seals can often be spotted in the vicinity, also taking advantage of the fine salmon fishing.

There are some protected anchorages in Henderson Inlet in 30 feet of water, just south of Cliff Point. The south half of the inlet tapers to the characteristic mudflats, home to some clams and oysters.

Johnson Point Marinas   Map 64

Fishing • Boating

Facilities: Marinas, 1-lane paved launch ramps with boarding floats, sling launch, boat rentals, fast food

🚗 From I-5 Exit 109 (Martin Way, Sleater-Kinney Road NE) head west on Martin Way for ½ mile, and turn north on Sleater-Kinney Road NE. In 2 miles turn northeast on South Bay Road NE, which bends to the north in ½ mile and becomes Johnson Point Road NE. Continue north on Johnson Point Road NE for 3¾ miles to 78th Avenue NE. *Puget Marina:* Turn east on 78th Avenue NE. In 1 mile go north on Walnut Road NE which bends west to reach the marina in ½ mile. *Zittell's Marina:* Continue north on Johnson Point Road NE 1½ miles beyond 78th Avenue, turn east on 92nd Avenue NE, and reach the marina in ½ mile.

🛥 Both marinas are on the east side of Johnson Point at the southwest end of Nisqually Reach.

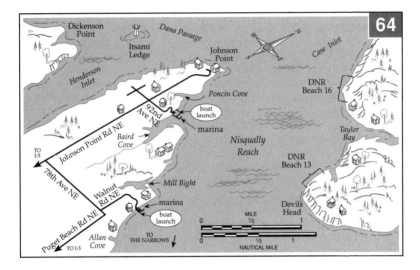

There are no public beaches between Tolmie State Park and Johnson Point, but boat access to this favorite fishing area is available via two marinas on the east side of the point. Puget Marina, off 78th Avenue, is south of Mill Bight. Parking, a concrete launch ramp with a boarding float, an L-shaped float, marine service, and gas are available. Only the outer leg of the float is usable at minus tides. No public access to the tidelands is permitted here, but there is a fantastic view of Mount Rainier over Nisqually Reach.

Zittell's Marina, off 92nd Avenue on Baird Cove, offers floats, fuel, groceries, marine repairs, fishing supplies, a sling launch, boat rentals, restrooms, a galley and grill, and a paved launch ramp with a boarding float.

Woodard Bay Natural Resource Conservation Area (State DNR)
Map 65

Hiking • Wildlife • Historic and nature interpretation

Facilities: Trails, picnic tables, toilets, hand-carry boat launch, interpretive signs

Area: 600 acres; 24,000 feet of shoreline on Woodard and Chapman Bays

🚗 From I-5 take Exit 105 (City Center), and then head north on Plum Street, which in ¾ mile becomes Bay Drive, which in turn becomes Boston Harbor Road NE in 2 miles. Continue north for 3 miles, then head northeast on Woodard Bay Road NE to reach the DNR property in 1¾ miles.

🚣 Chapman Bay is closed to boaters. Woodard Bay is open to paddlecraft from April 15 to Labor Day; a hand-carry boat launch is just inside the conservation area gate on Whitman Road NE.

Two small fingers, Chapman and Woodard Bays, fan out from the west side of Henderson Inlet, south of Dickenson Point. Parking is available along the deadend spur, Whitman Road NE, at the west end of the bridge. ❀ Paddlers

Woodard Bay is a quiet backwater that attracts paddlers.

should look out for a swift current under the bridge at maximum tidal flow. At minus tide this portion of Woodard Bay dries—plan trips accordingly. Portions of the area are fenced for safety and to protect the wildlife.

The old access road to the log-booming area, Whitman Road NE, is gated just beyond Woodard Bay Road NE. The remainder of the road and a trail that explores the woodland on the west side of the property are open to foot traffic. Whitman Road leads ½ mile north to the head of a grass field above

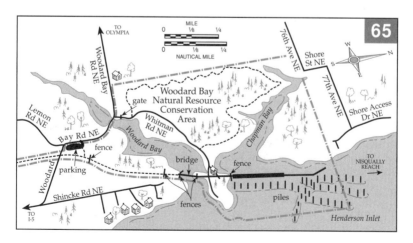

Lumber in Woodard Bay

The first settler in the Henderson Bay area was Harvey Rice Woodard, for whom Woodard Bay is named. He filed a donation land claim for 320 acres on the bay in 1854, cleared some acreage, and moved his family to a farm on the site. The Indian Wars of 1855–1856 drove the family to the safety of Olympia, where they remained. Woodard sold off the property in segments to loggers, and then land speculators bought and platted portions of the property in anticipation of a Northern Pacific Railroad termination at Olympia. When the NP went to Tacoma instead, the speculators folded (or were convicted of fraud) and the tidelands were purchased by an oyster company. Eventually most of the property was acquired by the Weyerhaeuser Company.

The lumber company was attracted to the bay by its need to find an economical means of getting timber from its large forest holdings near Vail, in southern Pierce County, to its major lumber mills in Everett. The waters of Woodard and Chapman Bays were deep enough that log booming and rafting could go on at any tide level, and the bays were well protected from storms. The company built private railroad lines to the bay and, beginning in 1928, unloaded an average of 140 railroad cars of logs a day here. The logs were secured into rafts and towed to the Everett mills.

By the 1970s the Everett mills had become obsolete, and the logs from Weyerhaeuser's timberlands were more profitably exported to the Far East via the Port of Tacoma. All log storage activity in Woodard Bay ceased in 1984, and in 1988 the state DNR purchased the land for a Natural Resource Conservation Area.

the log-boom railroad track. Interpretive displays describe this unique log-booming operation and name some of the wildlife that might be seen at the site. In the bay to the north, only the pilings remain, a faint memory of the bay's past log-boom activity. Harbor seals haul on out remnants of the old log-boom workings, bald eagles nest in snags, and clams and ghost shrimp regenerate in the shoreline mud of the bays. The area might be closed in spring to protect pupping seals.

A trail leaves Whitman Road a short distance beyond the gate for a climb west, through woods, along the conservation area boundary. Pause at trail-side benches to listen to the chorus of bird calls in the surrounding woods. The trail continues north, and then rounds a corner to an overlook of the crooked finger at the end of Chapman Bay. Here the path heads east through oak, cedar, alder, and damnable stinging nettles; views of Chapman Bay always appear through the trees. After dropping past a swampy spot, the way returns to the road near the caretaker residence.

A second trail along the old logging railroad track leaves a parking area south of Woodard Bay and follows the south shore of the bay for ½ mile to a gated trestle with views of the booming grounds and Henderson Inlet.

chapter ten

Case Inlet and Pickering Passage

LONG AGO, AT THE TIME OF THE CONTINENTAL GLACIERS, there was no division between Hood Canal and lower Puget Sound. As it retreated, the last Pleistocene glacier left behind a 2-mile-wide, 400-foot-high pile of till that now separates the northern tip of Case Inlet from the remote end of Hood Canal. As it is, the wide channel of Case Inlet heads northward resolutely for 15 miles toward the heart of the Kitsap Peninsula and fizzles out in a mudflat. For the recreation seeker, however, this geological quirk is a blessing; the remote inlet remains the most pristine of South Puget Sound waterways. The only town is the small community of Allyn, situated where SR 302 skirts the west shore of North Bay. Three parks offer public recreational facilities, while numerous coves and tiny bays provide shelter for cruising boats.

South Sound waterways lie in the shadow of the Olympic Mountains.

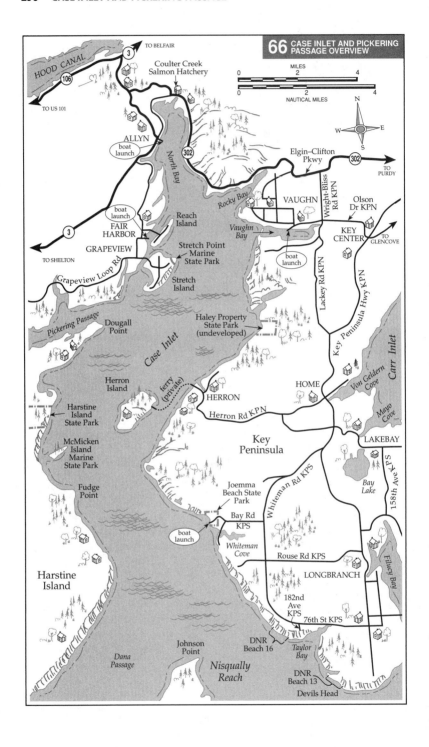

HOOD CANAL

TO BELFAIR

3

106

TO US 101

Coulter Creek
Salmon Hatchery

ALLYN
boat
launch

North Bay

302

Elgin–Clifton
Pkwy

302

TO
PURDY

boat
launch

FAIR
HARBOR

3

TO SHELTON

GRAPEVIEW

Grapeview Loop Rd

Reach
Island

Rocky Bay

VAUGHN

Vaughn
Bay

boat
launch

KEY
CENTER

TO
GLENCOVE

Wright-Bliss
Rd KPN

Olson
Dr KPN

Stretch Point
Marine
State Park

Stretch
Island

Lackey Rd KPN

Key Peninsula Hwy KPN

Pickering Passage

Dougall
Point

Case Inlet

Haley Property
State Park
(undeveloped)

Carr Inlet

Herron
Island

ferry
(private)

HERRON

HOME

Von Geldern
Cove

Harstine
Island
State Park

Herron Rd KPN

Key
Peninsula

Mayo
Cove

LAKEBAY

McMicken
Island
Marine
State Park

Bay
Lake

158th Ave KPS

Fudge
Point

Joemma
Beach State
Park

Whiteman Rd KPS

boat
launch

Bay Rd
KPS

Whiteman
Cove

Rouse Rd KPS

LONGBRANCH

Filbey Bay

Harstine
Island

182nd
Ave
KPS

76th St KPS

Johnson
Point

Dana
Passage

DNR
Beach 16

Taylor
Bay

Nisqually
Reach

DNR
Beach 13

Devils Head

MILES
0   2   4

NAUTICAL MILES
0   2   4

N
W   E
S

KEY PENINSULA SHORE
Map 66

Inside Case Inlet and along the eastern shoreline, Mount Rainier, which dominates the skyline in Carr Inlet and Nisqually Reach, drops from sight behind the Key Peninsula. Now the tourist is rewarded with broad panoramas of the Olympic Mountains. On land, an especially fine view of the Olympics is from SR 302 northbound between Vaughn Bay and Coulter Creek.

Devils Head and Taylor Bay   Map 66

Boating • Paddling • Fishing

From SR 16, 3 miles north of Gig Harbor, take the SR 302/Purdy exit and follow Purdy Drive (SR 302) north for ³/₄ mile to Purdy. Head southwest on SR 302, which becomes Key Peninsula Highway KPN for 12 miles to the community of Home. At a Y-intersection 1.5 miles south of Home bear southwest on Whiteman Road KPS, and follow it for 5 miles to where it bends east and becomes 76th Street KPS. In ¹/₂ mile turn south on 182nd Avenue KPS to reach road end in a short distance.

Taylor Bay is 1³/₄ n.m. northeast of the marinas on Johnson Point, where boats can be launched.

The Key Peninsula terminates in an abrupt 200-foot-high promontory called Devils Head. Immediately north of Devils Head the shore is indented by Taylor Bay. ❋Cruising boats can find some limited anchorages near the mouth, although the bay shallows rapidly and all the shoreline is private. A hand-carry boat launch can be found on the north side of Taylor Bay at the end of 182nd Avenue KPS. Depending on the tide level, a scramble down the boulder bank might be required.

Fishing near Devils Head

Two public DNR beaches, accessible only by boat, are north and south of the bay. DNR Beach 13, with 1300 feet of shoreline, lies between Devils Head and Taylor Bay. This is one of the nicest DNR tidelands in South Puget Sound, with a broad gravel bar fronting a grassy meadow. As with most DNR beaches, property above the mean high tide level is private.

Immediately north of Taylor Bay lies DNR Beach 16. The narrow, 2500-foot-long beach is driftwood and gravel at its upper reaches, with sand at low tide. Open to the sweeping waters of Nisqually Reach, beach life here is limited to some piddock clams and sea cucumbers.

Joemma Beach State Park   Map 67

Camping • Picnicking • Boating • Paddling • Fishing • Clamming, crabbing • Hiking • Beach walking

Facilities: 19 standard campsites (2 disabled accessible), 3 primitive campsites, CMT campsite, picnic shelter, picnic tables, toilets, 1-lane paved launch ramp, dock and floats, 5 mooring buoys, trail

Area: 122 acres; 3000 feet of shoreline on Case Inlet

Follow the directions to Whiteman Road KPS, as described for Taylor Bay. Follow Whiteman Road for 2½ miles to Bay Road KPS, signed to the park. Head west on Bay Road to reach the park in ¾ mile.

Joemma Beach is on the east side of Case Inlet, just north of Whiteman Cove, 4½ n.m. north of Devils Head.

North of Taylor Bay, the Case Inlet shoreline skirts steep bluffs for 2 miles before arriving at the next indentation, Whiteman Cove. Joemma Beach State Park, immediately north of Whiteman Cove, holds the only land-access campground on this side of Case Inlet. The park makes a nice overnight stop for campers and cyclists touring the Key Peninsula, as well as for boaters and paddlers cruising or fishing in the inlet.

For boaters, the park offers an excellent 500-foot-long dock with space on

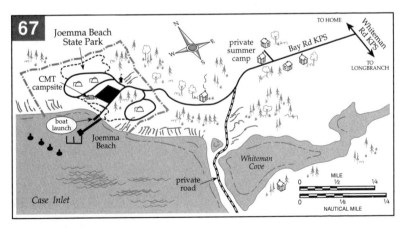

Dungeness crab can be caught off the dock at Joemma Beach State Park.

floats for about twenty boats. Additional moorage is provided by five buoys north from the end of the dock. The floats are removed from late September to May to prevent storm damage.

For many years this site, then known as Robert F. Kennedy Recreation Area, was a rustic gem, with primitive campsites and a dilapidated boat float that appealed only to the desperate. The DNR-owned facilities were beautifully remodeled and then transferred to state parks and renamed Joemma Beach—a combination of the names of Joe and Emma Smith, who lived here between 1917 and 1932.

Two campground loops lie just inside the gate; both have water faucets and toilets; each has one site for disabled campers, and some have water views. Primitive and CMT sites are on the hillside between the northern loop and the picnic shelter.

A short trail on the northeast side of the park wanders through second-growth forest; trailheads are along the northern campground loop road. The smooth beach, which slopes out gradually, is peppered with small rocks and has little exposed sand except at extremely low tides. To the north, steep bluffs of glacial till rise 150 feet.

South, the rocky shore continues to Whiteman Cove, where the bluff tempers somewhat to 20 to 50 feet high. Wave action built up a sandspit at the mouth of the cove, and over time it has totally blocked the entrance. Today the cove is actually a lagoon with a road-topped bar.

Herron Island   Map 66

Just as Eagle Island is not named for eagles, Herron Island is not named for herons, abundant though they might be in the vicinity. The island's name honors Petty Officer Lewis Herron, barrel maker for the Wilkes Expedition. (It didn't take much to get a piece of real estate named after you in those days.)

The mile-long island on the east side of Case Inlet, 2 n.m. northwest of Joemma State Park, is completely private and is accessible only by the island's privately operated ferry. The mainland ferry slip is on Herron Road S, on a small point of land northeast of the island.

❀ Boats of any draft navigating behind the island should be wary of a shallow sandbar protruding northeasterly from Herron Island, but midchannel depths between the island and shoreline are at least 2 fathoms. Tidal currents are swift in the shallow channel.

Haley Property State Park (Undeveloped)   Map 66

Fishing • Picnicking • Paddling • Beach walking • Clamming

Facilities: Primitive CMT campsite
Area: 178 acres; 1980 feet of saltwater shoreline on Case Inlet
🛥 The property is on the east side of Case Inlet, 2 n.m. north of the Herron Island ferry landing and ³⁄₁₀ n.m. south of Dutcher Cove.

This property on the northeast shoreline of Case Inlet was purchased by the state parks from the Haley family, of Brown and Haley candy fame. Plans

Raccoon tracks on the beach mark the presence of a nocturnal visitor.

for park development met with resistance from abutting property owners, who opposed a full-fledged park with land access. The park remains undeveloped, and probably is all the more beautiful because of it. The heavily wooded site surrounds a drainage, whose stream was once dammed to form a freshwater lagoon just above the beach. The dam broke in a 1994 earthquake, and the lagoon disappeared. The surrounding woodland is home for otters, beaver, deer, foxes, osprey—and possibly Hobbits?

The park is accessible by boats that can be landed on the wide sand and gravel beach. A 30-foot-high light-colored bank marks the north side of Dutcher Cove; there are a few beachfront residences along the south side of the cove. The park property, 500 yards south of Dutcher Cove, can be identified by a wide, gently tapering beach below a gravel bar, topped by an old, weather-silvered totem pole at its north end. The beach is open to clam digging. See comments in the introduction regarding harvesting shellfish.

Vaughn Bay (Pierce County)   Map 66
Boating • Paddling

Facilities: 1-lane paved launch ramp

🚗 From Key Center, head west on 92nd Street KPN, which in two blocks bends northwest as Olson Drive KPN. At its four-way intersection with Vaughn Road KPN (to the south), Wright-Bliss Road KPN (to the north), and Hall Road KPN (to the west), continue straight ahead on Hall Road for ½ mile to its intersection with Van Slyke Road at the community of Vaughn. The ramp is one block downhill from the intersection.

🛥 Vaughn Bay is on the east side of Case Inlet, due east of Reach Island and 5¾ n.m. north of Herron Island.

The north end of Case Inlet splits into three fingers. The largest of these, North Bay, continues on for another 3 miles; two smaller, shallower coves, Vaughn Bay and Rocky Bay, reach eastward. The ¼-mile-long sandspit guarding the west end of Vaughn Bay is a public beach from the top of the spit to the low-tide line on its western side. The sand and gravel bar offers a variety of clams and some red rock crab.

Access to the spit is by boat only, but a public launch ramp is nearby on the north shore of Vaughn Bay. The ramp is not usable at a minus tide. ❋ The bay is shallowest along its north side, so after launching follow the south shore to about 200 yards from the entrance spit and parallel the spit north to the entrance before heading out into Case Inlet.

NORTH BAY AND ALLYN
Map 68

The northwest end of Case Inlet is known as North Bay. Here SR 3 from Belfair joins SR 302 at the small community of Allyn. ❋ The west side of North Bay is extremely shallow, so boats of any draft should favor the east side of the bay until due east of the public pier at Allyn. North from the public pier the bay dries to mudflats and commercial oyster beds at low tide.

North Bay Public Access (State DNR)   Map 68
Shellfish • Beach walking • Paddling

Facilities: Toilets
Area: 6000 feet of tidelands on Case Inlet (North Bay)

🚗 From SR 3, 3 miles north of Allyn, head east on SR 302. In 2½ miles, just north of a powerline, look for a public access area on the west side of the road.

What a nifty surprise! An inconspicuous public access on the east side of North Bay opens onto a broad beach extending north for nearly a mile toward the end of the bay. The gradually sloping cobble and sand beach offers extensive tidelands for shellfish gathering at low tide. At high tide it is possible to launch hand-carry craft at the site. The only amenities are a parking area and a pair of toilets. See comments in the introduction regarding harvesting shellfish.

Allyn   Map 68

Boating • Paddling • Fishing • Picnicking

Facilities: 1-lane paved launch ramp, public pier, floats, guest moorage, marine pumpout, portable toilet dump, waterfront park, picnic tables, picnic shelter, children's play area, toilets. *Nearby:* Groceries, fuel (service stations), restaurants

Allyn is on SR 3, 3¾ miles south of Belfair, or 21½ miles north of Shelton. The park is one block east of the highway at E Drum Street, near the north end of town.

Allyn is on the northwest side of Case Inlet, near its north end. ❀ The water is quite shoal a long distance out from shore; boats of any draft should not try to approach closer than the end of the long pier, except at high tide (and then cautiously).

At the north end of town the Port of Allyn has developed a very nice little waterfront park that includes a public dock and boat-launch ramp. A prominent sign beside the highway at E Drum Street identifies it.

A single-lane concrete launch ramp is 300 yards north of the dock; however, it is not usable at a minus tide when the water retreats well out into the bay. A second ramp along the south side of the pier is usable, but is no longer maintained. A broad lawn uphill from the parking lot holds picnic tables and a children's play area, while a tree-shaded lawn to the north boasts a covered pavilion and more picnic tables. The 550-foot-long dock is a popular fishing spot. Floats at the end of the dock have about 200 feet of

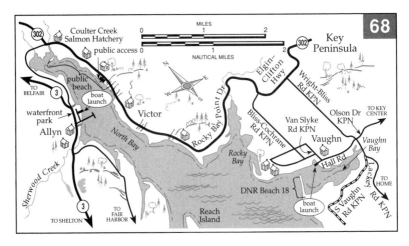

The quiet, protected water off Allyn is ideal for easy kayaking.

moorage space (overnight moorage permitted) and a water outlet but no power. One float has a marine pumpout station; a portable toilet dump is near the head of the pier. Boaters in need of supplies will find grocery, drug, and hardware stores a few blocks to the south.

Fair Harbor   Map 69

Boating • Paddling • Picnicking

Facilities: Marina: Gas, guest moorage, power, restrooms, showers, store (groceries, ice, fishing supplies, gifts), guest pavilion. *Adjacent:* Single-lane paved launch ramp. Parking and toilet nearby.

The marina and adjacent launch ramp are on Grapeview Loop Road, 3 miles from its north end. The road loops east from SR 3, with the north end near the Allyn city limits, and the south end another 6½ miles to the south.

The marina is best approached from the south, because at low tide the channel to the north holds only 1 foot of water. At high tide the 16-foot clearance of the Reach Island bridge is a hazard to be considered by sailboats. Boats entering the channels from either the north or the south should favor the west shoreline to avoid baring rocks midchannel and along the east side.

South from the community of Allyn, nestled against the western shore of Case Inlet, are Reach and Stretch Islands. Although they are largely private, the pair of islands do have some interest for land and water tourists. The more northerly Reach Island is also known by its realtor-hype name of Treasure Island. It is accessible by a bridge spanning the 200-yard-wide channel, but the entire island and shorelands are private.

Reach Island serves as protection for a small marina and launch ramp south of the bridge on an inlet locally called Fair Harbor. Although the marina caters mainly to long-term moorage, about 350 feet of guest moorage is available. Gas is available on the floats where there is also a small store (limited hours in winter). The two-lane concrete launch ramp north of the marina, operated by the Port of Grapeview, is for public use.

Stretch Island   Map 69

Picnicking • Paddling • Boating • Beach walking • Clamming • Fishing • Swimming

Facilities: *State Park:* 5 mooring buoys, no water, no toilets
Area: *State Park:* 4.2 acres; 610 feet of shoreline

The island can be reached by land via a bridge ½ mile south of the Fair Harbor Marina; at a sharp corner turn east from Grapeview Loop Road onto E Eckert Road, which crosses the bridge onto the island.

The state park is on the northwest tip of Stretch Island. The nearest launch ramps are at Fair Harbor or Allyn. There is no land access.

Stretch Island, ¼ mile south of Reach Island, also has no public property accessible from land but it does have a DNR beach and a small state park that is accessible from the water. At the turn of the century the island supported the beginnings of a western Washington wine industry and was known as Grape Island; the onshore community is Grapeview. Today grapes from Stretch Island vineyards are used primarily for juice and fruit leather, although a few boutique wineries operate here.

DNR Beach • The passage behind Stretch Island, which dries at low tide, is also constricted by the 14-foot-high fixed bridge. ✸Some protected anchorages can be found in the small cove on the southwest side of the island,

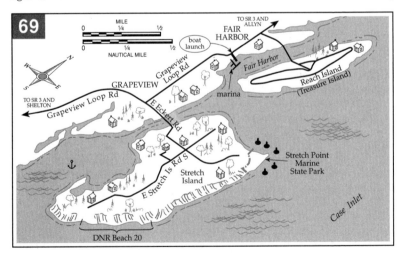

At Stretch Point State Park a giant driftwood log dwarfs a kayaker.

although it is exposed to weather from the south. Just around the southern tip of the island on the southeast side, an 1800-foot segment of tidelands is a public DNR beach accessible only by boat. The gravel beach below the steep clay bank offers some chances to gather oysters and mussels at low tide. Please respect adjoining private uplands and beaches

Stretch Point State Park • The small northeast tip of Stretch Island is a tiny day-use marine state park. Five mooring buoys placed around the point are within arm's reach of shore at minus tides, but because of the rapid drop-off they have adequate depth for most boats.

The gravel beach wrapping around the point provides an inviting picnic or swimming stop for passing boaters. At the heart of the point is a small, tree-ringed saltwater lagoon. The park has no drinking water or restroom facilities, so onshore camping is not permitted. There is no regular garbage pickup here; take all trash away with you.

HARSTINE ISLAND EAST SHORE
Map 70

Because most Harstine Island recreation sites are reached via the bridge over Pickering Passage, the island itself is included later in this chapter. However, those sites on the east shore of the island that can be reached by water from Case Inlet are described here.

Harstine Island State Park and DNR Beach 24   Map 70

Hiking • Paddling • Beach walking • Clamming • Fishing • Scuba diving • Picnicking

Facilities: Trails, picnic tables, toilet
Area: *State park:* 308 acres; 1600 feet of shoreline on Case Inlet. *Beach 24:* 5400 feet of shoreline

🚗 Eight miles north of Shelton turn east from SR 3 onto E Pickering Road. At an intersection in 3¼ miles continue east on E Harstine Bridge Road. The Harstine Island bridge is 100 yards east of this intersection. Cross the bridge and head north on E North Island Drive for 3½ miles to a T-intersection, and turn south on South End Road. In 1 mile turn east on gravel E Yates Road, and at a Y-intersection in 1 mile take the spur to the south into the park.

🛥 The park beach is on the east side of Harstine Island 1 n.m. north of McMicken Island. Nearest launch ramps are at Fair Harbor and Joemma Beach State Park.

Although its facilities are spartan, this small park provides easy access to one of the nicest beaches on South Puget Sound. From the parking lot a ¼-mile trail leads south through dense brush and second-growth trees. Picnic sites, each with a table on a gravel pad, are strung along the path. At the edge of a 100-foot-high forested bank, another ¼-mile-long trail drops down a ravine toward the beach. Log benches are provided for much-needed uphill rest stops along this steep section. At a junction near the bottom of the ravine, the path straight ahead climbs steeply back to the top of the bluff and loops back to the east side of the parking area. The beach trail to the right switchbacks downhill, reaching the gravel beach 1 mile north of McMicken Island.

The mile-long section of tidelands stretching north from McMicken Island is DNR Beach 24; most of the uplands are private. The gravel beach, which lies beneath a steep bank, tapers gently to sand and mud that contains a few clams and oysters, as well as a profusion of sand dollars. At extreme low tide the beach can be walked all the way onto McMicken Island. Portions of the shoreland are always soggy; wear boots or be prepared for wet feet.

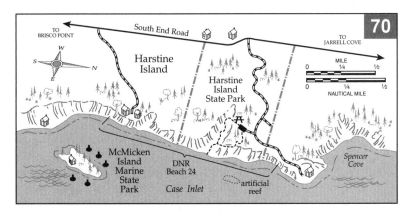

Huge cedars edge the trail at Harstine Island State Park.

For anglers, the most interesting feature of this beach is the artificial reef, composed of old automobile tires, placed offshore in 25 feet of water. It provides a haven for marine organisms that establish their homes on the rough surfaces, for tiny animals such as crabs and shrimp that seek shelter in the nooks and crannies, and for larger fish such as lingcod that come here to feed. Fishing and scuba diving in the vicinity are excellent.

McMicken Island Marine State Park   Map 71

Fishing • Boating • Paddling • Picnicking • Clamming • Beach walking • Hiking • Swimming

Facilities: 5 mooring buoys, composting toilet, no water
Area: 11.4 acres; 1661 feet of shoreline on Case Inlet

McMicken Island is on Case Inlet off the east side of Harstine Island. Nearest launch ramp is at Joemma Beach State Park 2½ n.m. to the southeast.

Here's an entire island to explore! With the exception of a triangular, fenced acreage enclosing some cabins and sheds on the south side of the park, all of McMicken Island is a state park. The fenced area is the property of the island's previous owner, who retained a lifetime lease as a contingency of sale of the island.

Mooring buoys float offshore, while a good holding bottom offers anchoring on either side of the island. ⚙ A large rock erratic, deposited by a Pleistocene glacier, is conspicuous at low tide on the south shore, but is covered at high water; use care anchoring here. Also exercise caution

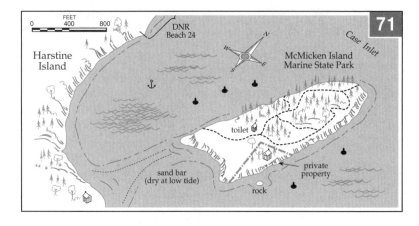

when passing on the west side of the island because the sandspit is barely covered at high tide.

Sandy beaches on the west end are quite shallow and warm enough in

A profusion of sand dollars is found on the sand spit that links McMicken Island to Harstine Island.

summer for saltwater wading and swimming. During low tide clamming is sometimes good, with red rock crab and some oysters available on the eastern end of the island. Although the island is joined to Harstine Island at low tide by a sandspit, approach to the island is limited to boaters or to hikers from Harstine Island State Park. When water covers the sandspit, DNR tidelands stretching north along the Harstine Island shore are within easy dinghy reach of the park moorages.

A composting toilet is just at the edge of the forest on the northwest corner of the island. There is no garbage pickup on the island, so be sure to carry yours away with you.

An unimproved trail system runs the length of the island through dense second-growth forest. One branch of the trail stays inland, while another skirts bluffs 50 feet above the beach on the southeast side. None of the trails have easy access to the shore. Signs warn that poison oak grows on the island. Beware!

PICKERING PASSAGE
Map 72

The ½-mile-wide finger of Pickering Passage bends around the west side of Harstine Island, connecting Case Inlet to the western channels of South Puget Sound. At its western end the waterway divides as it flows around Squaxin Island and becomes Peale Passage on the east and Squaxin Passage at its southwestern extremity.

Pickering Passage once offered an alternative route around Harstine Island when Harstine was reached from the mainland only by ferry. The ferry has now been replaced by a fixed bridge across the passage at Graham Point, which restricts that route to boats with a vertical clearance of less than 31 feet.

❁Tidal currents in the passage contradict logic; the flood tide current flows south, not north, reaching velocities of as much as 2½ knots near its southern end. Look out for an unmarked shoal that extends well into the passage at the point where it joins Hammersley Inlet. This shoal and the bridge are the only navigational hazards in the waterway.

McLane Cove • This gunkholer's delight, at the northwest end of Pickering Passage, just off the tip of Harstine Island, holds several anchorages, although there are no public shorelands. An old highway bridge once crossed McLane Cove midway, but the present highway skirts its northern end. The cove is at least 20 feet deep up to the point of the old bridge crossing. Anchorages are wherever one pleases.

Little McLane Cove is a delight.

Latimer's Landing (Mason County)   Map 72
Boating • Paddling • Fishing • Crabbing

Facilities: 1-lane paved launch ramp with boarding float, toilet

🚐 Eight miles north of Shelton turn east from SR 3 onto E Pickering Road. At an intersection in 3¼ miles continue east on E Harstine Bridge Road. Latimer's Landing is 100 yards east of this intersection.

🚤 On the west side of Pickering Passage immediately north of the Harstine Island bridge.

There are no public boat-launch facilities on Harstine Island itself; however, Latimer's Landing, an excellent boat-launch ramp is at the west end of the bridge leading to the island. This launch facility's ample gravel parking lot is just north of the west approach to the Harstine Island bridge. The single-lane concrete ramp, with an adjoining concrete boarding float, drops sharply into Pickering Passage. The ramp is usable at all tide levels.

HARSTINE ISLAND
Map 72

Although it is almost as large as Vashon Island, Harstine remains an area of sparse residences and summer homes, owing to its remote location in this far reach of South Puget Sound. Portions of the island are heavily logged, and a major real estate development, Harstine Point, is on the northern

The launch ramp at Latimer's Landing gives boating access to beaches in Pickering Passage.

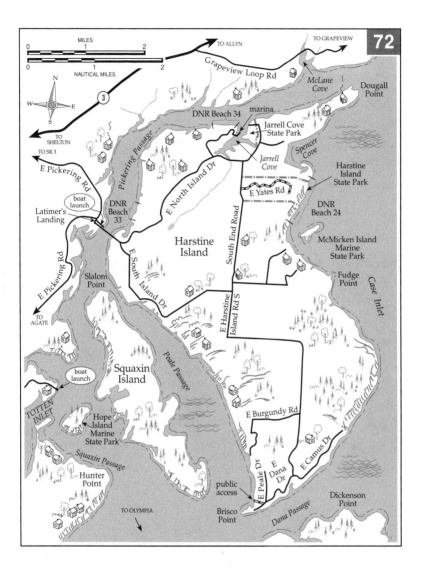

end. A beach with picnic shelters at Dougall Point and a moorage basin around the corner at Indian Cove, all part of this development, are for use by members only.

The island's shoreline is totally private, with the exception of a few isolated DNR beaches and two state parks. A small commercial marina lies on Jarrell Cove, just across from the state park. Beaches and other recreation sites that face on Case Inlet, on the east side of the island, are described earlier in this chapter.

Harstine Island DNR Beaches—West Side   Map 72

Two public DNR beaches are on the west side of Harstine Island, facing on Pickering Passage. The more southerly, DNR Beach 33, which is accessible only by water, is 1/2 mile north of the bridge, directly across from the boat launch at Latimer's Landing. The 1200-foot-long beach is narrow, with overhanging brush. The tidelands have potential harvests of a few clams and oysters.

Immediately west of the entrance to Jarrell Cove, DNR Beach 34 stretches for nearly 1/2 mile along Pickering Passage to the mouth of a tiny bay. A white post with a black top marks the western boundary—unless it has been vandalized. This beach, too, is narrow but less overhung with vegetation, making walking more pleasant. Gravel throughout its length, with a small, muddy bight midway at low tide, the beach also might have some oysters and clams.

Jarrell Cove Marina   Map 73

Boating • Paddling • Picnicking

Facilities: Guest moorage (power, water), gas and diesel, propane, trailer dump station, marine pumpout, portable toilet dump, groceries, ice, restrooms, showers, laundry, picnicking

🚗   Eight miles north of Shelton turn east from SR 3 onto E Pickering Road. At an intersection in 3 1/4 miles continue east on E Harstine Bridge Road. The Harstine Island bridge is 100 yards east of this intersection. Cross the bridge and head north on E North Island Drive for 2 3/4 miles, and turn west on E Haskill Hill

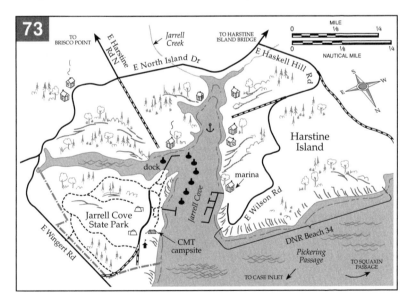

Road, which becomes E Wilson Road in ¾ mile, then arrives at the marina in another ½ mile.

🛥️ The marina is on the west side of the entrance to Jarrell Cove, on the north end of Harstine Island. Nearest launch ramps are at Latimer's Landing and Fair Harbor.

The only commercial marina on Harstine Island fills the west side of the entrance to Jarrell Cove with floats that provide some one hundred permanent and guest slips. The marina has fuel and groceries, as well as a couple dozen picnic sites on two tree-shaded grass flats overlooking the floats.

Jarrell Cove State Park   Map 73

Fishing • Hiking • Birdwatching • Camping • Picnicking • Boating • Paddling

Facilities: 18 campsites, CMT campsites, group camp, floats, 14 mooring buoys, picnic shelters, picnic tables, restrooms, showers (disabled access), trails, marine pumpout station, portable toilet dump, horseshoe pits

Area: 42.6 acres; 3506 feet of shoreline on Jarrell Cove

🚐 After crossing the Harstine Island bridge onto the island, turn north on E North Island Drive, and in 3.5 miles, at E Wingert Road, bear north to reach the park in another ¾ mile.

🛥️ The park is on the east side of Jarrell Cove, on the north side of Harstine Island, 2 n.m. southwest of Dougall Point. Nearest launch ramps are at Latimer's Landing 3¾ n.m. to the southwest and Fair Harbor 4½ n.m. to the northeast.

You might expect this remote little park on a far corner of the sound to be undiscovered, but it is one of the worst-kept secrets of the boating fraternity. On a sunny summer weekend it is often jam-packed, despite its generous mooring facilities. Off-season, however, the park is lightly used; that might be the best time to visit and quietly enjoy its charms.

The heart of the park is a meadowy camping area on a bluff above the cove. Campsites are informal (only four reservable), with picnic tables and concrete fireplaces scattered about. There are no surfaced pull-offs or hookups for trailers or RVs. A few walk-in campsites are on the west side of the park, just above the small float. At the far north end of this spot are CMT sites, reserved for visitors in hand-powered boats.

Many boaters come into the cove to take advantage of the park's excellent moorages and never go ashore. The small float on the northwest shore of the park can accommodate three or four boats. A larger float extends from the southwest corner of the park across the head of the western finger inlet. The float has about 10 feet of water alongside, and most of the buoys have 8 to 10 feet of water below them at a minus tide. When the floats and mooring buoys are filled, good anchorages can be found farther into the cove, ❄but be aware that the head of the cove is quite shallow.

Along the cove's eastern shore a narrow finger protruding inland invites exploration by dinghy. At high tide a thick growth of trees and vines dangle over the water's edge. At minus tide its character changes completely as the finger drains to a mucky mudflat. A heron rookery in the area is home to

The floats and anchorages of Jarrell Cove are a major cruising destination in South Puget Sound.

spindle-legged spectators who warily observe intruders. Heron nests, flat platforms of sticks, can be seen in some tall fir trees near the inlet. A variety of other waterfowl can often be spotted, depending on the season.

Several trails, some official and others just plain tramped, wind through the dense forest around the park's boundary. One leads to the land side of a mini-cove, but beach travel is impossible at high tide and unappealing in the mud of low tide.

Brisco Point   Map 72

Paddling

Facilities: Hand-carried put-in

🚙 From the Harstine Island bridge head south on E South Island Drive to a T-intersection with E Harstine Island Road South. Turn south on the latter; at a T- intersection in another 5 miles head south on E Dana Drive. At the intersection of E Dana Drive and E Peale Drive in ½ mile, continue downhill for 100 feet to a gravel road to the west (unmarked E Squaxin Drive). The road ends at the beach in about 200 yards (don't block adjacent driveways).

The road-end beach is on the southwest tip of Harstine Island on the northeast side of the entrance to the small lagoon behind Brisco Point. Nearest launch ramp is at Boston Harbor 1³/₄ n.m. to the southwest.

At the far south end of Harstine Island a county road deadends at the beach at Brisco Point. For those wanting to launch a canoe or kayak or other hand-carried boat, this access offers the possibility of an excursion up Pickering Passage with a car pickup at Latimer's Landing or Jarrell Cove.

The paved road continuing downhill to the southwest from the junction of E Dana Drive and E Peale Drive is private, but the steep gravel road dropping due west (Squaxin Drive) is a county road. It is narrow and deadends in about 200 yards at a bank above Peale Passage just north of Brisco Point. From here there are nice views out to Squaxin Island and of the pretty lagoon on the north side of Brisco Point. All adjoining property is private.

PEALE AND SQUAXIN PASSAGES
Map 72

After the populated shorelands of much of South Puget Sound, a cruise down Peale or Squaxin Passage comes as a bit of a shock. Both Squaxin Island and its little neighbor to the west, Hope Island, must appear today much as when early explorers saw them. Because neither island is connected to the mainland by bridges or ferries, they have escaped the real estate developers' chain saws and bulldozers. Squaxin Island has escaped development for an additional reason: it is entirely an Indian reservation, with the exception of a small section held by the state.

Squaxin Island

The 1,500-acre reservation on Squaxin Island was set aside for Native Americans of five tribes by the Medicine Creek Treaty of 1854. Prior to that time the tribes had inhabited the area around Sherwood Creek, some 10 miles to the north near Allyn. The island was one of three areas where South Puget Sound Natives were confined in order to give white settlers clear access to more desirable lands, an arrangement that ultimately precipitated the tragic Indian War of 1855.

Under the terms of the treaty, the tribes were given the collective tribal name of Squaxin, thus losing their distinction as politically autonomous groups. They were assigned to live on the 2,000-acre island; however, the lack of a source of potable water defeated their attempts to establish a permanent community or any type of commercial industry. The Natives had to bring water from the mainland, even for their cattle and horses. By the 1930s most had left the island to live on the mainland or Harstine Island.

❋The passage around Hope Island's east side, between it and Squaxin Island, is at least 9 feet deep, but peculiar shoaling patterns suggest cautious use by boats of any draft. Peale Passage, the water boundary between Squaxin and Harstine Islands, offers good bottomfishing along its shallower western edge. The passage is pinched to 100 yards wide at its northern end opposite Slalom Point. The center of the channel is maintained at a depth of 10 feet, but ebb currents of up to 2 knots can occur and tide rips are possible.

Hope Island Marine State Park   Map 74

Boating • Paddling • Camping • Picnicking • Beach walking • Clamming • Fishing • Hiking

Facilities: 4 campsites, CMT campsites, picnic sites, toilets, 5 mooring buoys, 1.5 miles of trail, caretaker cabin, no water
Area: 106.11 acres; 8541 feet of shoreline on Squaxin and Pickering Passages
⛵ Hope Island lies at the confluence of Totten Inlet, Hammersley Inlet, and Pickering Passage. Nearest launch ramp is at Arcadia ³/₄ n.m. to the northwest.

Hope Island was purchased in 1898 by Louis Schmidt, brother of Leopold Schmidt of Olympia Brewery fame, and he established a small farm on the island. The family had a son who was mentally and physically disabled, which might have been their reason for selecting such a secluded spot. The farm provided a self-sufficient life for the family; grapes were grown for a nearby winery, and foxes were raised for their pelts. In time, the family moved back to Germany. A few rusting farm implements, a decrepit windmill, fox pens, an orchard, and vestiges of an old vineyard are all that now remain.

In 1990 the State Parks and Recreation Commission acquired Hope Island, the last undeveloped island in South Puget Sound, saving the 106-acre, timbered island from development into residential lots and preserving it for the enjoyment of future generations. Due to lack of funding as well as opposition by neighbors, the state has moved cautiously with park development.

The bight on the southeast side of the park holds two mooring buoys; in a clearing above is a caretaker's cabin. Three more buoys are found along

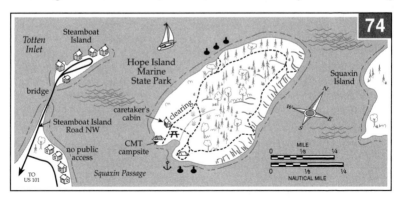

Fascinating Hope Island State Park is on the last undeveloped island in South Puget Sound.

the northwest shore. A toilet and CMT campsites are near the caretaker's cabin on the southwest end of the island.

An informal trail, said to have been beaten out long ago by two horses that were part of the farm, wanders north from the old garden and orchard. The path first passes through groves of second-growth Douglas-fir, alder, and then cedar. Vanilla leaf and grass form a lush understory. The woods wrap you in a buffer of quiet only faintly penetrated by the remote raucous sound of cars and boat motors. The trail finally reaches old-growth forest at the heart of the island.

The beaches are cobble, dropping steeply to sand at minus tide. The bank above the beach is steep and heavily wooded except on the southeast corner of the island, the site of the old vineyard. In a few places grapevines nearly as thick as a person's wrist can be seen entwined around firs, straining upward to reach the sun. A couple of campsites sit above the beach near the old vineyard.

chapter eleven

The Western Inlets and Budd Inlet

FOUR TAPERING FINGERS OF WATER fan out from Squaxin Passage, marking the most westerly limits of Puget Sound. The inlets—Hammersley, Totten, Skookum, and Eld—have limited public access, and roads seldom touch their shorelines; thus, they are best explored by boat. The city of Shelton on Hammersley Inlet is the only major population center in the region.

The long mudflats at the heads of these four Puget Sound inlets are the finest oyster-growing grounds on the Pacific Coast. Here, sun-warmed water reaches temperatures suitable for the mollusk's complicated reproductive cycle, while icy winter water chills and firms their flesh to a gourmet succulence. There

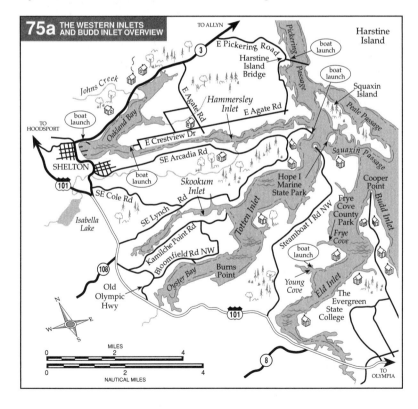

75a THE WESTERN INLETS AND BUDD INLET OVERVIEW

are very few free-for-the-taking oysters in the western inlets. The best way to sample them is to stop at a commercial oyster company; most sell fresh oysters retail and offer a tour of the facility to boot.

⚓ Rock or concrete walls enclosing oyster beds in the shoal portions of the western inlets, especially Totten and Skookum, are a navigational hazard that might cause damage to boats. Slender poles usually mark the boundaries of the beds, but do not rely on them. Consult navigational charts and keep a wary eye.

HAMMERSLEY INLET
Map 75a

Peter Puget passed right by the entrance to Hammersley Inlet without even seeing it, but settlers who discovered it fifty years later took one look at its shores, so thickly covered with prime trees that a person could scarcely

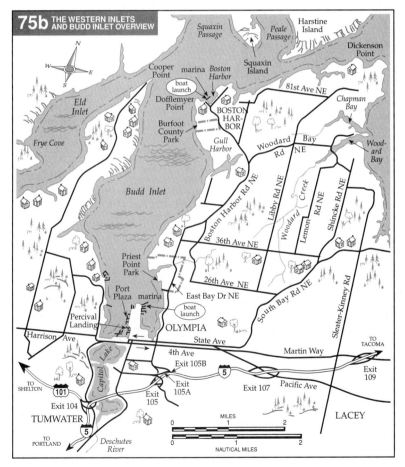

walk through them, and decided they had found paradise. Reports of timber resources sent back to Washington, D.C., were somewhat discounted as products of exuberant imaginations—it was staggering to think of that many board feet of lumber growing on a single acre of land.

Equally as important as the looming forests was the adjoining waterway that provided log staging areas with easy transportation of the harvest to mills, power to operate the mills, and a water transportation link for finished lumber down Puget Sound and on to the booming town of San Francisco. This was, indeed, a logger's utopia.

✸ Hammersley is the narrowest of South Puget Sound's major waterways; visits require cautious navigation to avoid shoals and to account for tidal currents ranging from 3 to 5 knots in some spots. The channel, scarcely 400 yards wide throughout, runs west for 6 miles to the town of Shelton, where it fishhooks back northeast for another 3½ miles and widens to form Oakland Bay. Nearly half of the length of the bay dries at low tide; log-booming grounds and private oyster beds fill much of its area.

Shelton   Map 76

Boating • Fishing • Shopping

Facilities: *Marina:* Guest moorage, power, marine pumpout. portable toilet dump, toilet, 1-lane dirt launch ramp, marine rail. *Shelton:* Restaurants, stores

🚐 Shelton is just east of US 101, 18½ miles north of Olympia, or at the south end of SR 3, 14 miles southwest from Bremerton.

🛥 Shelton is at the west end of Hammersley Inlet, and the southwest end of Oakland Bay.

Shelton was born as a mill town and remains so today, with the slender smokestacks of its lumber mills dominating the cityscape and piles of logs lining its waterfront. Shortly after the arrival of David Shelton in 1853, the

Logs fill the Shelton waterfront on Oak Bay.

first sawmill was built at the mouth of Mill Creek, midway along Hammersley Inlet, by lumber entrepreneurs Michael T. Simmons, Smith Hayes, and Nicholas DeLin, the same group that had built mills at Tumwater and on Commencement Bay. Soon after, other mills were built in the area—at Sherwood Creek on Case Inlet, at Johns Creek farther up Oakland Bay, and eventually within the Shelton Valley. As the supply of nearby trees dwindled, log flumes and then railroad spurs and trucks brought timber to the Shelton mills from the slopes of the Olympic Mountains.

Logged-over land spawned a second industry—growing and harvesting Christmas trees. The town calls itself Christmastown, U.S.A.—a justifiable claim, as some 2 million Christmas trees are shipped from here annually, going to markets along the Pacific Coast as well as to Hawaii, the Philippines, and Japan.

A public boat-launch ramp on Oakland Bay is just off Pine Street near some large fuel tanks. The dirt ramp is extremely soft and muddy, making it unusable at low tide. High tide permits cautious launching of shallow-draft boats. An adjacent marine rail might be intermittently functional. A much better launch facility, described in the section on Arcadia in this chapter, is maintained by the Squaxin Island Tribe at Arcadia.

❋The water approach to Shelton, down Hammersley Inlet, starts from the junction of Pickering and Squaxin Passages. The can buoy that for many

Olympia Oysters

As early as the 1860s settlers were harvesting the abundant little native Olympia oysters for commercial use. The small bivalve, with a shell rarely exceeding 3 inches, was prized for its delicate texture and slightly metallic flavor. At the turn of the century, the state acknowledged the importance of the industry when it first began to set aside tidelands for oyster cultivation. In 1902 seed stock was introduced from the larger Pacific oyster grown in Japan.

A combination of factors caused a serious decline in the beds that produced the Olympia oyster; the most serious of these was believed to be the construction of pulp mills and the resultant discharge of sulfite wastes. Overharvesting of the beds, runoff of muddy silt from onshore construction, and the predations of a small snail known as the Japanese oyster drill, which arrived along with the Japanese oyster, caused further damage to the stock. By the 1960s the annual commercial harvest of the native oysters had dropped to 10 percent of what it had been in the 1930s, and to 1 percent by the 1980s. Today their scarcity, coupled with the high labor costs of harvesting the tiny oysters, makes them the caviar of shellfish.

Pacific oysters proved to be more resistant to both pollution and predation and became the mainstay of the industry; however, with some pollution controls and more advanced oyster-growing technology, the delicate and delicious little Olympia oyster is regaining some of its former commercial prominence.

years marked a large shoal off Arcadia was so repeatedly knocked out by log rafts that the Coast Guard decided to quit replacing it—watch your charts and depth sounder near Hungerford Point to avoid the shoal. The channel squeezes between Cape Cod and the finger of Cape Horn and then follows the south shore to off Cannery Point. Another buoy that once marked deep water in this tenuous section has been abandoned, also because of log raft damage. Here the middle of the channel is deepest, but it again narrows at Libby Point. Bear close to Skookum Point to avoid shoals east of Church Point, and then head back to midchannel to bypass a shoal west of Skookum Point. Midchannel is reasonably deep and safe from here into Shelton. Strong tidal currents are best dealt with by entering the channel on a flood and exiting on an ebb. Refer to a navigational chart for the exact location of shoals.

The few marine facilities offered by Shelton are incidental to its major industry, lumbering. A 60-foot-long public float can be found at the Port

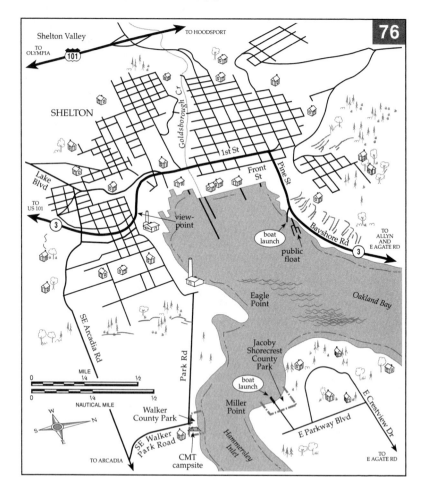

of Shelton moorage on the northeast edge of town. The moorage is near a group of large fuel-storage tanks that are easily spotted from the bay. The public float is sandwiched between private boat houses at the end of the pier adjacent the Shelton Yacht Club. The city center, with its numerous stores and restaurants, is a few blocks from the public float.

Walker County Park (Mason County) Map 76

Picnicking • Beach walking • Fishing

Facilities: Picnic shelter, picnic tables, fireplaces, restrooms, children's play area, quarter basketball hoop, CMT campsite

Area: 6.5 acres; 1650 feet of shoreline on Hammersley Inlet

🚐 Follow the main street (SR 3) south out of Shelton and up a steep grade with fine views over the lumber mills and Oakland Bay. Just beyond the top of the hill, turn east on SE Arcadia Road. In 1½ miles turn north on SE Walker Park Road and drop ½ mile down a wooded ravine to the park.

🛥 On the south shore of Hammersley Inlet, 1 n.m. east of Shelton

This pleasantly wooded park on a slight embankment affords a break in an auto or bicycle tour of the Shelton area. Picnic tables are in a grove of tall trees, with ample space for kids to romp and adults to relax. The park is open from 8:00 AM to dusk; camping is permited only at the CMT site.

The long gravel beach facing on Hammersley Inlet is accessible via remnants of an abandoned launch ramp that drops down to the shore. Small boats can be landed on the beach, but the approach is too shallow for boats of any draft.

Arcadia (Squaxin Island Tribe) Map 75a

Boating • Paddling • Fishing

Facilities: 1-lane paved launch ramp

🚐 To reach the ramp either drive 7¼ miles east of Shelton on SE Arcadia Road or drive 4 miles south of Shelton on US 101, and turn and drive 9 miles east on SE Lynch Road. From either direction, at the intersection marked by signs indicating "Squaxin Island Tribe Boat Launch," turn and drive northeast on SE Lynch Road for ¾ mile.

🛥 The ramp sits at the confluence of Pickering Passage, Hammersley Inlet, and Totten Inlet.

The Squaxin Island Tribe maintains a public launch ramp outside the channel of Hammersley Inlet at Arcadia, on the south shore of the entrance to the inlet. The wide, paved ramp is bordered on either side by private property. A dirt parking area, ample for more than twenty cars and trailers, is two blocks up the street.

The ramp's prime location at, or near, the entrances to several inlets, gives anglers ready access to excellent salmon fishing grounds. The area near the Steamboat Island bridge and a reef southeast of Hope Island are claimed to be fairly productive.

Jacoby Shorecrest County Park (Mason County Parks)   Map 76

Picnicking • Beach walking • Clamming

Facilities: Picnic tables, children's play equipment, launch ramp, toilet
Area: 2.75 acres; 320 feet of shoreline

🚗   Drive northeast from Shelton on SR 3 to the head of Oakland Bay. Here take E Agate Road south for 4 miles to the intersection with E Crestview Drive. Turn west and drive 2¼ miles, and then go south on E Parkway Boulevard to E Shorecrest Park Way and a parking area one block east of the park.

🚤   The park is on the north side of Hammersley Inlet, just before it hooks to the northeast.

This companion to Walker County Park lies on Hammersley Inlet at Miller Point. The park's main distinction is its boat-launch ramp, although it does have some picnic facilities and a very nice beach. The road into the park leads straight down to the water and the concrete launch ramp. There is no parking within the park itself.

The combination rock and sand beach has a trickling stream to fascinate youngsters. There might be some chances for clams, and possibly an oyster or two that escaped from the commercial oyster beds of Oakland Bay. To the west are nice views of the Shelton waterfront.

TOTTEN INLET
Map 77

This wide, shallow estuary was named for Midshipman George Totten of the Wilkes Expedition. It is also known locally as Oyster Bay, although that name technically belongs only to its southern extremity, where it tapers to mudflats.

There are no public beaches or access areas on Totten Inlet, so one rarely encounters much boat traffic, aside from the occasional angler. ❀ All of Oyster Bay west of Burns Point dries at low tide. Strong tidal currents might

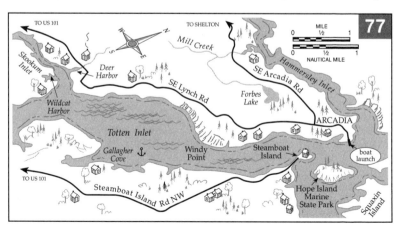

South Sound oysters are sorted and packed for sale.

be encountered where the narrow entrance to the inlet is choked by a spit protruding from its eastern shore, and there might be some tide rips where the passage joins Squaxin Inlet.

Tiny Steamboat Island, guarding the south side of the entrance to Totten Inlet, bristles with houses above its steep banks. The island is joined to the mainland by a long bridge over the top of a drying spit. The flanks of the island are popular for skin diving; give due respect to the tidal currents and whirlpools. The entire island is private and has no land access to the water, so divers must come in by boat.

Olympia Oyster Company   Map 75a

Point of Interest

🚐 Follow US 101 north from its junction with SR 8 for 5½ miles to the turnoff for the Old Olympic Highway, signed "To Oyster Bay, Kamilche, Kamilche Point." Continue on this road 1½ miles to Bloomfield Road NW. Turn east and drive 1 mile to where a large sign announces the Olympia Oyster Company.

🛥 Not accessible by boat. When traveling in the vicinity, use care not to trespass into the oyster beds, which are marked by poles.

Delicate little Olympia oysters, the caviar of mollusks, are grown in Totten Inlet. The Olympia Oyster Company, on the north shore of the inlet opposite Burns Point, welcomes visitors from 10:00 AM to 2:00 PM weekdays and has for sale both Pacific oysters and native Olympias. The company has been cultivating shellfish on their private tidelands since 1878. A tour of their facility is an interesting education in the harvesting and processing of these tasty little critters.

SKOOKUM INLET
Maps 75a and 77

Tom Sawyer would have loved it. Skookum Inlet is less a marine channel than a placid saltwater river that reverses its flow twice daily. You can picture Tom and Huck rafting down it. The upper portion of the narrow, 2½-mile-long passage dries to a mudflat at low tide, but two small coves at its entrance, Deer Harbor and Wildcat Harbor, are protected enough for a secluded, somewhat shallow anchorage. There are no public access points along the shoreline, and the road never comes close enough for views, so any exploration must be done by small boat or canoe—but that is the best way, anyway. The closest launch ramp is at Arcadia, 4 n.m. away near the entrance to Hammersley Inlet.

Around each bend of the waterway lies a new discovery—a moldering boat hull, a secret little tree-draped cove, an oyster farm looking just as it did sixty years ago. Enjoy the sights, but do not harvest any oysters. They belong to somebody.

✵ In Chinook jargon skookum means "strong"—bear that in mind when dealing with its tidal currents. At maximum flood and ebb, boats with small motors or those that are paddle-powered might have trouble making way. Plan trips accordingly.

ELD INLET
Map 78

The shores of Eld Inlet are lined with the bedrooms of Olympia. Water-ski boats and seaplanes rest on private floats; in summer sunbathers sprawl on lawns; the scent of barbecue mingles with the salt air. Yet for all the trappings of suburbia, the authors encountered in the waters of the inlet an inquisitive harbor seal who appeared to wonder what all these people were doing in *his* territory.

The only launch ramp on Eld Inlet is a small commercial ramp on Young Cove, a small indentation on the west side of the inlet, midway along its length. To reach the ramp follow US 101 north 1½ miles from its junction with SR 8. Turn off 101 at the Steamboat Island Road intersection. Drive a few blocks west on Sexton Road, head 1 mile north on Steamboat Island Road NW, and then northeast on Gravelly Beach Road NW for 1½ miles. Turn east on Gravelly Beach Loop NW and in ½ mile signs should indicate the ramp, a marine repair shop, and a boat builder, all on the same property. The ramp is concrete with a float alongside that sits on

Harbor seals are often curious about visitors.

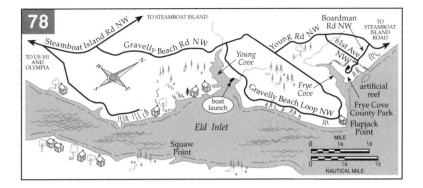

dry bottom at low tide. Launch fees are charged; there is no parking for cars or trailers in the vicinity.

Geoduck Beach (The Evergreen State College) Map 79

Hiking • Nature trail • Beach walking • Sunbathing

From I-5 take Exit 104 (US 101N, Aberdeen, Port Angeles), and in 3¼ miles take the (Mud Bay Road, The Evergreen State College) exit. Go north on Evergreen Parkway 2½ miles, past the main entrance to the college, and turn west on Overhulse Place, and in ½ mile turn south on Driftwood Road NW. Enter Parking Area F in ¼ mile; the trailhead is at the northwest side of the parking lot.

On the east side of Eld Inlet, about 6 n.m. south of Cooper Point

The 1000-acre campus of The Evergreen State College stretches along the eastern side of Eld Inlet. A mile-long nature trail leads from the campus down

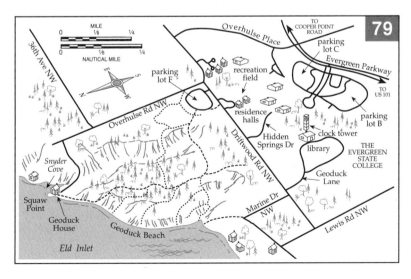

the wooded hillside to Geoduck Beach, the college's Marine Study/Ecological Reserve, which is used for both research and recreation. A trailhead sign shows major trails and several rather ambiguous boot paths to the beach. None of the trails are signed beyond this point, and many are difficult to find and follow without a guide or a woodsman's nose. Once at the beach, return trail locations are equally obscure.

Because the beach is used for research by the college's marine biology classes, shellfish and other marine life should not be disturbed. The beach was once known for collegiate nude sunbathing, but don't count on seeing any bare bodies.

Frye Cove County Park (Thurston County Parks)   Map 80

Picnicking • Scuba diving • Fishing • Clamming • Beach walking • Swimming • Views

Facilities: Picnic tables, picnic shelters, restrooms, trails, artificial reef, disabled access

Area: 90 acres; 2200 feet of shoreline

🚗 Drive north on US 101 from its junction with SR 8. In 1¾ miles turn north at the Steamboat Island exit, take Sexton Drive NW northwest for ¼ mile, and then head northeast on Steamboat Island Road NW. In 1 mile turn northeast onto Gravelly Beach Road NW, and follow it and Gravelly Beach Loop Road NW for 4¾ miles to the junction with Young Road NW. Head north on Young Road, and in ½ mile turn east onto 61st Avenue NW; reach the park boundary at the intersection with Boardman Road NW in ½ mile.

🚤 Frye Cove is on the west side of Eld Inlet, 3 n.m. south of Cooper Point. Nearest launch ramp is at Boston Harbor, 3¾ n.m. to the northeast.

Frye Cove is a pleasant little finger of water indenting the west shoreline of Eld Inlet just north of Flapjack Point. The cove itself nearly dries at a minus tide, exposing a mud-and-sand beach. A pretty little Thurston County

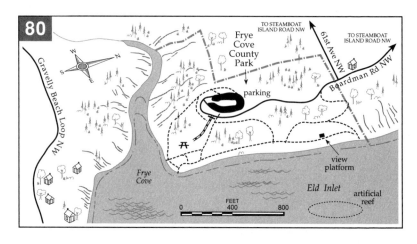

Moon snails can be found at Frye Cove County Park, as well as many other protected Puget Sound beaches. Left: *The shell can be as large as a baseball.* Right: *"Sand collars" are leathery shapes the snail makes by using mucus to cement together thousands of tiny snail eggs and grains of sand.*

park encompasses a substantial wooded acreage north of the cove, as well as most of the northern beach of Frye Cove and additional beach frontage on Eld Inlet itself.

Low tides bring excellent clamming in season, and the beach is also harvested for moon snails (if that mollusk is on your list of gourmet fare). An offshore artificial reef is an attraction for scuba divers and anglers. In a time when so many parks are becoming run down from lack of funds, this park is a special delight with its nice, new facilities.

The road ends in a large paved parking lot. A network of paths connect the parking lot with the cove, the beach, and the picnic area. Trails are well marked, broad, and well maintained; bank drop-offs are well protected by fence. Good views of Eld Inlet are from trailside benches and a wood-planked viewing platform.

BUDD INLET AND OLYMPIA
Map 75b

South Puget Sound ends with spectacular fanfare in Olympia, with the dome of the state capitol building dramatically punctuating the marine scene below.

✺ The northern half of the shallow inlet is uniformly 6 fathoms deep. Midchannel and halfway down the inlet, markers and lights on pilings indicate Olympia Shoal. These mark the beginning of shallow water, large portions of which dry to mudflats on a minus tide. Boats entering the inlet should follow the dredged ship channel west of Olympia Shoal, and then continue southeast from Butler Cove to the range markers near the head of the inlet. From here the channel buoys define the way south past commercial wharfs to the public moorages at Olympia.

Boston Harbor was named in the early 1900s by land speculators who platted it. It seemed a fine name for a soon-to-be industrial city. The boom never occurred here, of course, and today the community is a suburb of Olympia.

Back in the days when the favorite sport among the infant cities sprouting along the rim of Puget Sound was vying for political and economic plums, Olympia did pretty well. It was chosen as Thurston County seat in 1852, capital of Washington Territory in 1854, and, ultimately, capital of the new state in 1889. Its newspaper, which began publication in 1852, and the modest hotel that opened about the same time were both firsts in the territory.

Unfortunately, because early economic fortunes were tied inexorably to maritime trade, the city's bright hopes died on the vine. Its shallow harbor and distant location at the far end of the sound made it less attractive as a seaport than its neighbors' harbors downsound. Although still an active port that ships to Far East countries, its prime business became—and remains—government.

Government has spawned a worthwhile sideline—tourism. The capitol grounds, buildings, and numerous historic sites attract thousands of visitors annually.

Boston Harbor Marina   Map 81

Boating • Paddling

Facilities: Guest moorage, power, gas and diesel, CNG, 1-lane launch ramp with boarding float, restrooms, groceries, ice, marine supplies, boat rentals, deli, picnic tables

🚗 From I-5 Exit 105 (City Center) take Plum Street north for ¾ mile to Olympia Avenue, where it becomes East Bay Drive NE. Continue north for 7 miles, as

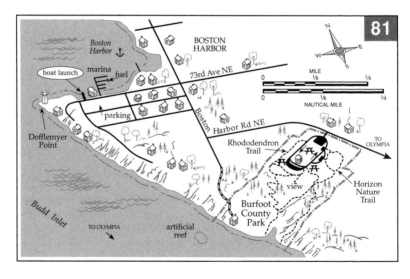

The Boston Harbor Marina has a pretty setting at the entrance to Budd Inlet.

the road becomes Boston Harbor Road NE, to a T-intersection where it turns sharply northeast. In ½ mile head northwest on 73rd Avenue NE and arrive at the marina in ¼ mile.

🚤 At the entrance to Budd Inlet, at the confluence of the inlet and Dana Passage, just east of Dofflemyer Point.

Just east of Dofflemyer Point, at the entrance to Budd Inlet, the small community of Boston Harbor overlooks a pleasant, protected harbor between Dover Point and Dofflemyer Point. The point is marked by a distinctive little concrete lighthouse; unfortunately, there is no land access to the beach on which it sits, so it must be appreciated from the water.

A popular stop for boaters is a marina with full marine facilities is on the east shore of Boston Harbor. Guest moorage is available, and there is some anchoring space nearby. Fresh seafood is available at the marina store, and picnic tables and gas grills at the head of the dock invite quick enjoyment of the larder. Just west of the marina the boat-launch ramp dips steeply into the water. Parking for vehicles and trailers is across the street.

Burfoot County Park (Thurston County)   Map 81

Hiking • Paddling • Beach walking • Picnicking • Swimming • Fishing • Scuba diving

Facilities: Picnic tables, kitchen shelters, trails, nature trail, children's play equipment, horseshoe pits, restrooms, artificial reef

Area: 50 acres; 1100 feet of shoreline

🚐 From I-5 Exit 105 (City Center) take Plum Street north for ¾ mile to Olympia Avenue, where it becomes East Bay Drive NE. Continue north, as the road becomes Boston Harbor Road NE, and in 6¾ miles reach the park entrance.

🛥 The park is on the east side of Budd Inlet, ¾ n.m. south of Dofflemyer Point. From the water the park can be recognized by the caretaker's house on a riprap-faced knob protruding out into the beach, as well as a conspicuous park sign at the base of the sand cliff above the beach.

The shores of South Puget Sound are full of steep and wild little ravines fronting lagoons enclosed by a baymouth bar. Some shorelines get a classy house perched high on the bluff and are enjoyed by a select few. This one got a county park and is enjoyed by tens of thousands of recreation seekers annually.

The park entrance opens on a large picnic area in a meadow. Other picnic sites are in the forest off the road loop. A sign at the small parking lot on the south side of the road loop directs hikers to the self-guided Horizon Nature Trail, a ¼-mile level loop through sun-sprinkled second-growth timber. Signs along the route point out features and distinctive flora of the forest, which was first logged in the 1880s.

Trails zigzag down the 100-foot ravine to the beach, meeting at the base of the ravine and then skirting the marshy lagoon on a planked walkway edged by spring-bright skunk cabbage.

For a pleasant hike through the upland woods, the Rhododendron Trail

In spring, the Rhododendron Trail at Burfoot County Park features (what else?) native rhododendrons.

leaves the north side of the loop road, paralleling the road, and then continuing through the dense undergrowth to finally join other trails.

The beach itself is yet another facet of the park—a broad gravel bar sloping gently into Budd Inlet, and behind it a driftwood-filled lagoon. Midway, on a flat grassy intrusion is the home of the park caretaker; the property in the vicinity of the house is not for public use. Summertime brings swimmers, waders, and sunbathers to the beach in droves, but even on chilly days the beach walk and marine panorama make the park a delight.

Priest Point Park (City of Olympia)   Map 82

Hiking • Picnicking • Fishing • Beach walking

Facilities: Trails, picnic shelters, picnic tables, children's play equipment, quarter basketball court, restrooms, floral garden, interpretive displays

Area: 312 acres; 1000 feet of shoreline on Budd Inlet

🚗 From I-5 Exit 105 (City Center) take Plum Street north for ¾ mile to Olympia Avenue, where it becomes East Bay Drive NE. Continue north for 2 miles to the park entrance.

🚤 On the east shore of Budd Inlet at and south of Priest Point. It is only accessible by beachable boats at high tide.

The inland section of Priest Point Park, east of the arterial, is divided between the Samarkand Rose Garden, several wooded picnic areas, and a large wooded area laced with trails. The western portion of the park, which faces on Budd Inlet, is reached by crossing the concrete viaduct over Boston Harbor Road. A number of loop roads lead to picnic tables, play equipment, and parking areas. At the lower end of one loop a concrete and rock platform overlooks the south end of the inlet.

Several miles of trails wind through the park. Those in the northeast section are unmarked, except at their start points, and they branch profusely.

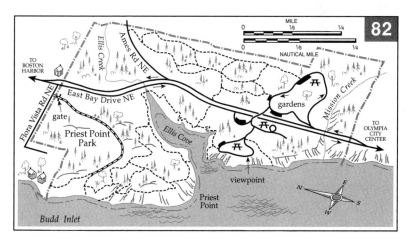

Stunning old-growth forest edges the trails at Priest Point Park.

The magnificent forest boasts huge old-growth Douglas-fir, grand fir, and stately western red cedar. Occasional benches lure you to a hiking respite to listen to birdsongs. But for the noise of traffic on Boston Harbor Road, you would feel you were in the forest primeval.

Trails on the west side of the park have bridges and boardwalks that bypass creeks and muddy spots, and a good deal of up and down as they drop deep into creek drainages and climb over adjoining wooded ribs. Wooden kiosks hold interpretive signs describing the ecology and history of the area.

Trail spurs touch the beach in several spots. Two are on opposite ends of a string of pilings that mark a long-forgotten bridge that once crossed Ellis Creek. Two more drop through breaches in the glacial till cliffs to reach the cobble beach on the north side of Priest Point. The beach at the south end of the park can be reached via several steep trails from the west section of the park.

The shallow tideflat extending into the estuary dries to a mudflat at the slightest suggestion of a low tide, permitting exploration of an expanse of pickleweed and other saltwater marsh vegetation. *Salicornia virginica*, or pickleweed, is an odd little plant, related to the tumbleweed, that is able to exist in the high salinity of tidal marshes. Its leaves are tiny scales along its jointed stems, and its greenish flowers, which appear in late summer, are clublike spikes at the tips of its branches.

Water approach to the park is difficult for boats of any draft because of extensive shoaling at low tide. Even inflatables might be wise to approach on a rising tide to avoid being mired in the muck until the tide changes.

Olympia   Map 83

Shopping • Museum • Capitol campus • Historic homes

🚗 To reach the city center from I-5, take Exit 105B onto Plum Street. Continue straight ahead to State Avenue and turn left (west) to reach the waterfront, or turn left (west) on Union Avenue to reach the capitol grounds.

🚤 Olympia sits at the south end of Budd Inlet.

A small peninsula splits the end of Budd Inlet into two similar bays, East Bay and West Bay. Facilities operated by the city and Port of Olympia provide touring boaters with some of the nicest guest moorages to be found on the sound—all within walking distance of downtown Olympia and the capitol grounds.

State Capitol • The state capitol building, one of the most impressive in the United States, was completed in the 1930s at a cost of over $7 million. The 187-foot-high dome is one of only two in the country that are constructed completely of stone. The building is open to visitors on weekdays during normal business hours; tours are available. Finish up with a visit to the conservatory and sunken gardens.

State Capitol Museum • The State Capitol Museum, eight blocks south of the capitol at 211 W 21st Street, has an outstanding exhibit on early Indians as well as displays on the history of the state capitol building. It is open from noon to 4:00 PM on Saturday and Sunday and 10:00 AM to 4:30 PM Tuesday through Friday; it is closed on Monday. The nearby residential district has several historic homes dating from the 1850s.

Olympia Farmer's Market • From April through December ships' larders or cyclists' panniers can be replenished at the Olympia Farmer's Market, an extravaganza of fresh produce, seafood, baked goods, and flowers. The market is at the corner of D Avenue and N Capitol Way, a few blocks north and east of Percival Landing. Vendors display their wares here during the day from Thursday through Sunday, 10 AM to 3 PM

East Bay   Map 83

Views • Birdwatching • Historic and nature displays • Picnicking

Facilities: *Swantown Marina and Boatworks*: Guest moorage, power, restrooms, showers, laundry, marine pumpout station, portable toilet dump, 2-lane paved launch ramp with boarding float, dry storage, picnic tables, barbecues, haul-out (Travelift), marine services. *East Bay Park*: View platforms, informational displays

🚗 From I-5 Exit 105 (City Center) take Plum Street north for ¾ mile to Olympia Avenue (to the east) and Marine Drive NE (to the west). Take Marine Drive west, then north for ¼ mile, passing the boatworks, and turn north on Market Street to reach the marina in another ¼ mile. Alternatively, from downtown Olympia, take N Capitol Way north to D Street, then head northeast on Marine Drive to

Market. *East Bay Park:* The park is on the northwest side of the intersection of Olympia Avenue and Marine Drive.

The marina is on the west side of the head of East Bay at the south end of Budd Inlet.

Swantown Marina and Boatworks (Port of Olympia) • At the south end of Budd Inlet, a large marine facility is on East Bay, on the east shore of the peninsula. Swantown Marina has ten floats for permanent moorage, serving over 650 boats; guest moorage on Dock A, the first dock south of the breakwater, can accommodate more than 50 boats. A two-lane concrete launch ramp with a boarding float is just inside the breakwater. Restrooms,

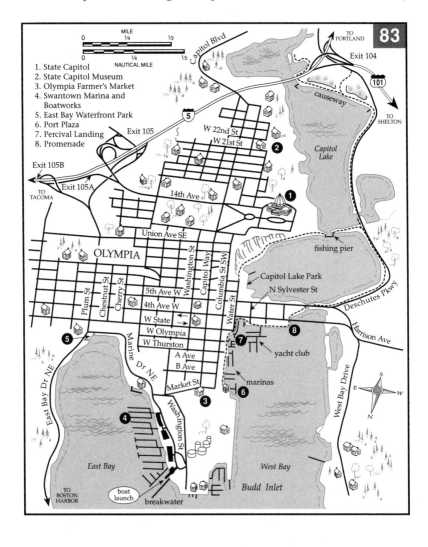

1. State Capitol
2. State Capitol Museum
3. Olympia Farmer's Market
4. Swantown Marina and Boatworks
5. East Bay Waterfront Park
6. Port Plaza
7. Percival Landing
8. Promenade

The capitol dome and boats at West Bay marinas serve as a backdrop for the tower views of Port Plaza.

showers, and laundry facilities are at the head of the guest floats.

The Swantown Boatworks, south of the marina itself, has haulout, work space, and a complete complement of marine services and supplies.

East Bay Waterfront Park (City of Olympia) • A pair of view platforms overlook the south end of East Bay. Informational panels describe and picture the historic use and improvement of Swantown Slough (East Bay). The various species of birds that might be seen at the site are shown, and several purple martin boxes mounted on offshore pilings offer some prospect of spotting birds.

West Bay   Map 83

Boating • Paddling • Views • Picnicking

Facilities: *Port Plaza:* Guest moorage, view tower. *Percival Landing:* Guest moorage, power, paddlecraft rentals, marine pumpout station, portable toilet dump, restrooms, showers, picnic tables, children's play equipment, informational displays

🚗 From I-5 Exit 105 (City Center) take Plum Street north for ¾ mile to State Avenue NE, head west on it, and in eight blocks turn north on Columbia Street NW. The park is on the water, five blocks to the north. Percival Landing is on the west side of Columbia Street NW.

🛥 *Port Plaza:* The moorage is on the east shore of West Bay, just south of the large cranes at the Port of Olympia docks. *Percival Landing :* On the east side of the extreme south end of West Bay, with portions of the park along the south end of the bay.

Port Plaza (Port of Olympia) • Attractive landscaping and a view tower present a foreground for a popular waterfront restaurant on West Bay. The

The boardwalk promenade at Percival Landing is great for a lunch break or an afternoon of boat watching.

two-story tower offers great views south over the moorages of West Bay with the capitol dome as a backdrop. A set of guest floats with about 180 feet of space fronts the park. There is water on the floats, and a seven-day limit to visitor stays.

Percival Landing (City of Olympia) • This beautiful park and public moorage is along the shore at the head of West Bay. The park's planked overlooks and grassy pockets are a lunchtime getaway for downtown Olympia office workers, who come here to watch boats, relax, and enjoy saltwater-inspired daydreams. The waterside promenade extends west to Capitol Lake. Kiosks on the boardwalk describe the history of Percival Landing, the industries that have developed here, and the shipping activities that the area has seen over the past 130 years.

Three sets of floats provide space for visiting boats. There is no water on the floats, but some have power. Overnight stays are limited to a maximum of seventy-two hours within a thirty-day period. ❋ Use care in the choice of moorage, as some portions of the floats come perilously close to the bottom at low tide.

About That Puget Sound Canal

Sometime in the 1850s a young U.S. Army lieutenant named Ulysses S. Grant, who was stationed at Fort Vancouver, suggested that Puget Sound be linked to the Pacific Ocean and the mouth of the Columbia River by a series of canals. Ever since that time Washington residents who enthusiastically endorsed the idea have formed commissions, and the project has been studied...and studied...and studied.

The state canal commission that reported to the legislature in June 1933 recommended a route that took advantage of the fact that, uniquely, Black Lake drains both to Puget Sound and the Pacific Ocean. The route of a canal was to begin at the head of Budd Inlet and follow Percival Creek to Black Lake. It would then go down Black Creek to the Chehalis River and west into Grays Harbor and the ocean. The lengths of Grays Harbor and Willapa Bay would be dredged for deep channels, and short canals cut through land would join Grays Harbor, Willapa Bay, and ultimately the Columbia River.

The canal proposed at the time incorporated more than a dozen locks and was large enough to accommodate oceangoing ships. The major motivation, during the 1930s, was the desire to transport timber from the Olympic Peninsula to Puget Sound markets; recreational uses were a secondary consideration. However, by the 1960s when another major government study took place, use of the canal as a recreational facility was a prime impetus. Developers envisioned throngs of pleasure boaters traversing the waterway, with "touristvilles" along the route providing services. Estimated cost of construction in 1965 was $500 million and, as in previous times, money for the venture was never appropriated.

As recently as 1972 the scheme again surfaced, but with soaring construction costs and increasing awareness of the environmental consequences of such dredging and 'dozing, it again died. It seems unlikely that this particular dream (or nightmare) will ever be realized. Thus, Budd Inlet remains not the beginning, but the end of Puget Sound, and the southernmost point of this entire maze of waterways.

chapter twelve

Hood Canal

IN PUGET SOUND COUNTRY, where inlets and bays and meandering channels are standard fare, this 1½-mile-wide watery finger is unique. Straight and true, it flows southward along the foot of the Olympic Mountains for over 50 miles before bending sharply to the northeast for the final 15 miles of its course. Hood Canal boasts some of the region's most spectacular scenery year-round, as seasonal changes paint the nearby rugged peaks, glacier-carved valleys, and timbered shorelines. Nine state parks and several other public parks distributed along the length of the canal make this an ideal destination for campers or for boats ranging from kayak to cruiser.

Although the nautical distance to Hood Canal from the major population centers on Puget Sound is less than the distance to the San Juan Islands, fewer boaters cruise here. While most boaters enjoy the solitude, it can also cause inconveniences—there are fewer commercial facilities to serve boating needs. The small towns of Seabeck, Hoodsport, and Union each have some marine amenities, grocery stores, and restaurants; a few additional commercial marinas are at other spots along the shore.

What's in a Name?

Capt. George Vancouver, who, on his voyage of discovery in May of 1792, was the first European to visit this body of water, named it Hood's Channel in his journal, but for some reason Hood's Canal was written on his charts, and "Canal" it has remained ever since. In reality it is a fjord—or as close to one as can be found here in Washington State.

The canal was carved by the advances of massive ice sheets that flowed across the area over a period of 1.5 million years. When warming weather caused the northward retreat of the glaciers about 15,000 years ago, several glacial lakes were formed, including Lake Hood. This lake drained to the east through Clifton Outlet into today's Case Inlet. As the glacial melt freed the Strait of Juan de Fuca of ice, the waters of the region dropped and rushed to this new avenue to the sea. Hood Canal took on its northerly saltwater opening of today, with its connection to Case Inlet but a memory. Most of the road cuts along the west side of US 101 show thick banks of sandy sediments laced with cobbles and gravel. This glacial till is a memento left behind by the melting ice sheets.

Opposite: *All the family takes part when digging clams in Hood Canal.*

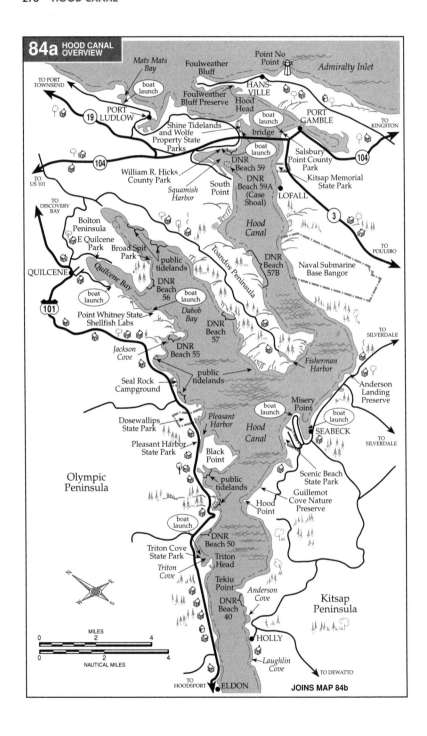

84a HOOD CANAL OVERVIEW

Mats Mats Bay
Foulweather Bluff
Point No Point
Admiralty Inlet
TO PORT TOWNSEND
boat launch
Foulweather Bluff Preserve
Hood Head
HANS-VILLE
PORT LUDLOW
19
boat launch
PORT GAMBLE
TO KINGSTON
Shine Tidelands and Wolfe Property State Parks
bridge
Salsbury Point County Park
104
104
TO US 101
William R. Hicks County Park
boat launch
DNR Beach 59
South Point
DNR Beach 59A (Case Shoal)
Kitsap Memorial State Park
LOFALL
3
TO POULSBO
Squamish Harbor
TO DISCOVERY BAY
Bolton Peninsula
E Quilcene Park
Broad Spit Park
public tidelands
Hood Canal
DNR Beach 57B
Naval Submarine Base Bangor
QUILCENE
Quilcene Bay
DNR Beach 56
boat launch
Toandos Peninsula
101
boat launch
Point Whitney State Shellfish Labs
Dabob Bay
DNR Beach 57
TO SILVERDALE
Jackson Cove
DNR Beach 55
public tidelands
Fisherman Harbor
Seal Rock Campground
Anderson Landing Preserve
Dosewallips State Park
Pleasant Harbor
boat launch
Misery Point
boat launch
SEABECK
TO SILVERDALE
Pleasant Harbor State Park
Hood Canal
Olympic Peninsula
Black Point
Scenic Beach State Park
public tidelands
Hood Point
Guillemot Cove Nature Preserve
boat launch
DNR Beach 50
Triton Cove State Park
Triton Head
Triton Cove
Kitsap Peninsula
Tekiu Point
Anderson Cove
DNR Beach 40
HOLLY
MILES
0   2   4
0   2   4
NAUTICAL MILES
Laughlin Cove
TO DEWATTO
TO HOODSPORT
ELDON
JOINS MAP 84b

US 101 parallels the west side of the canal for almost its entire length, with plenty of places for recreational access to the shorelands. The eastern shore is wilder, and roads touch down to water in only a few spots. Once around the Great Bend, civilization sets in with a vengeance on both sides of the canal, with elbow-to-elbow homes (both vacation and year-round) and a proliferation of "private property, no trespassing" signs.

Beaches along the canal are typically narrow, dropping off quickly to a depth of 80 fathoms or more. Low, sandy points, occasionally thrusting outward below the steep hillsides, extend for only a couple of hundred feet. The sole exceptions are the wide alluvial fans formed at the mouths of the major rivers draining the Olympics. Here mud and sand deposited by the rivers can extend out into the canal for as much as ¼ mile at minus tides. While shores along Puget Sound are generally gray, here they are a pleasing light tan, with a high-tide band of sparkling white oyster shells.

Because of the narrowness of the underwater shelf, very few docks, either public or private, are built at the northern end of the canal, and good anchorages can be found only at a few limited bays and coves. Stops must be planned accordingly. The underwater cliffs of this rapid drop-off are a magnet for scuba divers. They might be seen at many public beaches year-round.

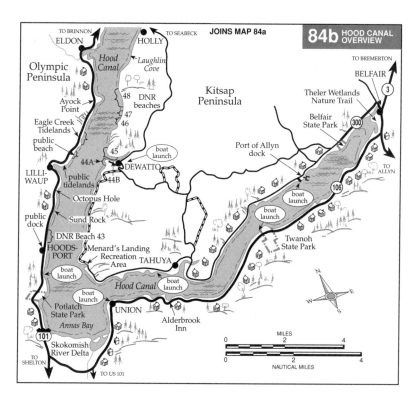

At the turn of the century, when settlements along the shoreline were primarily limited to logging camps, the camps relied on rafts anchored in deep water where the steamers of the Mosquito Fleet would stop to unload supplies. Barrels of crude oil for greasing the logging skids were rolled overboard and picked up by the logging boom man to be towed to shore. Horses or mules for the logging camps were pushed over the side to swim ashore.

❁ During times of extreme tide change, the tidal current in Hood Canal can exceed 2.5 knots, causing some problems for small boats. Although usually quite benign, weather can also be a concern, for the steep hills surrounding the channel serve as a funnel for winds, and storms can be furious.

The Table is Set

An old Puget Sound saying goes, "When the tide is out, the table is set." In Hood Canal, the tide doesn't even need to be out to harvest some of its seafood. The waters yield an abundance of fish to be taken either by rod or scuba gear. Oysters, clams, crabs, and spot shrimp are other forms of canal wildlife that lure thousands of eager gourmets each year. *No matter what seafood you hope to harvest, check Washington State Department of Fish and Wildlife regulations in their brochure or on their website.*

Cruise innocently into the canal on selected weekends in late May and early June, and you might think you have stumbled into a nautical convention. It is during that period that the one- or two-day-at-a-time, Hood Canal spot shrimp season opens, and residents and out-of-staters alike flock here to harvest this delicacy. Spot shrimp, which have white spots on their reddish-brown shells, are the largest species to be found in Puget Sound, reaching as much as 10 inches in size. They are caught in net traps called "pots" that are set in 200 to 300 feet of water. The best places for catching shrimp are in Dabob Bay and the south end of the canal from Hamma Hamma to Union. Special regulations apply to shrimp fishing in Hood Canal; a stiff fine can result for those failing to comply.

Another prime reason for visiting the canal is to invite to dinner one of the area's most important inhabitants—a succulent little gray critter that delights the palate and slides down the gullet with the greatest of ease—the Pacific oyster. The generally rocky beaches, however, dictate a lot of hard work for digging clams, except in the muddy alluvial fans at the mouths of rivers. The best chance for finding oysters and clams is at the public tidelands that are boat access only. Those beaches that can be reached from land are heavily harvested.

In recent years the canal has suffered the ravages of encroaching population. Seepage from onshore sewage drain fields and pollution from surface water run-off has resulted in major algae blooms that have lowered the oxygen content of the relatively stagnant waters in the canal to the point that marine life is being jeopardized, especially beyond the Great Bend. Control of human degradation of this priceless aquatic resource is essential for its survival.

Spot shrimp season on Hood Canal brings hundreds of boaters to favorite spots.

Bangor Vicinity • The presence of the U.S. Navy nuclear submarine base on Hood Canal at Bangor might cause some pleasure boaters to approach this section of the canal with trepidation. Boaters will encounter no problems while cruising in the vicinity of Bangor if they hold close to the western shore, staying well clear of the posted military areas lying on a 5-mile strip along the east shore. Movements of the submarines are not publicly announced, but on rare occasions one might be seen. The sight of one of these leviathans with a steel sail as tall as a four-story building cannot fail to stir awe. If a submarine is sighted, boats must keep 1000 yards away.

❀ A naval operations area is located in this portion of the canal from approximately Lofall to Hazel Point on the Toandos Peninsula and in Dabob Bay on the west shore. Such operations are rare; however, when they are underway, flashing green lights are shown when caution is required by boaters, and flashing red lights when the area is closed to navigation. If no lights are flashing, operations are not underway. Consult navigational charts for the exact location of the operations area and the warning lights. Boaters might also receive instructions by radio. Any total closure is usually only for a few hours. Failure to observe warning lights might result in a torpedo-sized opening in your hull.

TOANDOS PENINSULA
Map 85

This 12-mile-long forested spine separates Dabob Bay from the main channel of Hood Canal. The interior of the Toandos Peninsula offers little for tourists—the main road runs the length of the ridge, and a spur traces portions of the east flank. All views are obscured by dense forest, and the few road ends touching water are all on private property. A private camping club holds a large section of waterfront and timbered uplands along the southeast end.

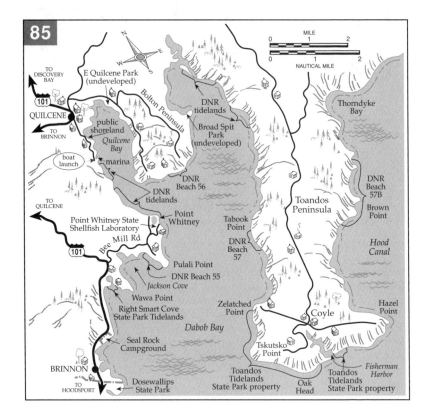

DNR Beaches 57B and 57 • Precipitous cliffs surrounding the Toandos Peninsula rise steeply for 200 feet, and below water the seawalls drop off as sharply to depths of 25 fathoms or more. Two narrow, cliff-bound DNR beaches on either side of the peninsula offer boaters several miles of shore access at low tide. DNR Beach 57B is a 12,050-foot strip on naval reservation property along the west shore of Hood Canal. It can be located by spotting the Brown Point light, which is approximately in the middle of the beach. Beach 57, facing on Dabob Bay, is a 3280-foot strip of tidelands running south from Tabook Point. Both of these rocky beaches hold oysters and a variety of clams.

Fisherman Harbor • Fisherman Harbor is a narrow slot in the bluffs at the foot of the Toandos Peninsula resembling, perhaps, a fjord for elves. Merely a cozy 200 yards wide, the cleft extends for ¾ mile between rocky walls.

Venturesome boaters enter Fisherman Harbor, but only during high tide; ❄ a sandspit extending from the west shore across the entrance is nearly bare at low water. After crossing the entrance shoal, turn to the west at a right angle, keeping within 10 or 15 feet of the sandspit—the shore drops off sharply on this side. Follow the spit for almost its full length, and turn north, following the west shore into deep water. Once inside, several tight anchorages can be found in adequate depths of water.

The tidelands for 700 feet on the east side of the entrance to Fisherman Harbor and those west from the entrance around the point to Zelatched Point are designated as Toandos Tidelands State Park. Oysters and clams can be taken at low tide on this 10,455-foot-long stretch of sand and gravel beach.

DABOB AND QUILCENE BAYS
Map 85

The forked arm of Dabob Bay, thrusting northward between steep, forested walls of the Olympics, provides a pleasant digression from Hood Canal's "main street." Here is found an even greater sense of remoteness; the intrusion of civilization is slight, and much of the shoreline remains just as natural as when it was first seen by early settlers.

Although to many people the names of Dabob Bay and adjoining Quilcene Bay are synonymous with gourmet oysters, the bays are also noted for their commercial production of oyster seed. The seed (juvenile oysters) is grown here in long net bags called cradles, which are suspended from logs floating in the water. The harvested seed is sold to oyster growers throughout the world. Quilcene Bay alone provides 75 percent of the oyster seed used by all West Coast commercial oyster growers.

Stores on Quilcene Bay have freshly shucked, commercially grown oysters for sale, or several public beaches on Dabob Bay are accessible by boat for those who thrill to stalking the wild ones.

Every year from the end of May to mid-June, Dabob Bay sees a major invasion by eager shrimp fishermen. The bottom configuration of the bay is especially suited to the lifestyle of shrimp, which spend their nights in 100 to 200 feet of water and move into deeper trenches during the day.

Because the tidal currents are weaker here than in the rest of Hood Canal, the steep, rocky underwater walls from Point Whitney to Seal Rock are prime scuba diving areas. Octopuses, lingcod, and free swimming scallops inhabit crevices in the basalt ledges.

An adult and two immature bald eagles perch in a tree snag along Hood Canal.

A young boater explores a public beach on the Bolton Peninsula.

Bolton Peninsula • The thickly forested knob of the Bolton Peninsula protrudes south between Dabob and Quilcene Bays. On the shores of the peninsula are two undeveloped, unnamed Jefferson County Parks properties. On the east side of the peninsula on Dabob Bay the park property is at Broad Spit, a hooked-shaped finger of land wrapping around a saltwater lagoon. Steep wooded hillsides inland have no public access. Beachable boats can take advantage of the shellfish largess in low-tide mud and sand.

On the west side of the peninsula the park property is on Quilcene Bay on the south side of the community of East Quilcene. There is no upland access, and the beach can become a wide mudflat at minus tides.

Quilcene Bay Public Accesses • Quilcene Bay dwindles out into a long, mucky tidal flat that doesn't lend itself to carefree boating. The town of Quilcene itself is at the head of the tidal flat and has no water access. Midway into Quilcene Bay, just where the water begins to shallow, is a public tideland and a waterside access. The only public boating facility is at Quilcene Bay Marina. A second launch ramp just north of the marina belongs to the local yacht club. Most of the beach on the west side of the bay from the marina south to Whitney Point, with the exception of Frenchmans Point, is DNR public beach below mean high tide level.

Indian George Creek Estuarine Restoration Site (DFW)   Map 86

Shellfish • Beach walking

Facilities: Paved parking, toilet, informational displays

🚙 From US 101 on the south side of Quilcene take Linger Longer Road east, and then south for 1¼ miles to reach two parking areas on the beach side of the road.

Indian George Creek, which drains into Quilcene Bay, had at one time formed an 8-acre estuary that was a vital ecosystem for fish, birds, and marine life. Sometime between 1939 and 1965 the stream was turned into a canal, roads were built over the estuary, and fill dirt was dumped along the shore, along with several derelict barges—an ecological disaster. A consortium of private, state, and federal organizations has recently returned the creek to its original channel and removed over 25,000 tons of fill material and the barges. Over time, tidal action should restore the estuary.

The more southerly of the parking areas offers access to DFW tidelands in the mudflats exposed at low tide. The tideland boundaries are marked by white fiberglass poles. Harvesting of clams and oysters is permitted here; all tidelands outside the marked area are private.

Quilcene Bay Marina (Port of Port Townsend)   Map 86

Picnicking • Boating • Swimming

Facilities: *Marina:* 1-lane paved launch ramp, gas, diesel, guest moorage (limited), marine pumpout station, restrooms, showers, picnic tables, fireplaces, RV parking (E), swimming beach. *Quilcene:* Groceries

🚗 From US 101 on the south side of Quilcene take Linger Longer Road east, and then south to the end of Linger Longer Road.

🛥 The marina is on the west side of Quilcene Bay, 1½ n.m. north of French-mans Point.

The Quilcene Bay Marina has a small basin with space for about fifty boats. Unoccupied slips are used for guest moorage; contact the marina in advance for availability and reservations. A small picnic area lies across the road from the marina, near the marina office and restrooms. RV parking is permitted on the spit above the marina. The single-lane concrete launch ramp inside the protection of the marina's rock breakwater is usable at most tide levels, but its snug proportions might give fits to less-experienced drivers.

The south side of the rock jetty spreads into a swimming area on a gradually sloping gravel beach (no lifeguard). The oyster company north of the marina offers fresh oysters for sale. For boaters in need of supplies, the town is a long but pleasant 1½ mile trudge along Linger Longer Road, with roadside blackberries in season, and some salty views across the end of the bay.

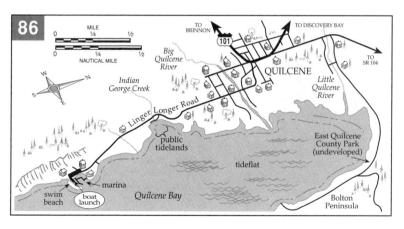

Point Whitney State Shellfish Laboratory   Map 85

Boating • Swimming • Shellfish • Fishing • Educational display • Picnicking

Facilities: 1-lane paved launch ramp, dock with float (closed pending repairs), restrooms, picnic table, laboratories

From US 101, 8¼ miles south of Quilcene, or 2¾ miles north of Brinnon, turn east on Bee Mill Road, signed to the laboratory. In 1½ miles continue northeast on Point Whitney Road to reach the laboratory in another mile.

Area: 10 acres; 2000 feet of shoreline

The laboratory is on the west shore of Dabob Bay at Whitney Point.

An interesting wayside stop along the western shore of Dabob Bay puts tourists in closer touch with the shellfish they hunt in Hood Canal. The labs located here are responsible for setting state regulations for the harvesting of shellfish and also raise juvenile geoducks for enhancing the local population. An interpretive display outside the building, near the restrooms, explains the biology of intertidal life and has a long shoreline diorama displaying a variety of marine life in their normal habitat.

A sandspit encloses a saltwater lagoon used to grow algae to feed the lab's shellfish. Although the lagoon is closed to shellfish harvest, the Dabob Bay side of the spit is open to the public for shellfish gathering, beach walking, and swimming. Because the bay is shallower than the rest of Hood Canal, the water here is generally much warmer. To the north, public lands continue to the cove south of Frenchmans Point, but on the south the open beach continues for only several hundred more feet onto the tidelands of the navy operations area, marked by a white wooden tower on the bluff.

Dabob Bay tidelands yield oysters ready for the dinner table.

Dabob Bay Public Tidelands
Map 85

Several strips of public land facing on Dabob Bay offer some chance for shellfish gathering.

DNR Beach 56 • A 2400-foot rocky tideland at the tip of the Bolton Peninsula is one of the best spots to find oysters, as well as clams. The beach, directly below Red Bluff, is easily located by spotting a house at the top of the bluff. The public shore is immediately east of a drainage flume coming down from that house.

Toandos Peninsula Beaches • Two of three DNR beaches on Dabob Bay are on the Toandos shoreline. One extends for nearly a mile south from Camp Discovery. A second beach, more than 1 mile in length, runs south from a finger peninsula near the head of the bay. Both beaches, which are bare at minus tides, are accessible only by boat. The third public shoreline wraps around the head of Tarboo Bay, at the north end of Dabob Bay, and is accessible only from the water. It is best visited at high tide—at low tide it is edged by a ¼-mile-wide mudflat.

Jackson Cove • Lying midway along the western shore of Dabob Bay, Jackson Cove has a section of rocky ledge offering at low tide some promise of oysters. The public area, DNR Beach 55, is a 2791-foot strip on the east side of the bay, lying along Pulali Point. Some clams can be found on the gravelly northern half of the beach. Boy Scout Camp Parsons is immediately adjacent to the beach, so it is heavily used by youngsters from the camp; there is no public access to the beach through the scout camp. Jackson Cove has space for several nice boat anchorages in a rocky bottom.

Right Smart Cove State Park Tidelands • This beach lies along the edge of the small cove west of Wawa Point. At one time a nearby landowner provided a pay launch ramp at the beach; however, strained relationships with various government agencies caused the road to the beach to be barricaded and liberally posted with "No Trespassing" signs. State Parks, in fact, has a legal easement for access to the beach, so walking to it is a legal, albeit a venturesome exercise.

DOSEWALLIPS AREA
Map 84a

Seal Rock Campground (Olympic National Forest)   Map 85

Scuba diving • Beach walking • Shellfish • Swimming • Walking • Paddling • Picnicking

Facilities: 42 campsites, picnic tables, fireplaces, restrooms, interpretive trails (barrier free), hand-carry boat launch
Area: 47 acres; 2700 feet of shoreline

🚐 On the east side of US 101, 10½ miles south of Quilcene, or 1½ miles north of Brinnon
🛥 On the west side of Dabob Bay, 1¼ n.m. north of the mouth of the Dosewallips River.

Near the mouth of Dabob Bay the Olympic National Forest dips down to touch saltwater. Here, along the shore, is Seal Rock Campground—the only Forest Service campground in the nation where oysters can be gathered. The camping area is at the north end of the park in fine, old growth. At the south end of the park, a barrier-free, interpretive trail winds uphill through the day-use picnic area, passing displays telling how the Natives used the bounty of the forest and beach before the arrival of European explorers.

Stairways lead to the beach from both ends of the day-use parking area. The upper beach ranges from cobble to boulders, all liberally covered with oyster shells. At low tide the beach tapers out gently for several hundred yards to gravel and mud.

A second marine interpretive trail follows the campground road north from the day-use area, and then slips down to the bank above the beach and continues north as a barrier-free boardwalk. Displays along the way tell the story of the balance between the three different ecosystems found in the park: forest, intertidal zone, and sea. The trail finally reaches the beach at the north end of the campground loop, where a short road stub permits launching hand-carried boats.

The park has no easy access for boaters; the only option is to anchor out and land small boats on the rocky beach.

Dosewallips State Park Map 87

Beach walking • Picnicking • Hiking • Fishing • Birdwatching • Shellfish • Wildlife watching

Facilities: 94 standard campsites, 40 RV campsites, 3 primitive sites, 4 platform tents, group camps, picnic tables, picnic shelters, fireplaces, restrooms, showers, trailer dump station, trails, wildlife viewing platform, interpretive signs
Area: 430.93 acres; 5500 feet of saltwater shoreline on Hood Canal, 5400 feet of freshwater shoreline on the Dosewallips River

The park straddles US 101, 1 mile south of Brinnon and 40 miles north of Shelton

The Dosewallips River, which originates in glaciers of the high Olympic peaks, meanders into Hood Canal at the mile-wide alluvial plain of Brinnon Flats.

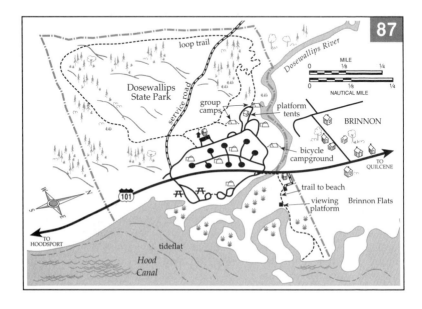

The estuary created here holds a thriving intertidal community of saltwater invertebrates, fish, and shorebirds. An access road that runs under the US 101 bridge leads to the older section of the campground, without hookups, east of the highway, along the Dosewallips River. Newer campsites, many with complete utility hookups, are on the west side of the highway in a grassy flat shaded by evergreens.

An upland trail starts near the park office at the entrance to the campground area and wanders through a forest of Douglas-fir, hemlock, and stumps of once-majestic cedar. By combining sections of trail with a fire road, three different loop trips are possible, ranging from 2 to 4¼ miles long. Walk quietly and perhaps spot blacktail deer, elk, raccoon, or skunk.

The marsh at the east side of the picnic area is heavily overgrown and laced with muddy channels that do not afford any easy access to the saltwater. To reach the beach, cross the river on a walkway along the east side of the bridge; on the northeast side of the bridge skirt the edge of an open field to the east to reach the trailhead. The trailhead can also be reached from the end of the first gravel road to the east just north of the bridge, which leads past a ranger residence. A gravel path leads to a viewing platform overlooking the Dosewallips estuary. Interpretive panels around the edge of the platform tell of the birds and other wildlife you might expect to see. The fenced channel to the east was once a haulout spot for hordes of seals, whose feces polluted the beach and caused its closure to shellfish gathering. The fencing caused them to move on, and the beaches are now safe for shellfish harvesting.

Shallow, mud-rimmed, saltwater channels give way to rock and cobble extending outward for another ¼ mile at minus tides. The vast tideflat lies waiting to be explored. Watch for great blue herons and eagles, as well as loons and other waterfowl frequenting the area, or join the mud-slogging crowd seeking the low tide treasures of clams and oysters. Access to the park by boat is difficult, due to the huge tideflat. Search the tideflats carefully to see how many kinds of life you can find, but treat every creature with care; each is a part of the web of life.

A family treks back from a clamming excursion on the Dosewallips estuary.

The best exploring is at low tide; wear rubber boots for wading channels and squishing through ankle-deep mud on the tideflats.

THE KITSAP PENINSULA SHORELINE
Map 84a

Traveling south along Hood Canal, the eastern shore, which is the Kitsap Peninsula, becomes wilder. Land accesses are limited to a few sites, joined together by isolated roads through the densely timbered hills of the peninsula. The common starting point for land trips is Bremerton, which can be reached by ferry from Seattle or via SR 16 from Tacoma.

Short sections of beach along the east shore between Misery Point and the Great Bend offer some limited opportunities for harvesting shellfish. Most have no upland access because of private land, and thus can be reached only from the water.

Anderson Landing Preserve (Kitsap County)   Map 84a
Hiking • Paddling • Shellfish

Facilities: Trails
Area: 68 acres; 2000 feet of shoreline on Hood Canal

From SR 3, 2 miles south of Silverdale, take the exit to NW Newberry Hill Road and head west on it for 3¼ miles to a T-intersection with Seabeck Highway NW. Head north on it and in 1¾ miles turn east on NW Anderson Hill Road. In ¾ mile turn north on Warren Road NW and reach the trailhead at the southwest corner of the park in ¼ mile.

The preserve beach is on the east side of Hood Canal 3¾ n.m. north of Seabeck at the mouth of Anderson Creek.

This property encompasses an upland second-growth forest, wetlands adjoining Anderson Creek and its tributaries, an estuarine wetland where the creek flows into the canal, and broad, shallow tidelands on Hood Canal. The site was settled in the 1890s by Norwegian immigrants; a dock built over the tidelands afforded access to a wagon road to Silverdale for steamer passengers, shrimp fishermen, and (during Prohibition) rum runners.

As of the publication of this book, upland forest trails to viewpoints are under development. Plans are to secure easements for accesses to Anderson Creek and the beach. Paddlecraft can reach the broad beach at low tide to harvest shellfish, including geoducks, found there.

Seabeck   Map 88
Boating • Fishing • Scuba diving

Facilities: Marina, boat launch hoist, boat rentals, guest moorage, bait and tackle, gas, toilets, groceries, restaurant, fast food

From SR 3, 2 miles south of Silverdale, take the exit to NW Newberry Hill Road and head west on it for 3¼ miles to a T-intersection with Seabeck Highway

NW. Head north on it; in 1¾ miles the road bends west along the beach to reach Seabeck in another 2¾ miles.

On Seabeck Bay on the east side of Hood Canal, due south of the south end of the Toandos Peninsula, and southeast of Misery Point.

One of the oldest towns in the state, Seabeck was founded in 1856 when a sawmill was established at the site. The town prospered as a lumber and shipbuilding center until a fire leveled the mill in 1886. Because the nearby timber supplies were nearly exhausted, rather than rebuilding at Seabeck, the operation moved to Hadlock. The population quickly deserted the town and the mill dock was used as a landing place for a small resort, which also failed after a short period. A church conference center now occupies a good portion of the town.

Today Seabeck is a favorite spot for anglers—the waters of the canal just west are one of the premium salmon fishing spots in the state, and prime shrimping areas are a short distance away. An artificial reef placed just northeast of the tip of Misery Point provides excellent fishing for rockfish, lingcod, and other bottomfish. Fishing from the marina dock is permitted, except during busy summer months. The smooth bottom of the bay, with its many old pilings, makes it a popular scuba diving site.

Seabeck Bay is the only noteworthy moorage spot south of Port Gamble along this side of the canal. The Native American name for it was *Kah-mogk*,

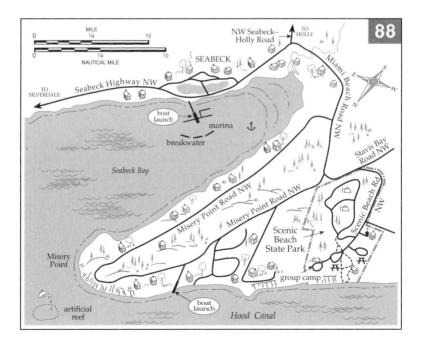

Olympic peaks watch over the moorage at Seabeck.

meaning "quiet waters." The bay is well sheltered on the west by the long finger of Misery Point; however, it has little protection from strong north-erlies. The marina located here has tried to solve this problem by chaining sections of old abandoned docks offshore from the marina—not pretty, but efficient.

Most of the parking in Seabeck is along the road; when shrimp season or fishing derbies are on, the space can be jammed.

Misery Point Launch Ramp (DFW)   Map 88

Boating • Paddling • Fishing • Scuba diving

Facilities: 1-lane paved launch ramp, disabled-accessible toilet, fishing reef

🚗 See directions to Seabeck, previously. ½ mile west of Seabeck head north on Miami Beach Road NW, and in 1 mile continue north on Misery Point Road NW for ½ mile to reach the ramp parking area.

🛥 The ramp and offshore reef are on the south side of Hood Canal midway between Misery Point and Scenic Beach State Park.

An excellent public launch facility between Seabeck and Scenic Beach State Park is heavily used by shrimpers and salmon fishermen. An artificial reef, placed to attract bottomfish, lies just a stone's throw to the northeast, off the tip of Misery Point. At minus tides the ramp ends above a soft sandy beach, where its use is questionable

The area is open for use between 4:00 AM and 10:00 PM Overnight park-ing and camping are prohibited. A spacious parking lot has room above the ramp for twenty cars with trailers. Additional parking is available in a large dirt field on the opposite side of the road.

Scenic Beach State Park   Map 88

Camping • Picnicking • Walking • Beach walking • Scuba diving • Views • Fishing • Boating • Paddling • Shellfish

Facilities: 52 campsites, group camp, picnic tables, picnic shelter, fireplaces, restrooms, trailer dump station, community center, children's play area, log cabin, volleyball courts, horseshoe pit, interpretive displays

Area: 88.24 acres; 1487 feet of shoreline on Hood Canal

See directions to Seabeck, above. ½ mile west of Seabeck head north on Miami Beach Road NW. At a Y-intersection in 1 mile continue north on Scenic Beach Road NW to reach the park in ½ mile.

Beachable boats can land at the park; it is on the south side of Hood Canal, ¾ n.m. west of Misery Point.

Scenic it is, with awe-inspiring views up the imposing glacier-gouged valleys of the Dosewallips and Duckabush Rivers on the west side of the canal, and north to Dabob Bay and the steep walls of the Toandos Peninsula. Sunsets silhouette the darkening peaks against a rosy sky, or morning mists engulf the phalanx of hills and peaks in nuances of gray.

In late May the scenic beauty is enhanced by masses of the pink blossoms of native rhododendrons. The park is said to have more rhododendrons than any other in the state; most bushes are to be found on the campground loops. Call ahead to the park ranger to find if they are at the height of their bloom, and enjoy them along the road on the drive to the park as well as in the park itself.

Campsites, on the southeast side of the park, are pleasantly isolated by tall western hemlock, Douglas-fir, western red cedar, and dense underbrush. The east picnic area lies above the beach in a small meadow with a scattering of tall evergreens. The trail to the beach can be found at the east side of the picnic area.

Farther west, across a marshy gully, is a large lawn and an orchard. Here, surrounded by carefully tended flower gardens and accompanied by a small gazebo, is the Emel House, built in 1912 and currently used as a community center. Interpretive programs are held here during summer months. The gorgeous views from the gazebo make this a popular wedding site. Joe Emel Sr. operated a resort and boathouse here named Scenic Beach. The log cabin on the east side of the

Wild rhododendrons edge a picnic table at Scenic Beach State Park.

gully is a replica of one that was built by his son. Following Emel's death, his 30 acres of property were purchased for a state park.

The park's gradually sloping beach is mostly gravel and cobbles below a steep, eroded bank, with access via a short trail from the picnic area. Very little beach is visible at high tide, however, as the water laps up against the bluff and bulkheads. This is a favorite area for scuba divers who swim out from shore. Hermit crabs, sea pens, sea cucumbers, and striped nudibranchs are but a few of the animals found on the sandy bottom. Extreme low tide reveals some of these creatures to beachcombers. This is also one of the better public oyster beaches on the canal.

Guillemot Cove Nature Reserve (Kitsap County) Map 89

Hiking • Paddling • Beach walking • Shellfish • Nature study • Picnicking

Facilities: Trails, toilets, parking, beach house, CMT campsite
Area: 164 acres; 1200 feet of shoreline on Hood Canal

See directions to Seabeck, above. West of Seabeck ½ mile head north on Miami Beach Road NW, and at a Y-intersection in 1 mile go southwest on Stavis Bay Road NW. In 4½ miles reach the trailhead. Parking is in a gravel lot on the opposite side of the road in another 100 yards.

Paddlecraft can land on the beach, which is on the east side of Hood Canal at the mouth of Boyce Creek, a little over 1 n.m. south of Hood Point.

Rhododendrons frame the access trail that begins at Stavis Bay Road NW; the path gradually switchbacks down the slope to meet a gravel road in ¼ mile. The road continues downhill to the south through second growth hemlock and maple, and then breaks into a clearing at an old barn in about a mile; the route straight ahead continues to a private residence.

A path crosses a bridge over Boyce Creek and in a few hundred yards reaches a rustic cabin (locked) at the beach. A CMT campsite sits in the brush behind the cabin. To the north the broad shallow mud fan at the mouth of Boyce Creek fronts a saltwater marsh. Several ¼-mile to ¾-mile trail loops, marked by wooden signs, branch off the lower clearings above the beach.

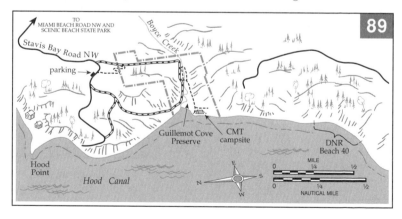

At Guillemot Cove, driftwood edges the mouth of Boyce Creek.

A roofed shelter in the hollowed-out stump of an old cedar is reached; this is said to have been the hideout of an early-day desperado.

DNR Beach 40 ● Exposed only at low tide, DNR Beach 40 is a 2145-foot strip of mud-to-sand, offering a chance for oysters, mussels, clams, and crabs to those who can beach a boat or anchor off and come ashore by dinghy. The beach lies north of Anderson Cove between a cluster of homes and a row of pilings 2500 feet farther north that extend far into the water.

Anderson Cove (State DNR)   Map 84a

Paddling

Facilities: Hand-carry boat launch

🚗 From Seabeck–Holly Road, 9½ miles south of Seabeck (½ mile north of Holly) turn west on the south end of Old Holly Hill Road; in about 300 yards there are pull-offs on both sides of the road at a gravel strip of beach leading into the cove.

🛥 On the east side of Hood Canal, ½ n.m. north of Holly, or 1 n.m. south of Tekiu Point.

As the Seabeck–Holly Road returns to the Hood Canal shoreline near Holly, a short loop to the west, Old Holly Hill Road winds down to the north shore of Anderson Cove. Waters of the shallow little cove reflect the snow-clad peaks of the Olympics across the canal. Hand-carried boats can be launched from the beach adjacent to the road at high tide. The tidelands off the small point on the north side of the cove are public below mean high tide level.

Kitsap Peninsula Public Tidelands   Maps 84a and 84b

Explorers in paddle-powered boats can land at several sites along the east shore of Hood Canal. Two have land access for hand-carry launching. These beaches are not heavily used, so the chances for finding shellfish are excellent. At the very least, solitude is assured. See comments in the introduction regarding harvesting shellfish.

Laughlin Cove (Kitsap County) • The no-bank cobble beach just north of Chinom Point holds two CMT campsites and a toilet; fires are not permitted. There is no feasible land access to the site. Paddlecraft can land at the beach on the east side of Hood Canal, just north of Chinom Point, 5¾ miles north of Dewatto Bay, or 2¼ miles south of Holly.

DNR Beaches 48, 47, and 46 • One long and two smaller beaches provide an opportunity to gather oysters and clams at low tide. All three beaches are cobble. Beach 48, immediately across the canal from Ayock Point, is 9072 feet long and lies below a steep, wooded cliff about 300 feet high. Beach 47, which is 900 feet long, lies 500 feet south of Beach 48 beneath extremely steep, timbered banks. Another 600 feet farther south is Beach 46, 1643 feet long, which lies below a recently logged area.

DNR Beaches 44A and 44B • Two short stretches of public beach are on the south side of Dewatto Bay. Both are gravel, sloping to sand and mud, where oysters, clams, and crab are found. Beach 44A, 514 feet long, surrounds a point at the southwest entrance to the bay. Beach 44B, 713 feet long, lies along the next curve of the beach, inward into the bay. This beach is accessible for hand-carry launching at a staircase on NE Dewatto Beach Drive. The bay itself is very shallow, with most of the inner bay drying at a low tide.

Dewatto Bay Launch Ramp (Port of Dewatto) • Adjacent an abandoned cinder block building near the head of Dewatto Bay, a single-lane gravel launch ramp dips gently into the bay. Unless the property is gated, or "No Trespassing" signs are erected, take advantage of the ramp and adjoining parking. The tidelands along the shore are public to the mean high tide level.

THE OLYMPIC PENINSULA SHORELINE
Map 84a

Pleasant Harbor   Map 90
Boating • Fishing • Picnicking • Paddling

Facilities: *State park:* Dock, picnic table, toilet. *Marina:* Guest moorage with water and power, wireless broadband, groceries, restaurant, gift shop, restrooms, showers, gas, diesel, laundry, fishing supplies, picnic pavilion
Area: *State park:* 0.8 acre; 100 feet of shoreline
🚗 Follow US 101 along the west side of Hood Canal to 1½ miles south of Brinnon. A paved road, signed to the marina, drops downhill to a road looping around the grocery store. The unmarked road to the state park leaves the highway at a deserted grocery store slightly less than ¼ mile north of the marina road. Parking for the park is at the end of the road.

Pleasant Harbor State Park has moorage on a float.

Pleasant Harbor is on the west side of Hood Canal behind Black Point; the entrance is from the north. The park float is the second dock inside the harbor; the next group of floats are private; the marina complex is at the south end of the harbor.

In summer evenings when nighthawks sweep across the bay, capturing insects in their open beaks, and the last rays of light glimmer across the darkening water, "pleasant" barely begins to describe this harbor—"superb" might be more apt. A bit more than ½ mile long and 300 yards across, this snug little evergreen-rimmed cove is one of the few well-protected niches on Hood Canal.

Pleasant Harbor shelters a short dock that is billed as a "state park" and a sizable commercial marina/resort complex. The second dock just inside

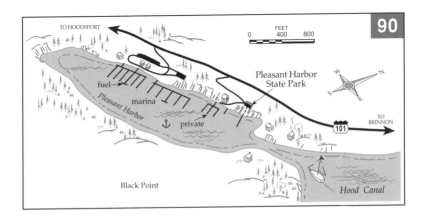

the harbor entrance is the principal facility of Pleasant Harbor State Park. The float has room for about six boats but has no power or water. The only other amenity of the park is a picnic table at the head of the dock and a toilet at the small parking area above. Private land bounds both edges of the property, leaving about 100 feet of beachfront for the park. Just beyond the state park float is a private marina, whose floats are plainly posted.

The commercial marina at the west end of the harbor more than compensates for the Spartan nature of the state park. Eleven long sets of floats are capable of accommodating more than 280 boats; 43 slips are provided for guests, and others in the permanent moorage area might be available. Onshore facilities provide most of the necessary amenities. If the marina is full, or if boaters do not want to take advantage of its facilities, the harbor has generous space to anchor in about 5 fathoms of water.

Triton Cove State Park   Map 84a

Boating • Paddling • Fishing • Picnicking

Facilities: 1-lane paved launch ramp with boarding float, disabled-accessible fishing pier, picnic tables, toilet, CMT campsite

Area: 28.5 acres; 592.7 feet of shoreline on Hood Canal

🚙 On the east side of US 101, 7 miles south of Brinnon or 7 miles north of Eldon, just north of the Mason County/Jefferson County line.

⛴ On Triton Cove, on the west side of Hood Canal, 3 n.m. south of the mouth of the Duckabush River.

This former trailer park north of Hoodsport was totally rebuilt by the State Parks and Recreation Commission after they acquired it. The original dock and float were replaced with a fishing pier, the launch ramp was relocated, and the launch ramp approach was modified to make it less steep and easier to use. It is a fine launching facility; however, the only shoreside amenities are picnic tables, a toilet and a large parking lot for cars and boat trailers. The park has been designated as a CMT campsite.

West Shore Public Beaches   Maps 84a and 84b

The glaciers that gouged out Hood Canal carved deeply into bedrock along its west shore, and the rocky ledges now lying underwater, paralleling the shoreline, are a scuba diving mecca, home to a kaleidoscope of marine animals that love niches and crannies. *Divers should be aware that although the tidal current might be weak near the surface, it can be much stronger at greater depths, as it flows through the subterranean canyons.*

Property owners along this portion of the canal zealously guard their tidelands and the tasty critters they harbor, and visitors will do well to heed posted property. Fortunately, a number of brief sections of beach lying just below US 101 are open to the public for gathering shellfish or for divers to enter the water.

Most of the alluvial fan of the Duckabush River is a DNR beach, but it holds little appeal because it becomes a mucky mudflat at low tide.

Duckabush River to McDaniel Cove • About 1½ miles southwest of the Duckabush River bridge, as US 101 swings close to the shoreline, is a 4000-foot-long public beach that extends to the southwest to the end of McDaniel Cove. The beach is very narrow and drops away steeply, except in the cove itself. Uplands above most of the beach are private, so it is best approached by boat.

DNR Beach 50 • The tideland lies 2 miles southwest of the outflow of the Duckabush River, and ½ mile southwest of McDaniel Cove. The north half of the 2610-foot-long strip has rock slabs tapering steeply into the water, making the beach almost nonexistent. The south half of the property is on the alluvial fan of Fulton Creek; the sand here harbors oysters, clams, geoducks, and crabs for the harvest at low tide. Although the beach is just below the highway, the bank is so steep that the upland approach is hazardous; it is best reached by boat.

Eagle Creek Recreational Tidelands • Directly across the road from a tavern on the south side of Eagle Creek, 2¼ miles north of Lilliwaup, are extensive tidelands that dry out about 2000 yards at a minus tide. The rocky beach is an excellent harvesting spot for oysters. There is parking for about fifteen cars on a wide paved road shoulder south of the Eagle Creek bridge. When the tide is out and oysters are prime, numerous cars are usually parked here. The beach north of the creek is private.

Beaches along Hood Canal yield oysters and clams for the dinner table.

Lilliwaup State Park Tidelands • As US 101 approaches Lilliwaup from the north, the highway bends west around Lilliwaup Bay. North of the bay, 1/2 mile from the town, the road curves southeast again, and a 4122-foot rocky stretch of public beach lies below the bluffs. Although the beach and adjoining bluffs are owned by state parks, the area is not developed. Parking is at an unmarked gravel pull-out above the bluff. A crude access trail has been worn into the bluff on the south end of the parking area. Very steep underwater rock walls below the beach are favorite scuba-diving sites.

Octopus Hole • This offshore rock ledge is an immensely popular scuba-diving spot. The rock ledge, in about 30 feet of water, is riddled with cracks and holes providing homes for wolf eels and octopuses. The area can be visited by divers of any skill level; tidal currents are minimal. The site is 3 1/4 miles north of Hoodsport and 1 1/4 miles south of Lilliwaup. Uplands are posted as "No Trespassing," but the site can be approached by boat from the water.

Sund Rock Marine Preserve • An offshore rock 1 1/2 miles south of Lilliwaup is of interest primarily to scuba divers. The top of the rock is exposed at all times, but it is the myriad ledges lying below the water, with their wealth of fish, numerous kinds of crabs, and colorful starfish, anemone, and nudibranchs that attract divers. A turn-out on US 101 just north of Virginia Avenue on the north end of Holiday Beach has parking for several cars. A short trail to the beach leads past an interpretive sign describing the sub-tidal ecosystems; respect private property flanking the path. *Watch out for poison oak.* A second pull-off 1/4 mile farther north is identified as a part of the marine preserve, but this is above 100-foot-high vertical cliffs, so there is no beach access here.

THE GREAT BEND: SOUTH SHORE
Map 84b

In this reach of Hood Canal the shore on either side is most often approached by land from Bremerton. Follow SR 304 west out of Bremerton to where it joins SR 3 as it skirts the north shore of Sinclair Inlet. Continue southwest on SR 3 for another 10 miles to reach Belfair, a small community at the far east point of Hood Canal. Here, at a T in the highway, SR 300 heads down the north side of the canal and in 1/2 mile, at a second Y, SR 106 heads down the south side.

If approaching from either the north or south via US 101, turn onto SR 106, 2 miles south of Potlatch State Park, or reach it via the Purdy Cutoff Road which leaves US 101 another 2 1/2 miles farther south.

Once past The Great Bend, the nature of the Hood Canal shoreline changes drastically, becoming wall-to-wall cabins, beach houses, and year-round homes, and the water becomes busier with small pleasure craft and water skiers. Pollution in the increasingly shallow water, along with the population density, make for slimmer pickings of shellfish at the few available public accesses. In short, here civilization has virtually conquered the natural state of the waterway.

Hoodsport   Map 91

Boating • Fishing • Shrimping • Scuba diving • Salmon hatchery

> **Facilities:** Groceries, ice, restaurants, fuel, scuba air fills, shopping, lodging. *Dock:* Guest moorage (no power or water), toilet, picnic tables.
>
> 🚗 Hoodsport is on US 101, 14 miles north of Shelton.
>
> ⛴ Hoodsport is on the west side of Hood Canal, just north of The Great Bend.

Hoodsport is the only town of any size on US 101 between Shelton and Quilcene. It marks the beginning of the Great Bend of the canal as it heads westward, and also the beginning of greater population. The community of around 600 residents is oriented to tourists, with numerous gift shops, restaurants, and motels catering to visitors touring the Olympic Peninsula. In late May, during shrimp season, the town is crammed with up to 20,000 sport shrimpers who descend on Hood Canal to set pots in offshore waters for the big crustacean.

Hoodsport Dock (Port of Hoodsport) • The Port of Hoodsport dock provides

guest moorage for pleasure boaters who want access to shoreside facilities. The floats at the end of the dock can accommodate a dozen boats; moorage is free, but limited to twenty-four hours.

At the head of the dock is a small park in memory of Ing Gronvold, a longtime resident who donated funds to the port for the construction of the public dock. There are picnic tables and three sets of stairs down the boulder bulkhead to the gravel beach.

Salmon Hatchery • A salmon hatchery operated by the DFW, immediately

north of Finch Creek in Hoodsport, is open for public viewing. Outdoor rearing tanks can be visited at any time. The 600-foot-long gravel beach in front of the hatchery is public and can be accessed from the north side. Saltwater fishing is restricted in a radius of 100 feet from the confluence of Finch Creek.

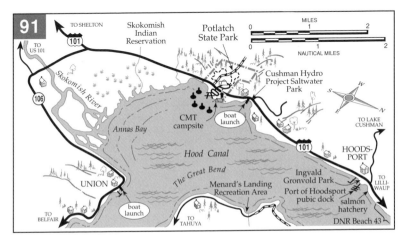

DNR Beach 43 • Lying immediately adjacent to the highway ¼ mile north of the center of Hoodsport, just north of the town limits, this beach is accessible from both land and water. The cobblestone beach is 2951 feet long; adjacent beaches are private. At low tide you might find oysters, clams, mussels, and crab, although the area is heavily used because of its closeness to the town. The beach also provides a scuba-diving access. Parking space along the highway at this point is very limited.

Cushman Hydro Project Saltwater Park (Tacoma Public Utilities)
Map 91

Picnicking • Fishing • Boating • Swimming • Scuba diving

Facilities: Picnic tables, fireplaces, restrooms, 2-lane paved launch ramp
Area: 4.7 acres; 1000 feet of shoreline on Annas Bay (Hood Canal)
🚗 The park is on the east side of US 101, 2½ miles south of Hoodsport, opposite the Tacoma Public Utilities generation plant.
🚤 The park is on the northwest side of Annas Bay at The Great Bend of Hood Canal

Tacoma City Light, which operates the large hydroelectric plant 2½ miles south of Hoodsport, provides this day-use picnic area and launch ramp immediately across US 101 from their facility. A large parking lot, ample for seventy-five to eighty cars and trailers, is adjacent to the highway. On the bank above the beach is a wide grass strip, trees, and some fifty picnic tables. Generator flywheels and other castoffs from the hydro plant are mounted at several places in the park as decoration and for kids to scramble on.

The long cobblestone beach is open for wading or swimming. A two-lane concrete launch ramp drops steeply from the southeast corner of the parking lot down to the water.

Potlatch State Park   Map 91

Camping • Picnicking • Swimming • Clamming • Boating • Paddling • Scuba diving • Hiking

Facilities: 17 standard campsites, 18 RV campsites, 2 primitive campsites, CMT campsite, picnic tables, fireplaces, restrooms, showers, trailer dump station, swimming beach, bathhouse, kitchen shelter, group day-use area, 5 mooring buoys, trail
Area: 57 acres; 9570 feet of shoreline on Annas Bay (Hood Canal)
🚗 On both sides of US 101, 3 miles south of Hoodsport.
🚤 On the southwest side of Annas Bay at the Great Bend of Hood Canal.

Potlatch State Park, a small facility along US 101, occupies the site of a former private resort. The park's campground lies on the west side of US 101, and the picnic area and beach on the east. A single campground loop has thirty-five sites (eighteen with hookups) and two primitive walk-in spots. The wooded campground isn't particularly spacious, so privacy between campsites is limited.

A short trail leaves the back of the campground, joins a service road, and then loops back to its beginning. The woodlands attract a variety of creatures such as squirrels, skunks, rabbits, and deer.

The picnic area is a large, open, grass field overlooking the beach. The beach below tapers gently into Annas Bay and varies from rock to gravel and mud. Offshore are five mooring buoys for visitors arriving by water. A CMT campsite is at the north end of the beach, just behind the kitchen shelter. Although clamming is a favorite sport here, the beach is heavily dug, and a sturdy shovel is necessary to find the few remaining shellfish down through the rocks and cobbles. Better to save the energy and leave them to repopulate. See comments in the introduction regarding harvesting shellfish. Seals are frequently seen cavorting in Annas Bay, and waterfowl frequent the salt marshes.

The Skokomish (meaning "River People") originally inhabited the river delta and adjoining valleys at the southern end of Hood Canal. The Point No Point Treaty of 1855 set aside a portion of their land as a reservation, which they were to share with the Toandos and Chimakum Tribes. Although the broad flat north of the Skokomish River delta was a traditional gathering site, it was not included as part of the reservation.

It was here that the Skokomish held some of their "potlatches"—ceremonies popular among Northwest Native Americans in which the host chief proved his

Great anchorages can be found off Potlatch State Park.

status and wealth by giving away or destroying vast amounts of his posses-sions. These elaborate ceremonies often required years of preparation, with dances and songs to be rehearsed, speeches to be composed, and offerings of furs, blankets, food, oil, ornaments, and slaves to be amassed.

Union   Map 91

Boating • Fishing

Facilities: Marina with limited guest moorage, groceries, ice, 1 lane paved launch ramp, toilet, restaurant, bait

🚗 5 miles east of US 101 on SR 106 or 24 miles southwest of Bremerton via SR 3 and SR 306.

🚤 On the south side of Hood Canal at the Great Bend.

The small community of Union lies on a point of land east of the delta of the Skokomish River, where Hood Canal makes its hook to the northeast. The town consists mostly of a few businesses catering to recreational boat traffic on the canal and tourists on the highway.

The marina at Union is private, but limited guest moorage might be avail-able with a call in advance. Immediately west of the marina is the Mason County public launch area, a two-lane concrete ramp. Adjacent parking is limited.

Alderbrook Inn   Map 84b

Swimming (saltwater and fresh) • Golfing • Boating • Paddling

Facilities: Resort, conference center, restaurant, swimming pool, hot tub, sauna, fitness center, shops, golf course, guest moorage, showers, marine pumpout station, portable toilet dump, tennis, trails, and rentals of paddle boats, small powerboats, and sailboats

🚗 Alderbrook is 13 miles southwest of Belfair on SR 106.

🚤 The dock at the inn is on the south side of Hood Canal, 2 n.m. east of Union.

Alderbrook Inn, one of the state's finest resorts, has complete lodging and conference facilities and a justifiably renowned dining room. Reservations are recommended for stays at the resort's rooms or cottages. Guest moorage with power and water is available on 1200 feet of dock. Moorage is free for boaters staying at the inn, or while dining there, but a fee is charged for oth-ers. A small additional charge is made for use of the indoor swimming pool. The closest spot for groceries or marine supplies is Union, 2 miles away.

Twanoh State Park   Map 92

Boating • Fishing • Swimming • Waterskiing • Hiking • Camping • Picnicking • Scuba diving

Facilities: 17 standard campsites, 22 RV campsites, group camp, restrooms, show-ers, picnic tables, fireplaces, kitchen shelters, dock with float, 6 mooring buoys,

2-lane paved launch ramp with boarding floats, marine pumpout station, portable toilet dump, swimming beach, wading pool, bathhouse, tennis court, horseshoe pits, trails, concession stand

Area: 182 acres; 3167 feet of shoreline

🚙 Take SR 304 southwest out of Bremerton to its junction with SR 3. Continue west on SR 3 for 9 miles to Belfair. Just west of Belfair follow SR 106 southwest for 7¾ miles to the park.

🚤 On the southeast shore of Hood Canal, 6 n.m. east of Union.

Flanked by miles of beachfront homes and near the population centers of Bremerton, Port Orchard, and Shelton, Twanoh State Park has many of the features of a well-developed city park, yet it manages to blend in the camping and hiking found in more remote state parks. SR 106 splits the park into two sections: on the south the camping and hiking area, and on the north the picnic grounds and beach. Campsites along the single loop road are fairly open, separated by second-growth cedar with sparse underbrush; some have full utility hookups, others only power. A group camp is on the ridgetop trail along the west side of the campground.

An interesting feature of the park is numerous large cedar stumps with springboard notches, remnants of the 1890s when the area was first logged. Many of the park buildings—built with large stones and heavy timbers—were constructed from 1936 to 1937 by the Depression-era Civilian Conservation Corps.

Although Twanoh is best known for its beach, most of the park consists of densely wooded hillsides above the small stream flowing through the

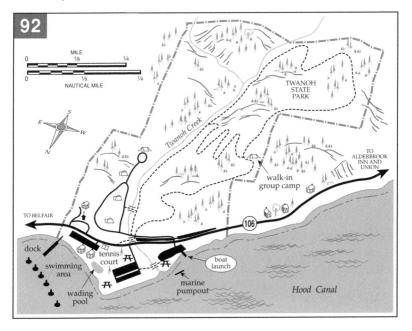

Picnic tables sit in the shadow of ancient firs at Twanoh State Park.

park. A 2-mile-long trail swings through this area, with a shorter 1¼-mile loop option. Both ends of the loop start at the parking lot west of the campground, and then travel through fir and hemlock forest. Near a creek, the moist forest sprouts devil's club, ferns, and moss.

A small creek divides the day use area in two; each section has a parking lot and picnic facilities. The two-lane concrete launch ramp is at the west section of the park. The eastern section has a roped-off swimming beach (unguarded); a shallow tide-filled wading pool for toddlers has been scooped out of the gravel beach near the swimming area.

At the southeast corner of the park, a 40-foot-long float extends off the end of a dock. The float is quite close to shore; approach cautiously at low tide. Six mooring buoys are spaced offshore for visiting boaters.

Theler Wetlands Nature Trail   Map 93

Hiking • Birdwatching • Nature study • Art work • Picnicking

Facilities: Information office, 2 miles of disabled-accessible trails, interpretive signs, toilets, picnicking, children's play area
Area: 135 acres

🚙 On the south side of Belfair and the west side of SR 3 look for the Mary E. Theler Community Center at 22875 SR 3. Parking and trailhead are at the center.

Three different environments are found at Theler Wetlands: a saltwater wetland, a freshwater wetland, and a freshwater swamp. The trail offers visitors an opportunity to experience firsthand the subtle differences of these different ecosystems. Interpretive signs along the paths provide more details about the plants and animals that inhabit the areas and their critical link in the ecological web that eventually affects the health and well-being of humans.

The saltwater marsh lies on the tideflat at the end of Hood Canal. The man-made freshwater marsh was originally created behind dikes as a place in which to compete hunting dogs. The dikes were also used to reclaim farmland, which is now being used to protect and enhance the estuary. The freshwater alder/cedar swamp is basically a forested wetland; here the forest growth cycles of these tree species are seen.

The longest wetland trail is about 3 miles, round trip. The way is nearly flat, either on a gravel path atop old dikes or on boardwalks over marshy areas. A quick circuit of all of the trails takes about one and a half hours, but more time should be spent to listen to the marsh sounds and watch for marshland birds and waterfowl such as red-tailed hawks, red-winged blackbirds, Virginia rails, barn swallows, mergansers, and many more. With luck you might also spot river otter, raccoon, muskrat, or beaver.

A tiny barn swallow rests on a railing at Theler Wetlands.

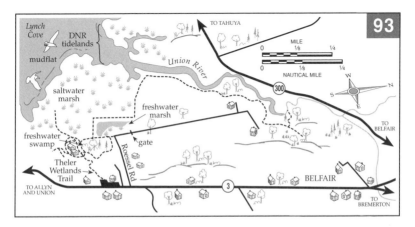

THE GREAT BEND: NORTH SHORE
Map 84b

Belfair State Park   Map 94

*Picnicking • Camping • Beach walking • Swimming • Kite flying • Crabbing •
Fishing*

Facilities: 134 standard campsites, 47 RV campsites, 3 hiker/biker sites, disabled-accessible restrooms, showers, picnic tables, fireplaces, swimming beach (unguarded), bathhouse, trailer dump station, horseshoe pits, children's play area, interpretive display

Area: 62.7/ acres; 3720 feet of shoreline on Hood Canal

🚗 Follow SR 304 southwest out of Bremerton to its junction with SR 3. Continue southwest on SR 3 for 11 miles to Belfair then turn north on SR 300. In ¼ mile SR 300 heads southwest and in 3 miles reaches the park.

🛥️ Because of the shallowness of the water, only small boats can approach the park beach, and even those with care, lest they become mired.

The farthest reach of Hood Canal dwindles down to a shallow tideflat that bares at the hint of a minus tide. Belfair State Park, the largest park on the canal, is at this end. The large park provides an interesting combination of freshwater and saltwater shoreline, as two good-sized streams, Big and Little Mission Creeks, flow through it to reach the canal. The advantage of the tideflat is that water flowing over it warms more quickly than that in deeper portions of the canal, making it ideal for summertime wading and swimming. A saltwater lagoon formed in a diked-off area with a tide gate at the mouth of Big Mission Creek provides an even warmer and more protected bathing spot.

Camping is in two distinct areas. The loops of the older section of the park are in old-growth Douglas-fir and rhododendrons; however, these sites

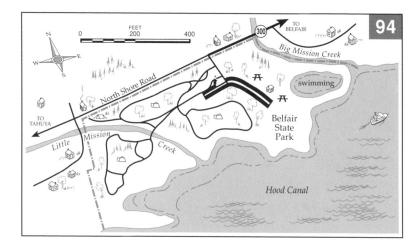

Belfair State Park has terrific places for kids to splash.

have no RV hookups. Many of the campsites in the newer section of the park have hookups, although they are more in the open. Camping is permitted year-round, although the park hours vary by season. Picnic sites are on the east side of the park, scattered along a grass strip between the parking lot and Big Mission Creek.

A rock bulkhead defines the park shoreline. The beach below is gravel baring to sand and mud at low tide. Seagulls, ducks, and geese populate the shore, while woodpeckers and a variety of other birds inhabit the wooded upland areas.

The tiny peninsula that juts out from the shoreline on the west edge of the park, according to Native American legend, carried supernatural powers that caused people loitering there to become possessed. Its Native American name meant "Snail Woman," an evil person who carried a large basket on her back and who stole children and ate them (no child psychologists back in those days!). She was transformed into the tiny snails with shells on their backs that can be found there today.

Allyn Dock and Launch Ramp (Hood Canal) (Port of Allyn)   Map 84b

Boating • Paddling

Facilities: Dock with float, guest moorage with power, marine pumpout, 1-lane paved launch ramp with boarding float, toilets

Area: 150 feet of shoreline on Hood Canal

🚙 Follow SR 304 southwest out of Bremerton to its junction with SR 3. Continue southwest on SR 3 for 11 miles to Belfair then turn north on SR 300. In ¼ mile SR 300 heads southwest and in 3 miles becomes North Shore Road. Reach the dock and launch ramp in another 1½ miles.

The Allyn dock on Hood Canal is small, but it has well-maintained facilities.

The dock and ramp are on the northeast side of Hood Canal, 4¼ n.m. northeast of Twanoh State Park (1½ n.m. west of Belfair State Park).

West from Belfair State Park, a small bulge of land provides a site for a dock and launch ramp operated by the Port of Allyn. The ownership seems a bit incongruous, because the town of Allyn lies 8 miles away on Case Inlet, at the end of Puget Sound, but one cannot complain of the existence of this fine, well-maintained facility.

The launch ramp and dock are separated by a two-block-long section of private beach homes. A smaller supplemental parking area is across the road to the north. The dock extends out to a U-shaped float that has room for about ten boats. A marine pumpout is provided on the float. Although the area is intended primarily for day use, overnight moorage is permitted. All adjacent beach is private. From land, the dock can be identified by a sign, "Caution, Pedestrian Crossing—Launch Ramp Ahead." Parking and a toilet are at a pull-off across the road from the head of the dock.

Tahuya   Map 84b

Boating • Paddling • Fishing • Camping • Waterskiing

Facilities: *Nearby:* Dock and floats, bait, ice, groceries, guest moorage, 1-lane paved launch ramp, boat rentals, restrooms, showers, laundry, rental cabins, RV camping, cottages

From SR 3 at Belfair turn north on SR 300. In ¼ mile SR 300 heads southwest and in 3 miles becomes North Shore Road, which reaches Tahuya in another 12½ miles.

Tahuya is on the north side of Hood Canal on the Great Bend, 2 n.m. east of Ayers Point and 1¾ n.m. northeast of Union.

The community of Tahuya surrounds a pretty little bay at the mouth of the Tahuya River. A commercial resort ½ mile west of the residential area has a launch ramp and a dock with floats. The melodious name *Tahuya* is a Native American word meaning "that done," referring to some memorable (but since-forgotten) event that took place here long ago. An alternate meaning is that the word also means "oldest people." The Twana Tribe that inhabited the area is considered the oldest on Hood Canal.

Menard's Landing (Port of Tahuya)   Map 84b

Picnicking • Beach walking • Paddling • Shellfish

Facilities: Pavilion, picnic tables, toilet, hand-carry boat launch
Area: 0.12 acres plus 2 acres leased from the DNR; 66 feet of shoreline on Hood Canal

See directions to Tahuya, above. Menard's Landing is on North Shore Road 3 miles west of Tahuya.

The park is on a small boat basin at Ayers Point on the north side of Hood Canal at the Great Bend.

A small section of land owned by the DNR, but leased by the Port of Tahuya, is at the far southwest point of the Kitsap Peninsula, just across Hood Canal from Hoodsport. The area consists mainly of a tiny peninsula covered with stumps and driftwood at the mouth of Rendsland Creek. Funds from the agency's Aquatic Lands Enhancement Account were used by the Port of Tahuya to develop a delightful little park, Menard's Landing, at the site. Driftwood and native plantings surround a small graveled flat with picnic tables, rustic log benches, and a small pavilion. A narrow gravel ramp leads down to a saltwater finger from Hood Canal where hand-carried boats can be launched. Parking is across the road to the east.

Appendixes

A. Emergency Phone Numbers and List of Contacts

All Western Washington counties use 911 as the number for fire and police emergencies. For nonemergency situations, contact the local sheriff or police department at their business number.

Other important contacts:

U.S. COAST GUARD

Seattle:

Search and Rescue Emergencies: 911 or (800) 982-8813
Other business: (206) 220-7000
Cellular Telephone Emergency Access: *CG (*24)
Museum: (206) 217-6993

RADIO CONTACTS

Marine VHF:

Coast Guard distress or hailing: Channel 16
Coast Guard liaison: Channel 22
Coast Guard Vessel Tracking Center: Channel 14 (1 watt only)
Marine Operator (Tacoma): Channel 28
Marine Operator (Seattle): Channels 25 and 26
NOAA Weather Service: Channel WX1
Citizens Band: Distress: Channel 9

Other Contacts:

Marine Toxins/PSP Hotline: (800) 562-5632. Website: *ww4.doh.wa.gov/ gis/mogifs/biotoxin.htm*
Whale Hotline (to report sightings or strandings): (800) 562-8832. Website: *www.whale-museum.org*

Washington State Parks

General information regarding the state parks is available from Washington State Parks and Recreation Commission, P.O Box 42650, 7150 Cleanwater Drive, Olympia, WA 98504. Phone: (360) 902-8500. Fax: (360) 753-1594. Telephone for the deaf: (360) 664-3133. Information Center: (360) 902-8844. Website: *www.parks.wa.gov*

Campsite reservations for reservation parks can be made by calling (888) 226-7688 between 7:00 AM and 8:00 PM, PST, except Christmas Day and New Year's Day, or anytime on the State Parks website.

Washington State Department of Fish and Wildlife

Natural Resources Building, 1111 Washington Street SE, Olympia, WA

98501. Mailing address: 600 Capitol Way North, Olympia, WA 98501-0191. Phone: (360) 902-2200. Website: *www.wdfw.wa.gov*

Washington Water Trails Association

4649 Sunnyside Avenue N, Suite 305, Seattle, WA 98103-6900. Phone: (206) 545-9161. Fax: (206) 547-0350. Website: *www.wwta.org*

B. Nautical Charts, Maps, and Tide Tables

Charts

Sketch maps in this book are intended for general orientation only. When traveling by boat on any of the Northwest's waters, it is imperative that the appropriate nautical charts be used. The following small-craft folio covers all areas that are included in this book. These charts, as well as more detailed ones, can be purchased at map stores or many marine supply centers.

NOAA chart folio 18445 SC, *Puget Sound—Possession Sound to Olympia Including Hood Canal* (1:80,000)

Maps

USGS topographical maps are not necessary for any of the hiking described in this book; however, the 7½-minute series maps are both useful and interesting.

City maps or various books of street maps, especially *The Thomas Guides*, are helpful for navigating through metropolitan areas.

Tide Tables (all published annually)

Tide Tables—20__, West Coast of North America and South America. NOAA

Tidal Current Tables—20__, Pacific Coast of North America and Asia. NOAA

20__ Current and Tide Tables for Puget Sound, Deception Pass, the San Juans, Gulf Islands, and the Strait of Juan de Fuca. Island Canoe, Inc., Bainbridge Island. (Extract from the above NOAA tables for local areas.)

Index

About the Authors

Marge and Ted Mueller are outdoor enthusiasts and environmentalists who have explored Washington State's waterways, mountains, forests, and deserts for more than forty years. Ted has taught classes on cruising in Northwest waters, and both Marge and Ted have instructed mountain climbing. They are members of The Mountaineers and The Nature Conservancy, and have served on the Board of Directors of Friends of Washington State Parks. They are the authors of twelve regional guidebooks.

The Muellers can be contacted at *margeted@comcast.net.*

THE MOUNTAINEERS, founded in 1906, is a nonprofit outdoor activity and conservation club, whose mission is "to explore, study, preserve, and enjoy the natural beauty of the outdoors...." Based in Seattle, Washington, the club is now the third-largest such organization in the United States, with seven branches throughout Washington State.

The Mountaineers sponsors both classes and year-round outdoor activities in the Pacific Northwest, which include hiking, mountain climbing, ski-touring, snowshoeing, bicycling, camping, kayaking, nature study, sailing, and adventure travel. The club's conservation division supports environmental causes through educational activities, sponsoring legislation, and presenting informational programs.

All club activities are led by skilled, experienced instructors, who are dedicated to promoting safe and responsible enjoyment and preservation of the outdoors.

If you would like to participate in these organized outdoor activities or the club's programs, consider a membership in The Mountaineers. For information and an application, write or call The Mountaineers, Club Headquarters, 300 Third Avenue West, Seattle, WA 98119; 206-284-6310. You can also visit the club's website at *www.mountaineers.org* or contact The Mountaineers via email at *clubmail@mountaineers.org*.

The Mountaineers Books, an active, nonprofit publishing program of the club, produces guidebooks, instructional texts, historical works, natural history guides, and works on environmental conservation. All books produced by The Mountaineers Books fulfill the club's mission.

Send or call for our catalog of more than 500 outdoor titles:

The Mountaineers Books
1001 SW Klickitat Way, Suite 201
Seattle, WA 98134
800-553-4453
mbooks@mountaineersbooks.org
www.mountaineersbooks.org

The Mountaineers Books is proud to be a corporate sponsor of The Leave No Trace Center for Outdoor Ethics, whose mission is to promote and inspire responsible outdoor recreation through education, research, and partnerships. The Leave No Trace program is focused specifically on human-powered (nonmotorized) recreation.

Leave No Trace strives to educate visitors about the nature of their recreational impacts, as well as offer techniques to prevent and minimize such impacts. Leave No Trace is best understood as an educational and ethical program, not as a set of rules and regulations.

For more information, visit *www.LNT.org*, or call 800-332-4100.

OTHER TITLES YOU MIGHT ENJOY FROM
THE MOUNTAINEERS BOOKS

Kayaking Puget Sound, The San Juans, and Gulf Islands: 50 Trips on the Northwest's Inland Waters, 2nd Ed.
R. Carey Gersten and Randel Washburne
All-inclusive guide to the world's best kayaking area.

**A Waterfall Lover's Guide
to the Pacific Northwest**
Gregory A. Plumb
The comprehensive field guide to
viewing hundreds of spectacular
waterfalls in Washington, Oregon, and
Idaho.

Nature in the City: Seattle
Kathryn True and Maria Dolan
For suburbanites, city slickers, and
newcomers, this book reveals the
best places for nature lovers to see
deer, eagles, and seals or find flower
gardens and other hidden, wild gems
without leaving the Seattle area.

The Outdoor Knots Book
Clyde Soles
Guidelines and know-how for selecting
the best rope and knots for any activity.
Author Clyde Soles is former senior
editor of *Rock & Ice* Magazine.

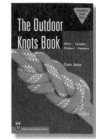

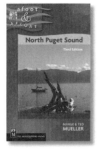

Afoot and Afloat: North Puget Sound and the Strait of Juan de Fuca, 3rd Ed.
Marge and Ted Mueller
Co-authors Marge and Ted Mueller have explored the
Northwest for more than 40 years. They are the authors
of all five titles in the *Afoot and Afloat* series as well
as *Washington State Parks*, 3rd edition, and *Exploring
Washington's Wild Areas*, 2nd edition.
